sababa

sababa

Fresh, Sunny Flavors from My Israeli Kitchen

<><><><><><><>

ADEENA SUSSMAN

AVERY
AN IMPRINT OF PENGUIN RANDOM HOUSE
NEW YORK

AVERY

an imprint of Penguin Random House LLC
penguinrandomhouse.com

Copyright © 2019 by Adeena Sussman
Photographs © 2019 by Dan Perez
Shuk photos pp. 13 top R, bottom L–R; 14, top R; 17, top L–R;
80, center R, bottom L–R; 262, all photos; 297 © by Eyal Yassky Weiss
Styling by Nurit Kariv

Most Avery books are available at special quantity discounts
for bulk purchase for sales promotions, premiums, fund-raising,
and educational needs. Special books or book excerpts
also can be created to fit specific needs. For details, write
SpecialMarkets@penguinrandomhouse.com.

Library of Congress Cataloging-in-Publication Data

Names: Sussman, Adeena, author.
Title: Sababa : fresh, sunny flavors from my Israeli kitchen / Adeena
    Sussman.
Description: New York : Avery, an imprint of Penguin Random House,
    [2019] | Includes index.
Identifiers: LCCN 2019004726| ISBN 9780525533450 (hardcover : alk.
    paper) | ISBN 9780525533467 (ebook)
Subjects: LCSH: Jewish cooking. | LCGFT: Cookbooks.
Classification: LCC TX724 .S87 2017 | DDC 641.5/676—dc23
    LC record available at https://lccn.loc.gov/2019004726
    p.   cm.

Printed in Germany
10 9 8 7 6 5 4 3 2 1

Book design by Ashley Tucker

FOR JAY

Contents

FOREWORD

As I climb the four flights of stairs up to Adeena Sussman's light-filled apartment a few blocks from the Carmel Market in Tel Aviv, I get a feeling that I'm hard-pressed to reproduce anywhere else. It starts with her hug, warmer and more genuine than most (although her husband Jay's isn't too shabby, either), and seems to presage the irrepressible hospitality that awaits. The smell of freshly baked bread begins a few floors down and leads directly to her kitchen, where the island countertop seems perpetually laden with a bounty of tasty delights. All the senses are engaged.

On a recent visit, there were perfect Persian cucumbers no bigger than my finger, sliced lengthwise and sitting beside a dish of coarse sea salt and a wedge of lemon. There was a pitcher of ice-cold fresh almond milk, scented with vanilla and sweetened with silan—a treat to drink by itself or mixed with the cardamom–scented cold brew coffee sitting next to it. Beside that was a carafe of freshly squeezed mixed citrus juice—whatever was lying around, she said.

This is an understatement on two counts. First, it's winter in Israel, and a riot of oranges and grapefruits and pomelos are practically bursting out of their skins at the market. And second, there's nothing effortless about Adeena's cooking. She only makes it look that way.

The location of her apartment is also no accident. When Adeena permanently relocated to Israel a few years ago (she was raised in Northern California but has traveled to Israel extensively her entire adult life), the Shuk HaCarmel loomed large in her decision about where to live.

There ought to be a word for the Instagram envy I feel watching her feed, which is like a technicolor flipbook through the seasons. She is on a first-name basis with her fishmonger, and knows where to get the absolute best strawberries during their season. She has a coffee guy and a butcher and a spice guy. The market is practically an ingredient in her cooking—a style that prioritizes pristine produce and simplicity over luxury ingredients and fussiness, earnest technique over shortcuts or fancy tricks. In fact, the lengths to which Adeena goes to blanket her guests in hospitality is an integral part of what makes her food sing. The love you take is equal to the love you make.

This is evident in the bread that sits on the counter, taunting me. She was up until midnight

the night before getting it ready for the oven. Now it is hiding inside a lidded aluminum tin (like the ones Danish butter cookies mysteriously appear in every holiday season). This is kubaneh, the Yemenite Sabbath bread that bakes overnight so that the butter and flour slowly caramelize into something wheatier and yeastier and richer than it has a right to be. It is a dish that gives definition to the landscape of Israeli food—born in poverty, brought to the country by Yemenite immigrants, and embraced by Israelis of all backgrounds.

Adeena removes the cover and flips the kubaneh out onto a platter, followed by a chorus of oohs and aahs. We discuss the importance of hand-grating the tomatoes for *resek* (a classic kubaneh accompaniment) and how the eggs in their shells nestled in the dough turn creamy from the slow, overnight bake. My eyes widen with joy (and a bit of pain) while devouring a hunk of kubaneh slathered with her homemade schug, the fiery green Yemenite chili paste. And all the while I keep asking myself, how does she do it? How does she make the most incredible kubaneh? How does she turn everything she touches into gold?

Well, now we know. The pages of this book ooze with her passion for the romance and beauty of Israeli cuisine. The recipes are soulful, elemental, and stunningly delicious. Her aesthetic jumps off the pages in the way she coaxes beauty out of simplicity. This is not just a cookbook. It is a study in the alchemy of converting the ordinary into the extraordinary.

In some ways, Adeena and I are opposites. I was born in Israel but grew up in the States. She was raised in the States but chose to make Israel her home. But we have both devoted our professional lives to exploring the wonderfully complex and constantly evolving nature of Israeli cuisine. I do it in our restaurants and Adeena does it for the home cook. She is Israeli by choice, and in that I think she has a unique perspective on what is special about this culture and this cuisine.

I wish that all of you could score an invite to Adeena's apartment in Tel Aviv and bask in the sun-drenched warmth of her food and company. This book is not a hug from Adeena Sussman. But it might as well be.

—Michael Solomonov with Steven Cook

INTRODUCTION

In a city full of night owls, I am among the earliest of risers. Tel Aviv is a place of sizzling days that can leave you wilting, of beach jaunts and afternoon naps and dinners out after the sun slips behind the Mediterranean Sea. But on mornings like this, just after the light begins to drift in through the wispy shades, the city feels like it belongs only to me. So I leave my husband sleeping and sneak out of the bedroom, grab my two-wheeled plaid shopping cart, slip out the door, and make my way the short distance between our apartment and the entrance to the Carmel Market, known in Hebrew as Shuk HaCarmel or, quite simply, the shuk.

A tree rustles, gently shaken by an ocean breeze from down the road. A bus trundles down our block as a surfer, his wetsuit peeled back like a banana down to his waist, walks barefoot toward the waves. I turn the corner and, just like that, the main artery of the shuk is visible ahead, a ragtag tableau of tarps and awnings ascending half a kilometer in front of me.

It always feels like an impossibility that in a town of 350,000 food-obsessed denizens, my flip-flopped feet could be the first to touch this asphalt that will be walked on by thousands by day's end. But right now, it's just me and the morning workers getting ready for the day ahead. I watch my step as vendors hose down the floors in front of their stalls one last time before the day begins. A mini forklift drops a pallet of spring garlic, its long stalks still attached, near the sidewalk. I sidestep a giant crate of watermelons to make my way inside. There are onions and beets waiting to be claimed, too, the boxes reminding me of those newspaper bundles you see being thrown off trucks in old movies. Except here, the headlines waiting to be unfurled are edible ones.

I'm on the hunt for herbs for my daily carafe of tea: mint, lemon verbena, maybe some sage. The fragile leaves fare better when I rescue them at the beginning of the day, before the heat takes its toll. The morning crew at the first produce stand on the left is sorting through tomatoes, tearing wilted leaves from bunches of lettuce and letting the sacrificial dark-green outer layers fall to the floor to join a fast-accumulating mountain of trimmed herb stalks, errant grape vines, corn husks, and carrot tops.

People aren't quite up to speaking yet; there is so, so much conversation ahead. A man walks around with a round metal tray, balancing glasses of milky coffee, delivering standing orders for vendors clearly seeking fortification for the day ahead.

Sababa is a state of being, where everything is cool as can be. It means, quite simply, "everything is awesome."

Early in the week, new produce trickles into the market, trucked in from all over Israel. If I hang around long enough, drink a coffee, and catch up with my friend Miki at his little café around the corner, I can watch the shuk come to life. In a country that can be traversed by car from top to bottom in six hours, of blink-and-you-miss-them micro-seasons, where people look at you funny if you ask for a peach a week out of peak, where you learn that avocados are ephemeral, and eventually know the exact week in the summer that the watermelons get mealy, it's best to stay close to the market. So I shop early; I shop often. I shop like this because I can.

"Hetzi kilo," (half a kilogram), I say to the cherry vendor, whose head barely clears the glistening pyramid of reddish-purple fruit piled in front of him. He hands over the goods as the fish vendor perched on a nearby corner upturns a Styrofoam crate full of ice onto the sidewalk before her.

"Sababa?" I ask, using the local turn of phrase that perfectly describes what I love about this food

in this country at this moment. *Sababa*, derived from the Arabic word *tzababa*, technically means "great" or "wonderful," but has come to define a state of being, where everything is cool as can be. It's an invitation to agree on a "yes" in a country where, as the old joke goes, two people generate three opinions. *Sababa* means, quite simply, "everything is awesome."

When it comes to Israeli food, everything really, truly is *sababa*. People around the world have developed an insatiable appetite for these sunny, spicy flavors, and a desire to learn how to re-create them at home. It's a moment that has blossomed into a movement with staying power, one anchored in an effortless blend of the new and the familiar and a desire to get to know a faraway land that—quite literally—brings so much to the table.

And for me it all begins here in the shuk. It may be quiet now, but within an hour it will be a place of happy action as people come to eat, drink, and shop. As the first Middle Eastern pop song blares, people start to trickle in: a line cook picking up the errant ingredient for his restaurant's mise en place; a woman grabbing a single apple on her way to work; an early treat from the one vendor ready to hand-crank orange juice into a glass.

I guess you could say I came to Israel for love but stayed for the shuk. I met my now-husband, Jay, on a blind date, arranged by our mutual friend Jessica, while he was in New York for work. Within a few months, we were shuttling back and forth over the Atlantic, and a year later I was one-way ticketed for better, for worse, for life. Tasked with finding a larger apartment for the two of us to live in and knowing that moving to Tel Aviv would be an adjustment, Jay surveyed dozens of places before signing a new lease for us. I had no idea what to expect the first time I ascended the sixty-nine steps with my heavy bags, and when I opened the door to our fourth-floor apartment on an early December day, I cried.

It had giant Belgian windows, slate-gray marble kitchen countertops over huge double-width drawers, and a deep, wide balcony overlooking a ragtag assemblage of low-slung buildings cloaked in brilliant-pink bougainvillea, and it took in more natural sunlight in an hour than my tiny Upper West Side co-op saw in a month. The kicker was the location, steps from this market. We went to the shuk the next morning, and I never *stopped* going. The shuk became my constant companion, the organizing principle of my days, a comforting routine that has evolved into a way of life and a habit of cooking joyfully from this country's bounty.

It's not that Israel or its cuisine was new to me. In some ways, I had spent a lifetime preparing for this move, immersing myself in the insanely delicious and incredibly diverse culture of Israeli food. My American parents spent a year here while my father did graduate work in Jerusalem, and I missed being born here by two months. At the age of nine we took a month to explore the country. Within twenty-four hours I went from drinking Tropicana from a carton in suburban California to a place where juice was pressed from oranges and pomegranates that had been split open before me to reveal colors so vibrant they seemed artificially enhanced. I had my first shawarma, the meat crowned with lamb fat and spiked with garlic, its crisped exterior carved with a long serrated knife straight into a warm pita bread. The crunch of falafel became a Pavlovian temptation.

Over countless visits and extended stays—including a five-year stint in Jerusalem after college and frequent visits to Tel Aviv—I had become all the more smitten with the edible life here. Israel's food scene had gone from notoriously sleepy, with an endless onslaught of hummus, tahini, and falafel (repeat), to something altogether different. An always-hungry population expanded their repertoire beyond these time-honored staples, though by no means leaving them behind. As the world opened up, Israelis did, too, with chefs and eaters venturing abroad to see what the world had to offer.

The thing is, Israel has always had the goods: olive oil extracted from fruit grown on politically contested but topographically blessed steppes. Cheeses formed from the milk of goats, cows, and sheep who graze on lands that have been tended by shepherds since biblical times. I started tasting dishes that reflected a harmony of local ingredients prepared with a wider-reaching embrace of global influences, the inevitable outcome of cooking for and by a population with so many distinct immigrant traditions.

Until the recent past, a chicken roasted with za'atar, the skin crisped up to perfection, might have been a stretch for an American home kitchen. Today, it's just the kind of dish we instinctively want to eat. Shakshuka used to be little more than a tongue-twisting tangle of syllables (for the record, it's shahk-SHOO-kah). Now, the combination of garlicky, rich tomato sauce, roasted

The shuk became my constant companion, the organizing principle of my days, a comforting routine that has evolved into a way of life.

peppers, and skillet-baked eggs—with almost as many variations as there are Israelis—has been adopted as a pitch-perfect, all-day, eminently customizable culinary darling.

And in a society where the market rules, the week's freshest produce—be it lush ripe figs, perfumed persimmons, or juicy grapes—are found on restaurant menus, layered between slices of local fish crudo and adorned with little more than grassy local olive oil, flakes of sea salt, and thin rings of hot green chilies.

And so, in a new city with a world-class resource for all the raw materials steps from my house, I started mining the Israeli pantry for ingredients and spices, using homegrown and regional staples in ways that reflected my own tastes. My own style developed, one that included dishes that could be ready in twenty minutes, combined

I hope you love these recipes as much as I do, and I hope, more than anything else, that it's all *sababa.*

with others that took a little more effort or needed to be cooked for hours; some that honored my Ashkenazi (Eastern European) Jewish heritage and others learned from Arab and Jewish Israelis who reflected this country's multicultural, multiethnic culinary melting pot.

Kitchen stalwarts like tahini, silan (date syrup), harissa and schug (hot sauces from North Africa and Yemen, respectively), and za'atar, the spice blend with an ancient pedigree and endless modern kitchen applications, became my go-to staples. As I settled in, I discovered surprising ways to use them at home, taking inspiration from the population of immigrants from more than one hundred lands who call Israel their home. I've had the privilege of cooking with some of these people at their homes and mine, and some of those recipes are here, too.

This book is a reflection of the things I like to make from the bounty I've found right outside my door. This is by no means a comprehensive guide to the foods of Israel, but rather a window into how I like to cook right now. Using the same flavor-packed staple ingredients that I do will give your cooking a lift, every day, hopefully opening up new doors to delicious. I hope you love these recipes as much as I do, and I hope, more than anything else, that it's all *sababa.*

Kefach Shbeta (top left) is one of the only vendors in the shuk to sell *baladi* (roughly translated from Arabic as "native" or "heirloom") vegetables. His father had a larger produce business in the Arabic city of Tira, about 45 minutes north of Tel Aviv, but Kefach began selling from a *basta* in the shuk for more than twenty years. I come here for the lovely bell-shaped eggplants with creases on the bottom; fat, round green cabbage; crunchy cucumbers with the blossoms still attached; and tiny zucchinis perfect for stuffing. Avrahem Koren (bottom right) of Merkaz Hadagim in the shuk, is where I buy their house-smoked salmon and cured fish.

A Brief History of Shuk HaCarmel

As Shuk HaCarmel nears the one hundredth anniversary of its loose beginnings, it continues to be a vital strand of Tel Aviv's connective tissue. According to Tel Aviv historian and tour guide Yossi Goldberg, legend has it that the land edging the top of the shuk was purchased by Russian Jews before World War I. After losing their fortunes during the Bolshevik revolution, they managed to immigrate to Palestine and discovered that their property actually had value. A few years before, the Yemenite Quarter had been established on land owned by Aaron Chelouche, a prominent French–North African Jew who lived in nearby Jaffa. In the early 1920s, as Tel Aviv grew, pushcart vendors began hawking produce and dry goods on Allenby Street, near what is traditionally considered the top of the shuk.

Over time more vendors flocked to the area, filling in the storefronts and setting up *bastot*, the free-standing stalls that line both sides of the shuk. Arab vendors from Jaffa, which at the time was still part of Tel Aviv, began setting up stalls in the southernmost portion of the shuk, and the northern portion remained more Jewish, though everyone coexisted in relative harmony. The shuk had the freewheeling feeling of a Levantine market, very much opposed to the modern vision of a European-style capital the founders of the city were trying to establish. The poet Esther Re'ev described the market as a place of "camels with backs weighted down with watermelons."

Around this time, there were efforts to consolidate vendors at another market on Bezalel Street, a few blocks northeast, but eventually vendors and customers settled on Independence in 1948 and the founding of the modern state, when many Arabs fled or were expelled from nearby Jaffa, and the shuk became predominantly Jewish-owned. Many other iconic institutions have been uprooted by gentrification and development, but the shuk has held fast to its traditions and neighborhood, defying the odds to remain the city's main produce market. In the process, restaurants and bars have opened in and around the shuk, and there have been hole-in-the-wall Yemenite eateries on the outskirts of the shuk for decades. There have been rumors that renovation and redevelopment are on their way; the shuk could use better sanitation and a unified canopy to protect it from the elements. But many vendors and customers, myself included, fear what will happen if modernity takes hold too fast. Only time will tell.

Pictured, clockwise from left: Cardamom–Kissed Schug (page 35);
24–Hour Salted Lemon Spread (page 34); Preserved Lemon Paste (page 40);
40–Minute Amba (page 36); Honey Harissa (page 37)

SPICES, CONDIMENTS, AND OTHER KITCHEN STAPLES

BEFORE YOU START

I keep my kitchen stocked with staples that open up limitless cooking opportunities. The ragtag collection of recycled jars that now line the side of my fridge and fill my spice drawer are cooking tools I've tried to make easy for you to re-create at home. They will set you up to make many of the recipes in this book . . . or to feel free to make up new ones of your own. Each store-bought spice or homemade spice blend recipe is an express lane to building flavor, revealing a small slice of Israel's multicultural kitchen, and more often than not I find myself throwing one or more into a dish to instantly amp it up by several decibels. Rather than make many, I focus on those I find the most versatile. That way they get used up, rather than languishing in a dark cabinet or on an obscure refrigerator shelf. If you make these kitchen building blocks, I can guarantee you'll never go hungry . . . or get bored. Just one judicious shake, smear, or dollop can take a dish in an unexpected direction, lending intrigue and depth. Refer to the Shopping Guide at the end of the book for resources on where to get many of the spices, as well as store-bought versions of many of the condiments I provide recipes for.

Baharat

This sneakily versatile spice mix has moved its way up to the top of my rotation because it works equally well in sweet and savory dishes. Until I did more research, I thought it was merely a mix of dark spices like pepper, cinnamon, and cloves. But when I spent a day cooking with Druze women in the Galilee (see page 198), I learned that some versions have an underpinning of green herbs like marjoram. Baharat's base is made up of the warm spices most of us know from the baking pantry but also a generous helping of black pepper and cardamom to ground it with earthier notes that make your taste buds stand up and pay attention. Like so many mixes, there are different versions that hail from different countries, regions, and family traditions—but I've settled on mine as the most versatile.

6 tablespoons ground cinnamon

3 tablespoons finely ground black pepper

2 tablespoons ground allspice

2 teaspoons ground cardamom

2 teaspoons freshly grated nutmeg, or dried

½ teaspoon dried marjoram (optional)

1 teaspoon ground ginger

1 teaspoon ground cloves

Makes
¾ cup

Active Time:
5 minutes

Total Time:
5 minutes

In a bowl, combine the cinnamon, pepper, allspice, cardamom, nutmeg, marjoram (if using), ginger, and cloves. Store in an airtight container for up to 6 months.

Dukkah

Pronounced *do'ah* in its native Arabic, dukkah, which hails from Egypt, is more of a topping than a spice blend. Nutty, toasty, and downright addictive, it's traditionally served alongside labaneh with olive oil for dipping with bread. But I find I use it more to top salads for a bit of subtle crunch, throw a little bit into my schnitzel blend, or, when no one's looking, I pinch it between my fingers and eat it out of hand. Hazelnuts really do add something special, but the same amount of almonds, pistachios—even peanuts—are also amazing here.

1 cup hazelnuts, preferably blanched

½ cup raw white sesame seeds

3 tablespoons whole coriander seeds

3 tablespoons whole cumin seeds

2 teaspoons freshly ground black pepper

1 teaspoon sugar

½ teaspoon kosher salt

Makes
2 cups

Active Time:
10 minutes

Total Time:
30 minutes

Preheat the oven to 325°F.

Place the hazelnuts on a rimmed baking sheet and toast until the nuts are lightly browned, 9 to 10 minutes. Remove from the oven and cool completely. If the nuts have skins on them, rub them between two clean kitchen towels to remove and discard as much of the loose, papery skins as possible (if you don't get them all, it's OK).

While the hazelnuts are roasting, toast the sesame seeds in a medium, dry skillet over medium heat, stirring often, until golden and fragrant, 3 to 4 minutes. Transfer to a plate to cool. Add the coriander and cumin seeds to the same skillet and toast until fragrant and the seeds begin to pop, 1 to 2 minutes. Transfer to a separate plate to cool. Grind the cumin and coriander in a spice grinder until powdery and transfer to the bowl of a food processor. Add the hazelnuts, pepper, sugar, and salt and process until the mixture looks like fine sand, being careful not to overprocess the nuts into paste, 15 to 20 seconds. Transfer to a bowl and add the sesame seeds. Store in an airtight container in a cool place for up to 1 month.

Israeli Everything Spice

My take on this new shake-it-on staple includes dried lemon peel, za'atar, sumac, dried red pepper flakes, and a bunch of different whole seeds, which lend Middle Eastern intrigue to whatever they touch. I use this spice mix on the outside of my bagel-ish bread (page 82), but it's great wherever a little Everything is required—Israeli cottage cheese being my favorite.

2 tablespoons minced dried onion

2 tablespoons minced dried garlic

2 tablespoons raw white sesame seeds

1 tablespoon za'atar

2 teaspoons nigella seeds or black sesame seeds

2 teaspoons finely grated dried lemon zest*

1 teaspoon cumin seeds

1 teaspoon caraway seeds

1 teaspoon Maldon sea salt or kosher salt

½ teaspoon dried red pepper flakes

○○○○○○○○○○

Makes
⅔ cup

Active Time:
10 minutes

Total Time:
10 minutes

○○○○○○○○○○

In a small, dry skillet over medium heat, toast the minced onion, garlic, and sesame seeds, stirring often, until toasty and golden, 3 to 4 minutes. Transfer to a small bowl, cool slightly, then add the za'atar, nigella seeds, lemon zest, cumin and caraway seeds, salt, and red pepper flakes. Store in an airtight container for up to 1 month.

*To make the dried lemon zest, use a wand-style Microplane grater (see Shopping Guide) to finely zest a lemon onto a plate. Microwave for 90 seconds, or let the lemon zest dry, uncovered, stirring every 3 to 4 hours until completely dry, 12 hours. Store in a sealed glass jar for up to 1 year.

Hawaiij

This spicy, turmeric-heavy blend, traditionally stirred into soups, was introduced to the Israeli kitchen by Yemenite immigrants. In her excellent book *Bone Soup and Flipped Bread*, Sue Larkey writes that hawaiij varied by region in Yemen, with northerners preferring a pepper-forward blend and southerners, who had access to a wider variety of spices due to commerce and trade, introducing other spices into the mix. Hawaiij is a flavor lightbulb in a pot of chicken soup, brightening it and clearing sinuses with every sip of golden broth. I don't stop there, though—its flavors are great on pargiyot (chicken thighs) and especially harmonious with rich cuts of red meat, where the spice cuts through the fat (see my Hawaiij-Braised Short Ribs with Roasted Kohlrabi Mash, page 244). I like to toast whole spices and grind them for this recipe, but by all means feel free to use dried, which work great, too.

¼ cup whole black peppercorns or freshly ground black pepper

¼ cup cumin seeds or ground cumin

2 tablespoons cardamom seeds or ground cardamom

2 tablespoons coriander seeds or ground coriander

3 tablespoons ground turmeric

Makes
¾ cup

Active Time:
10 minutes

Total Time:
10 minutes

If using whole spices, in a large, dry skillet combine the peppercorns with the cumin, cardamom, and coriander. Toast over medium-low heat, stirring, until the seeds begin to pop and the spices are fragrant, 3 to 4 minutes. Transfer to a plate to cool. Place the toasted spices in a spice grinder or mortar and pestle. Add the turmeric and grind until fine. (If using dried spices, toast the ground pepper, cumin, cardamom, coriander, and turmeric in a dry skillet over low heat, stirring constantly until fragrant, 2 to 3 minutes; transfer to a plate to cool.) Hawaiij can be stored in an airtight container for up to 6 months.

Za'atar Spice Blend

An herb with a pedigree that goes back to the Bible, za'atar, or hyssop leaf, is at the heart of the blend of the same name. Herby, tangy, nutty, and slightly salty, the blend elevates every dish it touches. Every spring, when za'atar grows in abundance, Arab and Palestinian women dry reams of it on rooftops and patios before grinding it with sesame, salt, sumac, and, occasionally, thyme for a homemade version they use all year. There are different styles of za'atar all over the Middle East; some are much tangier due to the amount of sumac added; some have more sesame seeds or salt. I found making my own to be a revelation, because I could control exactly how much of each element I wanted in the mix. Microwaving herbs to dry them is another discovery; it removes the moisture while leaving the herbs bright green. You can sometimes find za'atar fresh at farmers' markets or well-stocked Middle Eastern stores, but fresh oregano is a worthy stand-in; dried herbs also work really well here, too.

1 cup picked fresh za'atar or oregano leaves (or 6 tablespoons dried oregano)

3 tablespoons dried marjoram

3 tablespoons toasted sesame seeds

4 teaspoons dried thyme

1 tablespoon ground sumac

1 teaspoon fine sea salt

Makes
around 1 cup

Active Time:
15 minutes

Total Time:
15 minutes

If using fresh za'atar or oregano, arrange it on a towel-lined plate and microwave in 15-second intervals, stirring between intervals, until dry and crumbly, 2 to 2½ minutes. Crumble the leaves by hand or in a spice grinder until almost fine (the way dried herbs look), then combine in a medium bowl with the marjoram, sesame seeds, thyme, sumac, and salt. Store in an airtight container for up to 3 months.

Other Spices

Fenugreek

A staple in Yemenite cuisine with origins in India, fenugreek has a bitterness that helps cut through the richness of other foods. Its gelatinous quality gives the condiment chilbeh (page 66) its unique texture, and lends slick body and sheen to amba (page 36).

Turmeric

I love dried turmeric's sunny hue and dusky, earthy flavor accents. I add it to soups and stews to deepen both flavor and color.

Dried Persian Limes

Sour, funky, citrusy, and smoky, the flavor of dried limes, known here as *limon parsi*, and *limu omani* in Arabic, is unmistakable. Though traditionally used in Persian soups and stews, I spread the wealth by pulverizing them in a spice blender for a seasoning I use on my Sour Lime and Pomegranate Chicken Wings (page 234). They come in both black and white versions (see photo, right); their color depends on the fresh variety (sometimes actually lemons) and drying method.

Nigella Seeds

Though they look like sesame seeds from afar, a closer inspection reveals tiny black bits with rough edges. Traditionally used to top many breads like Yemenite kubaneh, they taste mildly like onions and garlic, so think twice before substituting them for black sesame seeds in a dessert.

Sumac

Ground from the beautiful fuchsia-hued berry of the same name, sumac, has a tanginess reminiscent of sour citrus. Arab and Israeli chefs, particularly in the Galilee region in Northern Israel, find multiple uses for its pleasing pucker, from soups and kebabs to a colorful flourish on my dips and spreads.

A Few Other Notes

Salt

Kosher salt, named for its original use—koshering meat—is my standard salt throughout this book. I prefer Diamond and have designed my recipes to use it. If you use Morton, cut the amount in half wherever it is called for.

Yeast

The two types of yeast commonly used in Israel are fresh, which come in little cubes you crumble or as instant-dry (rapid-rise) yeast that doesn't need to be "activated" like the active dry yeast common in the United States. Since it's easy to find in the U.S. and very reliable, I use instant (also referred to as rapid-rise or quick-rise) yeast in all my baking recipes. I like to buy the yeast in a jar and keep it in the freezer, where it lasts for at least a year.

Vegetables

I chose to keep this book light on vegetable weights. In cases where it's important, I specify a weight.

Flour

I use unbleached all-purpose flour as my basic go-to for all baking recipes. If you like to weigh your flour, use 130 grams (4.6 ounces) per cup as your guide. I measure my flour using the simple scoop-and-level method: Scoop out of the bag using a tablespoon and shake it into your measuring cup, being sure not to pack it down. Keep scooping and shaking until the measuring cup is slightly overflowing. Then use a knife to "level" the measuring cup.

Salt-Brined Dill Pickles

My favorite pickles in the whole wide world are the small, canned, salt-brined Israeli pickles made on Kibbutz Yavneh, about an hour south of Tel Aviv. Salty and crispy-briny, they're a staple in falafel and sandwich stands all over the country. But since the flavor of those is hard to re-create—they're factory-canned under pressure—I reverted to a super-simple, salty, dilly pickle that you can scale up to make as many as you like; this recipe yields enough pickles for a small crowd, but you can increase the recipe amounts and vessel size all the way up to the impressive 5-gallon jar I filled and photographed here. Using filtered water for pickling prevents the garlic from turning blue, which can happen when trace metals in some tap water react with components in the garlic. Feel free to improvise, adding more garlic, dried chilies, and spices if you like. To facilitate proper pickling, it's important to keep the pickles completely submerged in the liquid; you can buy glass fermentation weights on Amazon, or lodge a small, nonreactive bowl on top of the pickles to keep them from bobbing above the surface.

12 to 14 small Persian or Kirby cucumbers (1¼ pounds)	1 dried hot red chili pepper, such as chile de arbol	½ teaspoon whole black peppercorns
5 peeled garlic cloves	1 bay leaf	½ teaspoon mustard seeds
3 dill sprigs	¼ cup kosher salt	½ teaspoon coriander seeds
		Filtered water

Makes
12 to 14 pickles

Active Time:
10 minutes

Total Time:
3 days

Scrub the cucumbers under warm water to remove any excess wax or dirt, place them in a large bowl, cover them with ice water, and chill for 30 minutes (this helps the pickles stay crisp). Pack the pickles tightly into a clean, wide-mouthed 3-quart glass jar (you can also scale down to smaller jars, as long as the cucumbers will fit) with a tight-fitting lid, preferably with a rubber gasket. Fit the garlic, dill, dried chili, and bay leaf into the jar, finding crevices and pockets between the cucumbers if possible. Sprinkle the salt into the jar, then sprinkle in the peppercorns, mustard seeds, and coriander seeds, moving the jar a bit so they fall into the bottom of the jar.

Fill the jar almost to the top with filtered water and swirl it a bit to dissolve the salt. Top off with water, then try to use a small dish or fermentation weight (see Shopping Guide)—whatever will stay wedged inside the mouth of the jar—to ensure that the pickles are below the water line; this is essential for proper pickling. Seal tightly and let sit on the counter to brine; the pickles will be slightly salty and crisp after 1 day; slightly softer after 2; and soft, funky, and even slightly fermented at 3 days, at which point you can move them to the refrigerator for storage (you can also leave them out for longer if you like really fizzy, salty, fully sour, and softer pickles).

24-Hour Salted Lemon Spread

This little bit of lemony magic (see photo, pp. 20–21) comes courtesy of Jonathan Borowitz, the chef of M25 steakhouse in the shuk. Jonathan serves it on a sexy little plate of spreads and spicy things you can use to dab your burgers, steaks, and other meats. I asked for a little extra to take home so many times, he finally just offered up the recipe for what he calls "pure lemon." Unlike real preserved lemons, which take a minimum of two weeks to "cook" in salt and sunlight, here chopped lemons are salted for twenty-four hours along with garlic and jalapeños, then blended into a chunky-smooth spread that maintains both the bright qualities of fresh citrus and the pleasing bitterness of the rind. I use it on everything from sandwiches and kebabs to Lemony Chili and Tuna Pasta (page 216). Look for smooth, thin-skinned lemons, which have less bitter white pith.

3 large or 4 medium lemons (1 pound), preferably thin-skinned, scrubbed

3 large garlic cloves, thinly sliced

1 small green jalapeño, seeded and chopped (or 2 for a spicier spread)

3 tablespoons kosher salt

2 tablespoons canola or other neutral-flavored oil

Makes
1½ cups

Active Time:
15 minutes

Total Time:
about
24 hours

Trim the tops and bottoms from the lemons and slice each one into 8 wedges, then trim and discard all the visible white membranes from the tips of the wedges and remove and discard the seeds. Cut each wedge crosswise into 3 chunks and toss them in a medium nonreactive bowl along with the garlic, jalapeño, and salt. Cover and refrigerate for 24 hours, tossing every 8 hours if you can. Transfer the contents of the bowl to the bowl of a food processor and puree with the canola oil until just about smooth, 30 seconds to 1 minute. Stored in an airtight container, the 24-Hour Salted Lemon Spread will keep in the fridge for up to 1 month.

Cardamom-Kissed Schug

One of Yemen's greatest contributions to Israeli cuisine, schug (see photo, pp. 20–21) is a riot of tender green herbs, dried spices, and fresh hot chilies blended into an incredibly versatile condiment that is a must smeared inside a falafel sandwich or on my Schug-Marinated Baby Lamb Chops (page 250). Almost twenty years ago my friend Gil Hovav, who is half Yemenite, first let me in on the genius idea of adding cardamom, and it's been my ace in the hole ever since. Chilies can really vary in their spiciness; really hot ones will yield a three-alarm schug, but after a day or two in the fridge the heat begins to mellow slightly. Some schugs contain a lot of oil, but this one is almost all veg and spice. The small amount of oil in the recipe (not to mention a bit of lemon juice) helps the schug preserve its color and last longer, especially before it's broken into for the first time. Don't worry; even if the schug darkens in the jar, and though it may fade in flavor slightly, it's still good for up to a month.

2 cups tightly packed fresh cilantro, leaves and tender stems

2 cups tightly packed fresh parsley, leaves and tender stems

20 garlic cloves (about ⅔ cup)

10 to 12 medium jalapeños (about 6 ounces) or 6 to 8 medium serrano peppers, stemmed and coarsely chopped but not seeded

2 teaspoons kosher salt

2 teaspoons ground cumin

2 teaspoons ground cardamom

2 teaspoons freshly ground black pepper

2 teaspoons freshly squeezed lemon juice

1 tablespoon extra-virgin olive oil, plus more to cover

Makes
2 cups

Active Time:
15 minutes

Total Time:
25 minutes

In the bowl of a food processor, combine the cilantro, parsley, garlic, jalapeños, salt, cumin, cardamom, black pepper, and lemon juice and pulse 15 to 20 times, then process until smooth, about 1 minute, stopping and scraping down the bowl once if necessary. The mixture may seem a bit pulpy at first, but it will come together. If you need to, add water by the tablespoonful to get the contents of the processor running. Drizzle in the olive oil and pulse very briefly. Transfer the schug to one 2-cup jar with a tight-fitting lid (or two 1-cup jars with tight-fitting lids) and cover with a very thin slick of olive oil. Stored in the refrigerator, schug lasts for up to 1 month.

40-Minute Amba

Brought to Israel by Iraqi Jews who had originally become familiar with pickled mangoes while living in India, amba (see photo, pp. 20–21) has earned a place of pride as the weirdest, most delicious condiment on the falafel bar. With a slick viscosity (courtesy of fenugreek) and a yellow hue (thanks to turmeric) that can vary from sunshine yellow to vintage 1970s kitchen and is like nothing else you've ever eaten, amba's distinctive funk is a love-it-or-hate-it proposition. Some recipes call for starting with ripe mangoes, but that gives you a base sweetness you need to counteract with lots more spice and salt; I'm going for maximum amba punch, so I curry extra favor in the shuk by scooping up rock-hard specimens no one else seems to want. I came up with the method to make a great amba in a little more than half an hour; many of the Israeli recipes I've seen call for pickling the unripe fruit days in advance, but my way (and the stealthy addition of fish sauce) allows you to bring almost as much of that distinctive tang to dinner on less than an hour's notice.

1 large or 2 medium completely unripe, green-skinned mangoes, such as Tommy Atkins variety (about 1 to 1¼ pounds)

1 medium onion, finely diced

1½ tablespoons chopped jalapeño, with seeds

2 tablespoons kosher salt, plus more to taste

3 medium garlic cloves, chopped

1 tablespoon ground turmeric

1½ teaspoons yellow mustard seeds

1 teaspoon ground fenugreek

½ teaspoon ground cumin

½ teaspoon sweet paprika

3 tablespoons freshly squeezed lemon juice

1 teaspoon fish sauce

Makes
a generous
2 cups

Active Time:
35 minutes

Total Time:
40 minutes

Peel the mango, discard the peels, and grate on the large holes of a box grater straight into a medium saucepan. Add 2 cups water, the onion, jalapeño, salt, garlic, turmeric, mustard seeds, fenugreek, cumin, and paprika. Bring to a boil, then reduce the heat to medium-low and cook, stirring occasionally, until the mango and onion have softened and the liquid has reduced slightly, adding water by the tablespoonful if the amba seems super thick or on the verge of burning, 20 to 25 minutes. Remove from the heat, cool slightly, and stir in the lemon juice and fish sauce. Transfer the mixture to a blender or the bowl of a food processor. Puree until smooth and glossy, 20 seconds. Stored in an airtight container in the refrigerator, amba lasts for 1 month.

Amba Mayo

To make the luscious spread that goes in my egg salad (page 62), with Shawarma Pargiyot (page 229), and improves almost any sandwich, simply whisk together ¾ cup mayonnaise with ¼ cup 40-Minute Amba (or store-bought amba). Stored in an airtight container in the fridge, it lasts for up to 1 month.

Honey Harissa

Harissa (see photo, pp. 20–21), a fiery-red condiment with roots in the Maghreb (the North African region that includes Nigeria, Tunisia, and Morocco), can vary wildly in heat and flavor. Some are milder and almost fermented in flavor, while others are practically too hot to handle. I like my harissa to get used up, so I make it a little mellower, starting with roasted peppers and adding in roasted garlic and even a drop of honey. That gives you more latitude to use it in sandwiches, mixed into mayo or yogurt, or as a seasoning for a soup or a stew. Of course, if you like your harissa super spicy, just add more dried hot peppers.

5 smallish whole dried hot peppers, such as chiles de arbol

2 large red bell peppers, or 2 whole jarred fire-roasted red peppers,* drained, rinsed well, and patted dry

5 garlic cloves, unpeeled, or 5 cloves Garlic Confit (page 293)

1 teaspoon caraway seeds

1 teaspoon coriander seeds

1 teaspoon cumin seeds

1 teaspoon sweet paprika

2 tablespoons freshly squeezed lemon juice

1 teaspoon honey

1 teaspoon kosher salt

Makes
1½ cups

Active Time:
20 minutes

Total Time:
1 hour
15 minutes

If you're using fresh bell peppers and garlic, preheat the oven to 450°F. Place the whole dried peppers in a bowl, cover with hot water, soak for 30 minutes, then drain and discard the water.

While the chiles are soaking, arrange the peppers on a rimmed baking sheet and roast until puffed and blackened in spots, flipping with tongs halfway through, 25 to 30 minutes total. During the last 10 minutes of cooking, open the oven and throw the garlic cloves on the tray to roast along with the peppers. During the last 5 minutes of roasting, place the caraway seeds, coriander seeds, and cumin seeds on a piece of foil and roast them in the oven until fragrant (check them starting at 3 minutes in case they toast a little ahead of schedule). Remove the spices to cool, then remove the bell peppers and garlic from the oven. Using the tongs, place the bell peppers in a bowl, cover tightly with plastic wrap, and let cool for 30 minutes.

Transfer the caraway, coriander, and cumin to a spice grinder or mortar and pestle and grind until powdery. Uncover the bell peppers. Working over the sink, remove and discard the stems, seeds, and skins (but don't rinse the peppers!). Place the peppers in the bowl of a food processor and squeeze the roasted garlic out of its skins into the bowl along with the ground spices, paprika, soaked hot peppers (hold back on a hot pepper or two at the beginning if you're scared of a lot of spice), lemon juice, honey, and salt. Process until smooth, then transfer to a jar with a tight-fitting lid. Stored in an airtight container, the harissa will keep for up to 10 days.

*If you're starting with jarred peppers and Garlic Confit, simply toast the caraway, cumin, and coriander in a small, dry skillet over medium heat for 3 to 4 minutes, until fragrant, transfer to a plate to cool, and proceed as instructed.

Preserved Lemons

Limon mosif hamon ("lemon adds a lot"), my husband always says, and it's true: The food here just begs for a bright pop of acid, which further brings dishes to life. When lemons are at their peak in the winter months, I hoard and preserve them to last me all summer. My favorites for preserving, a technique that has its origins in Morocco and Tunisia, are small, thin-skinned ones locals call *limon sini*, or Chinese lemons, for reasons that aren't quite clear to me; the skins almost melt when preserved and the resulting preserves are almost like a savory jelly. For your purpose, standard full-sized lemons work really well. Try to find lemons that feel heavy for their size, which indicates lots of juice. Thin-skinned lemons mean less bitter pith to preserve. If you have the time, you can sterilize the jars and tops in boiling hot water, but I've found that washing them well in soapy hot water works just fine.

7 or 8 small lemons (2 pounds), scrubbed, plus additional lemon juice to fill

1 cup kosher salt, or more if needed

Makes
3 cups

Active Time:
20 minutes

Total Time:
2 weeks (includes minimum preserving)

Wash a 24-ounce jar and its lid in soapy water and dry well. Using a sharp knife, cut an *X* shape into each lemon so it is quartered but not cut all the way through; it should look like an open flower that can be closed with the palm of your hand. Working over a bowl, hold one of the lemons in your hand. Pack the salt inside, close it, and fit it into the bottom of the jar. Keep working with the lemons and the salt, fitting the lemons in as tightly as possible. Sprinkle more salt on the lemons as you go along. Juice will start to gush out of the lemons and fill the glass with liquid as you move your way up; this is what you want. Continue salting and packing the lemons until the jar is filled almost to the top with lemons and lemon juice. If you need to, add lemon juice to cover and fill the jar. Seal tightly, place the jar on a plate to catch leaks, and leave out in a sunny place for at least 2 weeks and up to 3 months, flipping the jar occasionally so the salt and lemon juice move around a bit. Transfer to the refrigerator, where the preserved lemons will last for up to 1 year.

To make preserved kumquats (pictured top right): Use the same scoring and salting method used for the lemons above, filling the jar up to the top with lemon juice. Preserve using the same method as above.

To make preserved lime slices (pictured top left): Layer the lime slices with kosher salt in a jar, then fill the jar to the top with fresh lime juice. Preserve using the same method as above.

Preserved Lemon Paste

Just trust me and make this (see photo, pp. 20–21). It's almost like preserved lemon aioli if you blast the blender enough, creamy and salty and just begging to be put on fish (Lemony Salmon with Fennel and Orange Salad, page 264) and sandwiches. Softer preserved lemons work best here.

1 cup Preserved Lemons (2 large preserved lemons, page 38, or store-bought), seeds removed, roughly chopped

1 teaspoon sweet paprika

½ cup extra-virgin olive oil

Makes
1½ cups

Active Time:
5 minutes

Total Time:
5 minutes

Combine the lemons and paprika in a blender or the small bowl of a food processor, turn on the machine, and drizzle in the olive oil until the mixture is creamy and emulsified, 1 to 1½ minutes. If you have a NutriBullet-style blender or attachment, just mix everything together and whirr for about 15 seconds for a super creamy spread; if you want to keep it low-tech, you can just chop the preserved lemons by hand as small as you can, drop them in a bowl, add the paprika, then whisk the olive oil in slowly. It'll be chunkier, and you'll have to whisk again with a fork before using, but it's still delicious.

Tomatoes

So attached are Israelis to their tomatoes that their retail price is considered a bellwether of food inflation. Stirred into soups and stews, sliced into salads, made into sauce—the possibilities, as well as colors as varied as a Pantone wheel, are endless. By far the most popular variety in Israel are small, candy-sweet cherry tomatoes, known here as *aguaniot sherry*. Varieties include the sweet mini Tamars, a baby version of Roma tomatoes, which also come full-sized; *eshkolit* ("grapefruit"); the standard round cherry tomato; Maggie, the Rolls-Royce of tomatoes with their super-red hue and concentrated tomatoey flavor; and lycopene or *menumar* ("leopard"), named after a small version of what Americans know as Tiger cherry tomatoes. Many are grown in hothouses, guaranteeing year-round consistency. Beefsteaks and funky heirlooms are only starting to gain traction here and are usually available only through CSAs (community-supported agriculture) and friends with home gardens.

Roasted Sheet Pan Cherry Tomatoes

In our house, we call the copious amount of cherry tomatoes, or *agvaniot*, we consume our "daily kilo," and aside from snacking on them or throwing them into salads, this is what I do with them the most. An olive oil–splashed roast in a hot oven yields a kitchen staple with a thousand applications, whether as a topper for Labaneh (page 44) or a star turn in Roasted Tomato and Labaneh Pappardelle (page 214).

2 pounds (6 cups) cherry tomatoes, rinsed and dried

2 tablespoons extra-virgin olive oil

½ teaspoon kosher salt, plus more to taste

¼ teaspoon freshly ground black pepper

Makes
3 cups

Active Time:
5 minutes

Total Time:
25 minutes

Preheat the oven to 425°F.

Dump the tomatoes on a large rimmed baking sheet, drizzle with the olive oil, and sprinkle with the salt and pepper. Give the baking sheet a shake to coat the tomatoes. Roast until the tomatoes are shriveled and some of the juice releases onto the pan, 20 to 25 minutes (you don't want to take these too far because then that juice will evaporate, and basically that juice adds the essence of tomato flavor straight from the heavens into anything it touches). Allow the tomatoes to cool, and make sure to scrape up and use the slightly jellied juices that collect on the pan.

Note

To use as a hummus topping (see cover for a pic): Spoon 1 cup of the finished roasted tomatoes and their juices over 2 cups prepared hummus of your choice. Top with toasted pine nuts and serve with Cardamom-Kissed Schug (page 35).

Labaneh

I always keep thick, tart labaneh, or strained yogurt, in my fridge to spread it on a plate underneath roasted vegetables (Lemony Cauliflower over Labaneh, page 126), for instance, or even to enhance desserts like my Labaneh Malabi Panna Cotta (page 334). Here in Israel, you can buy it by weight from the cheese monger, purchase it in prepackaged tubs, or—best of all—easily make it at home, which has several advantages. For one thing, you get to control what goes in the labaneh and how you season it (I keep it simple with salt). All you do is mix up the ingredients, tie them up in a clean cloth, and hang it over a bowl where it drips to your preferred level of viscosity depending on how long you let it drip, drip, drip. What's surprising is just how much of yogurt is actually water; try different brands of yogurt to see which works best for you and how much liquid emerges from each type. Though most labanehs call just for yogurt, my friend and colleague Tressa Eaton's mother-in-law, Roni Darom, adds a bit of sour cream, which lends extra creaminess; feel free to do so, or to just use more yogurt.

4 cups whole-milk yogurt

½ cup sour cream (optional), or more yogurt

1 tablespoon kosher salt, or more to taste

Extra-virgin olive oil (optional), for labaneh balls

Makes
1¾ to 2 cups

Active Time:
10 minutes

Total Time:
minimum
4 hours,
maximum 24

If you are hanging the labaneh, find your hanging spot and make sure there's room underneath it for a bowl to collect the drippings (unless you are hanging it directly over a sink or shower, which also works). If you are straining the labaneh over a bowl, fit an 8- or 10-inch mesh colander over a bowl and line it with a linen or flour sack kitchen towel or three layers of heavy-duty paper towels. In a large bowl whisk together the yogurt, sour cream (if using), and salt until smooth. Pour the yogurt mixture onto the cloth, gather up the edges, and tie them into a knot. Strain over the colander into the bowl, or hang on a hook over a bowl or sink until you achieve the desired texture (all of this is done at room temperature, not in the fridge).

4-Hour Labaneh: For looser labaneh, like the one I use in Labaneh Malabi Panna Cotta (page 334), strain for 4 hours.

8-Hour Labaneh: For thicker labaneh similar in texture to thick Greek yogurt and ideal for spreading under salads like Lemony Cauliflower over Labaneh (page 126), strain for 8 hours.

12-Hour Labaneh (pictured facing page, top right): To achieve something akin to thick cream cheese, or if you're making labaneh balls (see below), go anywhere from 12 to 24 hours.

To make labaneh balls (pictured facing page, bottom right): Roll the 12- to 24-Hour Labaneh into 1-inch balls (roll in za'atar if desired). Arrange in a clean jar, cover with olive oil, and seal with a tight-fitting lid. Stored in the refrigerator in an airtight container, labaneh keeps for 2 weeks; labaneh balls keep for 1 month.

Six Things to Do with Labaneh

Labaneh's tangy versatility works beautifully underneath simple preparations both savory and sweet. These are just six of the countless ways you can go here. I like to use the 8-Hour Labaneh here, but if you like a looser consistency by all means use the 4-Hour version.

Crispy Artichoke Hearts

Tahini Caramel, Berries, and Nuts

Warm ¼ cup Tahini Caramel (page 320) or store-bought caramel sauce with 1 tablespoon milk to thin slightly; cool to room temperature. Drizzle labaneh with caramel and top with sliced strawberries and roasted mixed nuts.

Caramelized Pineapple with Sumac

Dredge 1 cup thinly sliced pineapple in sugar. Caramelize in a skillet over medium-low heat until golden, 3 to 4 minutes per side. Add 2 tablespoons butter and swirl to melt; brown slightly. Cool and spoon over labaneh; sprinkle with sumac.

Beets, Beet Greens, and Black Quinoa

Separate greens and stalks from 4 small beets. Wrap beets in foil; roast at 400°F for 90 minutes; cool, peel, and quarter. Sauté thinly sliced garlic and beet stalks in olive oil until soft; add beet greens, a splash of water and salt; sauté until wilted. Top labaneh with cooked quinoa, beets, and greens.

Wild Mushrooms and Thyme

Heat a dry, heavy skillet over medium-high heat. Sear 1½ cups mixed wild mushrooms (don't crowd the pan) until charred and slightly wilted, 7 to 8 minutes. Add olive oil or butter, salt, pepper, and a thyme sprig and warm through. Spoon onto labaneh; garnish with thyme.

Crispy Artichoke Hearts

Quarter 4 whole, cleaned baby artichoke hearts (inner leaves attached) or canned or marinated artichoke hearts; pat them dry. Deep fry in vegetable oil until crispy and golden, 4 to 5 minutes. Drain on paper towels. Season with salt and pepper; serve over labaneh. Drizzle with olive oil and garnish with parsley.

Roasted Tomatoes

Spoon warm Roasted Sheet Pan Cherry Tomatoes (page 42) over labaneh.

Roasted Tomatoes

Beets, Beet Greens, and Black Quinoa

Tahini Caramel, Berries, and Nuts

Wild Mushrooms and Thyme

Caramelized Pineapple with Sumac

Pomegranate Molasses

Though you first start seeing them in the market as early as July, peak pomegranate season typically begins around Rosh Hashanah, the Jewish new year—usually in September—and lasts through January. By then the fruit, some type of which has been grown in these parts for thousands of years, is bursting with plump seeds, with every last one yielding a deep reddish, mildly tannic, and perfectly sweet-tart, earthy juice. Pomegranates represent many things in the Jewish tradition—fertility and abundance among them—and in the shuk, selling the juice is a year-round business. When the fruit is in peak season, the savviest vendors extract gallon after gallon of juice, freeze it, then defrost it to sell and serve until another year's worth of their most precious commodity arrives.

To evoke the essence of pomegranates year-round, make or buy pomegranate molasses; a small drizzle adds sweet-and-sour acidity wherever it's used. If you're buying, look for a pure product without artificial coloring; sometimes, if it's too brilliantly purplish-red, it may be too good to be true. I make my own, starting with (ideally) fresh or bottled pure pomegranate juice with a little honey added. The honey helps balance and round out the texture, since the juice needs time to slowly evaporate without burning.

4 cups pure pomegranate juice   2 tablespoons honey

Makes
1 scant cup

Active Time:
5 minutes

Total Time:
55 to
60 minutes

In a small (2- or 3-quart) saucepan, whisk the pomegranate juice and honey together. Bring to a low boil over medium-high heat, then boil until the syrup is reduced to 2 cups (I like to keep a measuring cup nearby and quickly pour the syrup in to gauge the volume), about 20 minutes. Reduce the heat to medium-low and let simmer, stirring occasionally, until the molasses begins to thicken and small bubbles form all over the top (this is how you know you're getting somewhere). Reduce the heat a little more and continue to simmer until the liquid is visibly thickened but not as thick as honey (it will thicken as it cools); the bubbles will become foamy and small—this is how you know you're just about ready.

Turn off the heat and slip a spoon into the molasses; it will still drip off the spoon, but if you run your finger over the back of the spoon, a distinct stripe will form. Transfer to a jar to cool. Stored in an airtight container, pomegranate molasses will last for up to 6 months.

BREAKFAST

It's unclear when Israeli breakfast became an institution, but its hearty yet healthy-ish stick-to-your-ribs ethos harkens back to the early days of Israel, when immigrants on kibbutzim (collective agricultural communities) needed fuel to power long days of physical labor. What's so fun about this meal is how customizable it is. There's usually some form of egg involved, several cheeses, olives, bread, jam, and coffee, but beyond that, the rest is up to you. Craving tahini swirled with silan? Go ahead, make a little bowl of it. Cheese sprinkled with za'atar and olive oil? Sure! One of my favorites is the classic breakfast pictured on pages 50–51: a simple omelet, slightly overcooked and flipped in the pan (sorry, Jacques Pépin), some crusty bread, delicious jam, butter, soft white cheese, fresh-squeezed juice, and, of course, a milky coffee. But there are so many ways to put your spin on the first meal of the day, all of them resulting in a good morning, or what Israelis call a *boker tov*.

Zucchini, Dill, and Feta Shakshuka

Believed to be translated from the Tunisian word for "shaken up," shakshuka started out as a breakfast dish for laborers, who would scoop up the saucy eggs, their yolks cooked all the way through, into pitas for a handheld breakfast. You can still find this kind of steam-table fare at some old-school joints and hotel breakfast buffets, but somewhere along the way restaurants and home cooks alike realized they had a winner on their hands: Freshly prepared tomato sauce is a willing canvas for whatever its maker chooses to add to it. Now there's hardly a restaurant in Israel that doesn't have it on the menu, or a home cook without a highly personal version. Everyone thinks their version of shakshuka is the undisputed best, and I would argue that each one is; shakshuka is a dish designed to make a cook look good. There's a forgiving, hard-to-mess-up sauce and a single-skillet presentation that's festive yet overridingly casual. In our house, we often have a skillet of "shak" sauce cooked and ready to rumble. That way, when friends come over (or Jay wakes up), we rewarm the sauce and crack in the eggs, and breakfast is practically ready. People generally leave the yolks a little runny, but do as you wish; by making shakshuka, you've already won breakfast—or, sometimes, lunch or dinner.

¼ cup extra-virgin olive oil, plus more for drizzling

1 medium zucchini, thinly sliced into rounds

Kosher salt and freshly ground black pepper to taste

1 medium onion, finely diced

1 large red bell pepper, seeded and chopped

3 large garlic cloves, thinly sliced

3 tablespoons tomato paste

1 teaspoon ground cumin

1 teaspoon sweet paprika

1 teaspoon ground coriander

¼ teaspoon cayenne pepper, or more to taste

6 medium very ripe fresh tomatoes, finely chopped by hand, or pureed in the bowl of a food processor if you like smoother shakshuka

One 14.5-ounce can crushed tomatoes

1 small, fresh, finely diced red jalapeño, plus more to taste and for serving

¼ cup chopped fresh dill, plus more for garnish

6 large eggs

1 cup (4 ounces) crumbled feta cheese

Pita or other bread, for serving

Serves 4

Active Time:
20 minutes

Total Time:
1 hour

Set a rack in the top third of the oven. Heat 2 tablespoons of the olive oil in a large oven-safe skillet over medium-high heat. Add the zucchini, season in the pan with some salt and black pepper, and cook, not stirring too much, until the zucchini has released its water and is golden and slightly charred around the edges, 3 to 4 minutes per side. Transfer to a plate.

Add the remaining 2 tablespoons oil to the skillet, then add the onion and bell pepper and cook, stirring, until the onion is lightly golden and softened but not too dark, 9 to 10 minutes. Add the garlic and cook 1 more minute. Add the tomato paste, cumin, paprika, coriander, and cayenne and cook, stirring, until the mixture is fragrant and the tomato paste is slightly caramelized, 2 minutes. Add the fresh tomatoes, canned tomatoes, and jalapeño. Bring to a boil, then reduce the heat to a simmer and cook until the sauce has darkened and thickened slightly, 20 to 25 minutes; season with additional salt and black pepper to taste.

RECIPE CONTINUES

Preheat the broiler during the last 5 minutes of cooking.

Stir in the dill and return the zucchini to the pan, stirring gently. Use a spoon to form 6 wells in the sauce, then crack an egg into each well. Sprinkle the feta around the skillet and cook for 3 minutes. Transfer the shakshuka to the oven and broil until the top of the sauce is slightly caramelized and the whites of the eggs are just opaque but the yolks are still runny, 2 to 3 minutes. Remove from the oven (use an oven mitt since the handle will be hot), top with fresh chopped dill and more jalapeño, and serve immediately, or cool to room temperature and serve, sandwich-style, stuffed into pitas or piled on top of bread.

Variations:

Cook 4 ounces of sliced merguez sausage along with the onions and peppers (omit the feta cheese if you're kosher).

——

In place of the dill, add ½ cup chopped mixed fresh herbs of your choice (basil, parsley, cilantro, etc.).

——

Drizzle tahini all over the top of the shakshuka.

——

Creamy Green Shakshuka with Crispy Latkes

I shop the shuk for produce the way some scour racks for clothes, poring over a table of greens for the frilliest kale, the chard with the loveliest shade of green, the spinach with the most beautiful tapered blossoms. I end up with arms so full that I get home and start cleaning and separating leaves from stems, eager to cook down the bounty so the rest can fit, albeit tightly, in the fridge. A great vehicle for this bounty is a skillet of green shakshuka, which always seems like a great idea in theory, but in practice has some technical issues: I wanted my green shakshuka base to hold together like a sauce the way its cousin, red shakshuka, does, almost becoming one with the eggs. I found my solution in an American steakhouse side: creamed spinach. By adding half-and-half to the cooked greens, it brings them together, taking on the earthy flavor of the vegetables while adding a little sweetness and creaminess. I took it a step further, making latkes that serve as the ideal landing spot for those golden yolks and sauce. You can make the sauce, cover it, move on to the latkes, and then, while they're frying to a crisp, warm the sauce, add the eggs, and finish the shakshuka.

GREEN SHAKSHUKA

⅓ cup extra-virgin olive oil

1 large onion, finely diced

3 large garlic cloves, thinly sliced

1 pound (about 16 cups) roughly chopped stemmed mixed green leaves (such as kale, spinach, chard), from 1½ pounds unstemmed mixed greens

¼ cup vegetable broth

1 cup packed mixed fresh herbs (parsley, cilantro, basil), finely chopped

1 teaspoon chopped fresh thyme, za'atar, or oregano

1 tablespoon finely chopped jalapeños

1 teaspoon kosher salt

¼ teaspoon freshly ground black pepper

⅛ teaspoon freshly grated nutmeg, plus more to taste

½ cup half-and-half (or ¾ cup if you're feeling the creamed-spinach vibe)

8 large eggs

CRISPY LATKES

2 very large Russet potatoes (2 pounds), scrubbed

1 medium onion

2 large eggs

½ tablespoon kosher salt

1 teaspoon freshly ground black pepper

½ cup vegetable oil

○○○○○○○○○○○

**Serves
4 to 6**

Active Time:
1 hour
15 minutes

Total Time:
1 hour
15 minutes

○○○○○○○○○○○

Set a rack in the top third of the oven.

Make the shakshuka: In a 12-inch oven-safe skillet heat the olive oil over medium heat. Add the onions and cook, stirring, until lightly golden, 9 to 10 minutes. Add the garlic and cook, stirring, 1 more minute. Raise the heat to medium-high, then add the greens in batches, stirring as they wilt and release most of their liquid, 2 to 3 minutes per batch (you don't want the greens to be completely dead, but they should have slumped and reduced in size significantly). Add the vegetable broth and cook until mostly absorbed. Stir in the mixed herbs, thyme, jalapeño, salt, pepper, and nutmeg.

RECIPE CONTINUES

Preheat the broiler.

Reduce the heat on the stove to medium-low, stir in the half-and-half, and simmer until the mixture unifies and thickens slightly, 1 to 2 minutes (at this point you can turn off the heat, cover the mixture, and make the latkes). Use a spoon to hollow out eight small wells for the eggs, and crack the eggs into the wells. Cook for 3 minutes, then transfer to the oven and cook until the whites are just opaque but the yolks are still runny, 2 to 3 minutes. Serve over latkes.

Make the latkes: Fill a large bowl with cold water. Using the large holes on the side of a box grater (or a food processor fitted with the shredder attachment), grate the potatoes and onions, transfer them to the water, and let them sit for 5 minutes. Place a clean kitchen towel on the counter near the sink. Pull the potatoes and onions out of the water, squeeze out as much water as you can back into the bowl, and let the water settle. Dump the potatoes and onions onto the towel, fold the towel over the mixture, and squeeze out and discard as much of the liquid as you can from the potatoes and onions. Gently drain the water out of the large bowl, tipping out all the water but leaving the white potato starch at the bottom. Add the squeezed potatoes and onions to the sludge in the bowl, then add the eggs, salt, and pepper and stir it all together.

Meanwhile, heat ¼ cup of the vegetable oil in a 10-inch skillet over medium heat (don't worry, they'll still crisp, without burning). Two or three at a time, spoon the mixture into the pan ⅓ cup at a time into 4-inch-round, ½-inch-thick latkes, pressing down gently, and fry until each side is golden and crisp, 3 to 4 minutes per side. Repeat with the remaining batter and oil; drain latkes on paper towels. Serve with the green shakshuka.

Israeli Cheeses

In a place described in the Bible as the "land of milk and honey," it's no surprise that Israelis eat a lot of cheese. For such a small country, there is a rich and robust cheese industry, both from large companies and small-batch producers. Whether mild and spreadable or salty and crumbly, there are enough delicious fresh cheeses to try something new every day for a month.

Breakfast is the classic meal for indulging in the country's huge variety of fresh and semi-hard cheeses, but they're used in dishes for every meal of the day.

Feta, which can range from crumbly to creamy, can be made with a variety of cheeses (sheep, goat, cow). Ha Me'iri, a sheep's milk feta, is a little creamier and less salty, made by the same family in the northern Israeli city of Safed (Tzfat in Hebrew) for more than 150 years. It's great pulled apart into pieces for use on sandwiches.

Salty, creamy-yet-crumbly **Bulgarian** cheese is great on salads and as a traditional filling for *borekitas*, Balkan filled pastries with flaky dough. The best Bulgarian cheese, available at better cheese shops in Israel, is Pinchas brand, made from cow's milk.

Jibneh and **Nabulsi** are delicious, slightly rubbery cheeses typical in the Arabic kitchen and used in desserts like knafeh (see page 339). If you can find so-called Syrian cheese in a Middle Eastern market, it's worth trying as a substitute.

Typically sold in a round shape with little raised, braille-like dots on top, **zfatit** (named for the city where it's made, Safed) has a smooth, slightly spongier texture, less dense and less salty than Bulgarian and feta cheeses. It's great in salads. Zfatit is also sold studded with nigella seeds.

You have to love a country where the lowest acceptable fat level in a container of **cottage cheese**, or just cottage, as it's referred to here, is 3%, with the dial easily moving up to 9%. Every Israeli home has a tub in the fridge, but unlike its American counterpart, it's not considered diet food. Cottage cheese here is creamy, with large curds and a good amount of salt.

Similar to German quark, *g'vina levana* ("white cheese") is creamy, tart, and smooth. It can be served alone as a savory, yogurt-like cheese or, more famously, in a less-sweet (but no less delicious) Israeli cheesecake (Fluffy Israeli Cheesecake with Fresh Plum Compote, page 323).

Sort of a cross between yogurt and buttermilk, **eshel**, cheap and nostalgic, is great with some chopped cucumbers or dates. To approximate eshel at home, combine two-thirds Greek yogurt with one-third buttermilk.

Thick and rich, *g'vinat shamenet* ("sour cream") comes in three fat percentages: 9%, 15%, and a whopping 27%. To give you an idea of how indulgent Israeli sour cream is, the average full-fat American sour cream contains 8% fat. The 15% and 27% fat cheeses are often used in baking and also ably do duty as a rich base for dips.

Labaneh is typically nothing more than yogurt and salt, strained to optimal thickness for a rich eating experience. Labaneh can be made with goat's, sheep's, or cow's milk cheese. In a break from tradition, I add a small amount of sour cream to my homemade labaneh (page 44) for richness.

Mini Sandwiches: Amba Egg Salad and Preserved Lemon-Date Tuna Salad

I'm an early riser—a watch-the-sunrise, shuk-not-open-yet kind of gal. By the time six thirty or seven rolls around, I need my "gateway breakfast," a mini-meal to tide me over until people with more normal sleeping patterns wake up and I can move on to the second first meal of the day. Thank goodness for little sandwiches that satisfy without sending me back to bed for a nap. I find them in great cafés that open early, seemingly just for me. They're almost always savory, filled with a tiny folded omelet, avocado, cheese, or—my two favorites—egg or tuna salad. Israel is not a canned-white-tuna land. Look for olive oil–packed, line-caught tuna, then load it up with bits of date, chopped preserved lemon, toasted nuts, and spice. Shredding eggs on a box grater makes my egg salad, mixed with Amba Mayo (page 36), light and fluffy. Make both salads in big quantities so you'll have enough for a few days, not to mention a third breakfast in a pinch.

AMBA EGG SALAD

⅓ cup Amba Mayo (page 36) or regular mayo

½ teaspoon kosher salt, plus more to taste

¼ teaspoon freshly ground black pepper, plus more to taste

6 large hard-boiled eggs*

2 tablespoons chopped fresh chives

PRESERVED LEMON-DATE TUNA SALAD

Two 5-ounce cans olive oil-packed tuna, lightly drained

½ cup finely chopped toasted almonds

½ cup finely chopped pitted Medjool or Deglet Noor dates (page 85)

3 scallions (white and green parts), finely chopped

2 tablespoons finely chopped Preserved Lemons (page 38)

2 tablespoons mayonnaise

1 teaspoon finely chopped hot red chili peppers

Zest and juice of ½ large lemon

½ teaspoon kosher salt, plus more to taste

½ teaspoon freshly ground black pepper, plus more to taste

TO ASSEMBLE

8 small seeded rolls

4 lettuce leaves

Tomato, cucumber, and radish slices

○○○○○○○○○○

Makes
8 sandwiches
(4 of each
variety)

**Active Time
(for both
salads):**
1 hour

Total Time:
1 hour

○○○○○○○○○○

Make the egg salad: In a large bowl, whisk together the mayonnaise, salt, and black pepper. Using the large-holed side of a box grater, grate the eggs directly into the bowl. Stir in the chives and season with salt and pepper to taste. Chill until ready to use.

Make the tuna salad: In a large bowl, combine the tuna, almonds, dates, scallions, preserved lemon, mayonnaise, chilies, lemon zest, and lemon juice. Add salt and black pepper, plus more to taste as needed. Chill until ready to use.

Assemble the sandwiches: Layer the egg or tuna salad on rolls with lettuce and slices of tomato, cucumbers, and radish.

*To hard-boil eggs, place eggs in a medium saucepan, cover with 2 inches heavily salted water, bring to a rolling boil, boil for 1 minute, turn off the heat, cover, and let sit for 10 minutes. Gently crack the eggs, drop them into a very cold ice-water bath, and cool for 5 minutes. Peel under cold water.

Kubaneh Bread with All the Fixings
(Weekend Project Alert!)

Once you make this magically fluffy, buttery bread, you'll understand why patience is a virtue. A cross between brown bread and brioche, kubaneh is designed to sidestep the prohibition against cooking on the Sabbath; the dough is prepared on Friday, then slow-baked overnight, permeating the whole house with the irresistible aroma of caramelized yeast and dough. I first discovered kubaneh while working on a story for the now-departed *Gourmet* magazine, when my research took me to the Tel Aviv suburb of Rosh HaAyin, where many Yemenite Jews settled after being airlifted to Israel in the years immediately following the founding of the modern state in 1948. I had tried several other Yemenite breads, including jachnun, a dense log of sweet, oily dough; pan-fried, flaky malawach; and lachuch (page 74), all of which have become comfort-food staples in Israel. But this one, introduced to me by sisters-in-law Ilana Tzana'ani and Daphna Sa'ad, was different. To make the bread, the dough is risen twice, divided, spread out gossamer-thin, lavished generously with softened butter, then rolled and shaped into snails that are sealed snugly into a tightly lidded vessel for a long and lazy overnight bake in the oven. My favorite way to eat it is to peel the eggs, tear off slices of bread, and dip them both into a table full of accompanying condiments: hand-grated tomatoes called *resek*, spicy schug, and chilbeh, a whipped fenugreek-and-herb sauce that Yemenites traditionally use to cut through the richness of food.

1 cup (2 sticks) unsalted butter, at room temperature, plus more for greasing

1 cup lukewarm water

⅓ cup sugar

3¼ cups unbleached all-purpose flour, plus more as needed

1 tablespoon instant (rapid-rise) yeast

1½ teaspoons fine sea salt

8 large eggs in their shells, rinsed and dried

1 tablespoon Za'atar Spice Blend (page 28 or store-bought)

Cardamom-Kissed Schug (page 35), for serving

Serves 8

Active Time: 2 hours

Total Time: 11 to 15 hours, depending on length of baking

In a microwave-safe bowl, heat ¼ cup (½ stick) of the butter until just melted, 20 seconds. In the bowl of a stand mixer, whisk together the water, sugar, and the melted butter. In a separate bowl, whisk together the flour, yeast, and salt. Add it to the mixer, fit the mixer with the dough hook, and knead, adding flour by the tablespoonful if needed, until a smooth, glossy, and only slightly sticky dough forms, 5 to 6 minutes. Remove the dough from the bowl, lightly butter the bowl, return the dough to the bowl, turn to coat, and cover with plastic wrap. Let the dough rise in a warm place until doubled in size, 45 minutes to 1 hour, then punch it down and let it rise for another hour.

Preheat the oven to 225°F.

Use a sharp knife to divide the dough into 8 equal pieces and set the remaining ¾ cup (1½ sticks) softened butter next to your work surface. Butter an aluminum kubaneh pot or 9- to 10-inch oven-safe pot with a tight-fitting lid and set aside.

RECIPE CONTINUES

Using about 2 teaspoons of the butter, liberally butter a 15-inch square on your work surface, then scoop up about 1 tablespoon of the butter into your hands and, using your fingers, spread a piece of the dough out into an 11 x 13-inch rectangle, working the butter into the dough as you go. The dough will be quite thin; don't worry if some parts rip or a few holes appear in the dough. Fold the dough lengthwise, then roll up like a jelly roll, then curl it into a snail. Repeat with the other 7 pieces of dough. Nestle them in the buttered pot. Nestle the eggs between the pieces of dough, sprinkle with za'atar, and seal the pot tightly (for extra insurance, cover the pot with foil before you place the lid on top). Bake until golden and fragrant, a minimum of 8 hours and up to 12; the longer you bake it, the darker it will become, and by the end the eggs will be hidden among the dough balls. Serve fresh from the oven, or at room temperature, with the eggs and all the condiments.

Resek (Grated Tomatoes)

Makes 3 cups

| 8 very ripe medium tomatoes (2 pounds) | ¾ teaspoon kosher salt, plus more to taste | Pinch sugar (optional) |

Using a box grater, grate the tomatoes into a bowl, discarding the skins. Add the salt, and a drop of sugar, too, if your tomatoes need a wintertime acidity assist.

Chilbeh (Fenugreek Relish)

Makes 2 cups

| 3 tablespoons ground fenugreek | 1 cup lightly packed fresh parsley leaves | 2 teaspoons Cardamom-Kissed Schug (page 35), or more to taste |
| 2¼ cups very cold ice water | 1 tablespoon freshly squeezed lemon juice | ½ teaspoon kosher salt |

In a medium bowl, stir the fenugreek with ¾ cup of the ice water. Soak for 20 minutes, letting the fenugreek settle to the bottom. After 20 minutes, drain as much water as you can from the bowl and repeat 2 more times so the fenugreek has soaked for a total of 1 hour. Place the fenugreek seeds and parsley in a blender or food processor. With the motor running, slowly drizzle in the remaining ¾ cup ice water and blend on high until the mixture is light and fluffy, stopping and scraping down the sides of the blender if necessary, 45 seconds to 1 minute. Add the lemon juice, schug, and salt and blend an additional 5 to 10 seconds. Store in an airtight container in the refrigerator for up to 5 days.

Golden Gravlax with Creamy Cucumber Salad

One of my favorite Friday shuk routines is stopping by Merkaz Hadagim to buy herring in cream sauce, smoked mackerel, and lox. I love watching as the proprietor, Avraham Koren, bends over a worn white cutting board, cuts slices of salmon with a flourish from whole sides that he and his brother cure at their facility nearby. Inspired by them, I've started to make my own at home. Coating the fish with turmeric gives the sliced gravlax a lovely golden edge, and the gentle fennel and dill flavors really come through. It may seem intimidating to do this at home, but once you coat and wrap the salmon, three days' time does the rest of the work for you. Serve this on open-faced sandwiches with all the trimmings.

GRAVLAX

One 2-pound skin-on, center-cut salmon fillet, preferably wild, pin bones removed, patted dry

¾ cup kosher salt

½ cup sugar

1 tablespoon crushed fennel seeds

1 tablespoon crushed black peppercorns

½ cup chopped fresh dill

1½ teaspoons ground turmeric

CREAMY CUCUMBER SALAD

6 medium Persian cucumbers, thinly sliced

1 tablespoon kosher salt, plus more to taste

⅓ cup 4-Hour Labaneh (page 44 or store-bought), or sour cream

2 tablespoons finely chopped fresh dill

1 tablespoon freshly squeezed lemon juice

½ teaspoon freshly ground black pepper, plus more to taste

TO ASSEMBLE

Rye bread

Butter

Store-bought herring

Capers

Makes
1½ pounds cured salmon

Active Time:
30 minutes

Total Time:
3 days

Make the gravlax: Line a large rimmed baking sheet with plastic wrap, leaving a generous overhang on all sides. (If you have larger, restaurant-style plastic wrap, that's great; but if you don't, layer standard-size plastic wrap so you'll eventually be able to tightly seal the salmon.) Pat the salmon dry on both sides.

In a medium bowl, combine the salt, sugar, fennel, and peppercorns. Sprinkle half the salt mixture on the plastic wrap, then sprinkle ¼ cup of the dill over the salt. Press the salmon skin-side down into the mixture so that it adheres.

Sprinkle the top of the salmon with the turmeric, then sprinkle the remaining ¼ cup dill, followed by the rest of the salt mixture, on top of the salmon. Using your hands, spread the mixture evenly over the top and sides. Bring the plastic wrap up around the sides of the salmon and wrap it tightly, wrapping it in one more layer of plastic so that it is tightly sealed. Cover the salmon with another baking sheet, weigh it down with a few heavy cans (a barbell works well, too), and refrigerate for 2 to 3 days.

RECIPE CONTINUES

When ready to use, make the cucumber salad: In a medium bowl, toss the cucumbers with the salt and let sit for 30 minutes. Drain the liquid from the cucumbers, and if you can, squeeze and discard even more excess liquid from the cucumbers with your hands. In a small bowl, whisk together the labaneh, dill, lemon juice, and pepper. Fold the dressing into the cucumbers and season with more salt and pepper to taste.

Finish and serve the salmon: Remove the salmon from the fridge and unwrap it, draining off any excess liquid and carefully scraping the salt mixture from the salmon. Thinly slice the salmon on the bias, cutting the slices away from the skin (the skin will get left behind) and serve with the cucumber salad, herring, rye bread, butter, and capers. The salmon will keep, sealed in plastic wrap, for up to 1 week. The cucumber salad will keep for 3 days.

Pitaquiles

When it comes to the limits of appetite, Israelis are overly optimistic. I'm guessing that's why store-bought pitas come in ten-packs, a few of which are bound to be left over. Once you're past thirty-six hours of purchase, it's either freeze, repurpose, or dispose—in other words, time to get creative. Chilaquiles, that hangover dish of old tortillas crisped and doused in a tangy sauce, hasn't made it to Israel yet; I've rarely even seen a tomatillo in these parts. But I built this dish by starting with a riff on my classic Roasted Sheet Pan Cherry Tomatoes (page 42), brightening them with hot peppers and other elements that allow the sauce to rightfully call Israel home.

3 pitas (do *not* split into 2 rounds each)

¼ cup plus 2 tablespoons extra-virgin olive oil

1 tablespoon Za'atar Spice Blend (page 28 or store-bought), plus more for sprinkling

Kosher salt and freshly ground black pepper to taste

4 cups (1½ pounds) yellow or orange cherry tomatoes

1 medium onion, sliced into thin wedges

5 garlic cloves

1 large whole jalapeño, plus more thinly sliced, for garnish

1 tablespoon freshly squeezed lemon or lime juice

4 large eggs

½ cup (2 ounces) crumbled feta cheese

¼ cup 4-Hour Labaneh (page 44 or store-bought), or Greek yogurt

2 tablespoons chopped fresh cilantro, for serving

Serves 2 to 3

Active Time: 35 minutes

Total Time: 55 minutes

Preheat the oven to 425°F.

Stack the pitas and, using a sharp or serrated knife, slice them in half through the middle, then slice the halves into ½-inch-thick strips crosswise. In a large bowl, whisk together ¼ cup olive oil and the za'atar and add salt and black pepper to taste. Add the pita strips and toss to coat. Arrange them on a rimmed baking sheet and set aside.

Place the tomatoes, onion wedges, garlic, and jalapeño on a large rimmed baking sheet, toss with the remaining 2 tablespoons olive oil, and season generously with salt and black pepper. Roast until the garlic cloves are softened and golden but not burned and some of the tomatoes have burst, 15 to 20 minutes. During the last 6 to 7 minutes of roasting the tomatoes, add the baking sheet with the pita strips to the oven and toast, stirring once midway. Remove both from the oven and cool slightly.

Place the cooled tomato mixture in a blender and add the lemon juice. Blend until smooth and season with salt and black pepper to taste. Place the sauce in a 10-inch skillet and warm over medium heat until bubbling, 2 to 3 minutes. Drop in the pita strips and shake the skillet. Warm the mixture for 3 to 4 minutes.

While the mixture is warming, cook the eggs sunny-side-up in a separate pan. Add the eggs to the skillet with the tomato sauce and pita and top with the feta and dabs of labaneh. Garnish with the cilantro and jalapeño rounds.

Cheesy Asparagus Sheet Pan Pashtida

The catch-all term for a variety of egg-bound casseroles, the word *pashtida* carries with it over a thousand years of Jewish history. In her book *International Savory Pies*, Israeli cookbook writer and food historian Ruth Sirkis traces it all the way back to the Talmud. Later, an agglomeration of terms—the Italian *pasticcio*, Latin *pasticia*, and the French and Dutch *pastate*—were molded into the modern Hebrew word—not that it was so easily welcomed into the Hebrew language. Eliezer Ben-Yehuda, who codified the modern Hebrew language, disliked *pashtidot* and refused to put the word in the first Hebrew dictionary. I make this crustless version of the pashtida, filled with asparagus and both sharp kashkaval—a hard cheese with flavors similar to a sharp white Cheddar—and mellow goat cheese, in a shallow, American-style sheet pan. It cooks quickly and evenly. When I'm having friends over, I leave the tray out at room temperature with a knife and let people cut exactly how much they want.

2 tablespoons extra-virgin olive oil

2 tablespoons unsalted butter, plus more for greasing

1 jumbo or 2 medium onions, diced

2 teaspoons kosher salt

½ teaspoon freshly ground black pepper

16 large eggs

¼ cup heavy cream or half-and-half

1 tablespoon chopped fresh thyme

2 cups (8 ounces) grated kashkaval or sharp white Cheddar cheese

¾ pound asparagus (longer, thinner stalks are preferable), tough ends snapped off and discarded

1 cup (4 ounces) crumbled goat cheese

Makes
15 pieces

Active Time:
40 minutes

Total Time:
1 hour
10 minutes

Grease a 12 x 18-inch rimmed baking sheet with butter and set aside.

Heat the olive oil and butter in a large skillet over medium heat. Add the onions, 1 teaspoon of salt, and ¼ teaspoon of pepper and cook, stirring, until the onions are lightly golden but not charred in any spots, 10 to 12 minutes. Remove the onions from the heat, cool them slightly, then sprinkle the onions evenly over the prepared baking sheet to cool to room temperature, about 10 minutes.

Arrange two racks in the center and top third of the oven and preheat to 300°F.

In a large bowl, whisk the eggs and cream with the thyme and the remaining 1 teaspoon salt and ¼ teaspoon pepper. Scatter 1¾ cups of the kashkaval evenly over the onions, then pour the egg mixture over the cheese, tilting the baking sheet back and forth a bit to evenly distribute the mixture. Arrange the asparagus evenly on top of the mixture however you want to (I like to do them alternating the direction of the tips). Dot with the goat cheese, sprinkle with the remaining ¼ cup kashkaval, and bake until the pashtida is set in most parts, but may have a small wet spot or two, 21 to 23 minutes. Turn on the broiler, move the sheet pan to the top third of the oven, and broil until the top is slightly browned, 1 to 2 minutes. Cut into equal-sized pieces and serve warm or at room temperature.

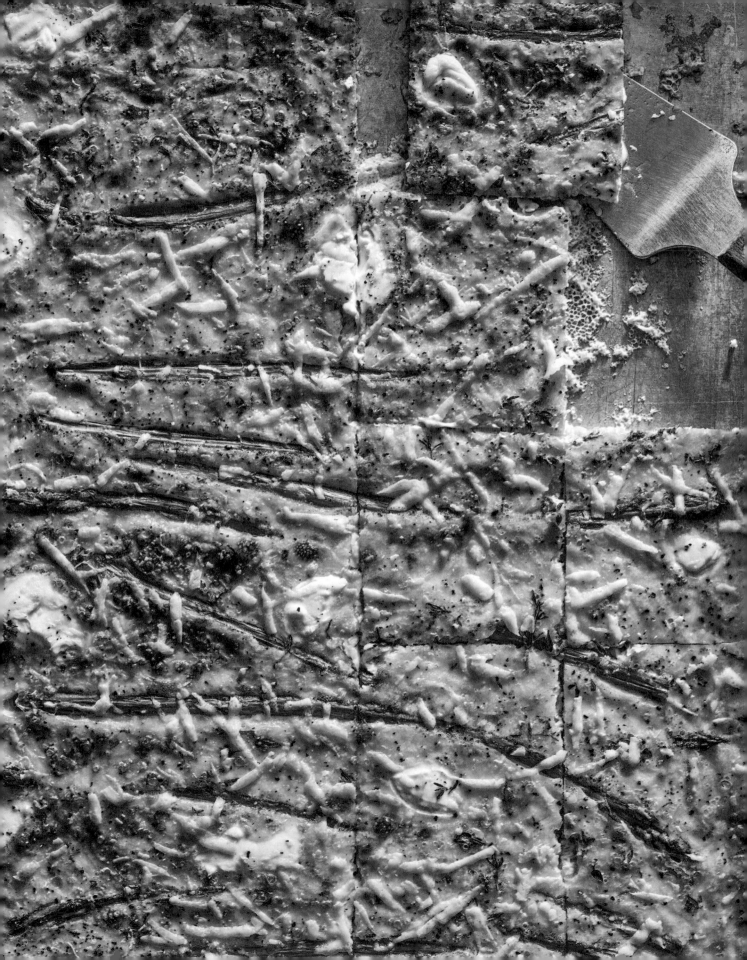

Lachuch (Yemenite Crumpet Pancakes)

Somewhere between a crumpet, a pancake, and an Ethiopian injera, lachuch gets its signature holes from a generous lashing of yeast and a quick ferment. Irit Aharon (opposite, bottom left), who grew up in the Yemenite Quarter and hosts visitors to the shuk for lachuch in a tiny space adjacent to the home she inherited from her Syrian mother and Yemenite father, graciously taught me how to perfect the recipe. If things go according to plan, the batter will cook, drying from the outside in, all the while developing its telltale holes. It's important to cool off the pan between pancakes; a too-hot surface will burn the bottom of the pancake before the top is cooked through. Many of the Yemenite soup joints near my house serve lachuch to mop up rich, spicy broth; for this, make the larger version. I often shrink them down to pancake size and top them with warmed honey and melted butter. Either way, you can't lose.

4 cups all-purpose flour

2 tablespoons instant (rapid-rise) yeast

1 teaspoon ground fenugreek

1 teaspoon baking soda

3¾ cups lukewarm water, plus more as needed

2 teaspoons fine sea salt

Vegetable oil, for cooking

Warmed honey and salted butter, for serving

Makes
10 large or
15 smaller
pancakes

Active Time:
45 minutes

Total Time:
1 hour
30 minutes

In a large, wide-bottomed bowl whisk together the flour, yeast, fenugreek, and baking soda. Slowly whisk in 3½ cups of the water, until the mixture is the thickness of pancake batter. Cover tightly with plastic wrap and rest in a warm place until the batter more than doubles in size, has thickened considerably, and is fluffy and spongy, 35 to 45 minutes. Uncover, gently whisk in the remaining ¼ cup water until the batter is the texture of a thick, pourable milk shake.

Line a large sheet pan with a clean kitchen towel and set aside. Have handy a small bowl filled with vegetable oil. Heat an 8- or 9-inch nonstick skillet over medium-high heat, then use a paper towel to wipe the inside of the skillet with a very thin sheen of oil. Working quickly, and keeping the batter covered between pancakes, ladle or pour ⅓ cup of the batter into the skillet and cook until the batter dries from the outside in and airy holes poke their way through the batter, covering the skillet during the last 30 seconds, 3 to 4 minutes. Slide the lachuch over onto the towel-lined baking sheet. Repeat with the remaining batter, running the pan under cold water and slicking the skillet with a bit of oil between pancakes. Store between pieces of parchment paper, wax paper, or flour sacks for 1 to 2 days (the bread is best eaten fresh and can mold quickly because it's so moist). Serve with a schmear of jam. Top with warm honey and butter.

Note

To make larger pancakes, which are great for mopping up soup or sauce, use ½ cup batter instead of ⅓ cup.

Right: Top, L–R: Yemenite lachuch, finished and in process, in the Yemenite Quarter near the shuk.
Bottom, L–R: Irit Aharon, Lachuch with warm honey and butter

Tahini

Prized for its versatility, nutritional value, and deeply satisfying nutty richness, tahini is something I use practically every day. Tahini is so popular here that Israelis are second only to the Chinese in per capita sesame seed consumption. Ideally made from nothing more than ground sesame seeds, it's Israel's answer to peanut butter but so much more versatile. Here, the best tahini is made in Arab and Palestinian factories with sesame seeds imported primarily from Humera, in Ethiopia, where they're grown in one of the most fertile soil microclimates on earth. To make tahini, sesame seeds are soaked in water (sometimes salted), then crushed so the hull separates from the tender inner germ. The seeds are then run through a centrifuge to separate and dispose of the waste before being roasted and finally ground between huge millstones to produce the tahini virtually every Israeli has in their cupboard. Though it's shelf-stable, the date of production is stamped visibly on many jars. The fresher the tahini, the less likely it is to separate, meaning you don't need to stir it before using. At Amrani, the spice and dry-goods shop I frequent in the shuk (see page 81), Noni, one of the brothers, always looks for the most recent dates for me. "See?" he joked recently on a ninety-degree day as he handed over a jar, "it's still warm."

Tahini and Olive Oil Granola

Olive oil comes in 5-liter jugs; why doesn't tahini? Once I poured some into my salty-to-sweet granola recipe, I never looked back, and you won't, either. It coats every grain with nutty richness and helps keep the mixture from becoming overly sweet. I use olive oil, which can lend a strong flavor depending on the variety you use; I love that assertiveness, but feel free to swap in coconut oil, vegetable oil, or a mixture. And while I love silan (date syrup; for more information, see page 85) here, it can burn resting directly against the sheet pan. So I cut it with maple syrup to make sure the whole tray turns the right shade of golden. In winter, I serve this granola over yogurt with tart pomegranate seeds and citrus; depending on the season, swap in the fresh fruit of your choice.

2½ cups old-fashioned rolled oats

¾ cup chopped pecans, or other nuts of your choice

½ cup finely shredded unsweetened coconut

¼ cup shelled pumpkin seeds (pepitas)

2 tablespoons sunflower seeds

2 tablespoons sesame seeds

⅔ cup pure tahini paste

½ cup extra-virgin olive oil

⅓ cup lightly packed light brown sugar

¼ cup maple syrup

¼ cup silan (date syrup)

2 teaspoons pure vanilla extract

1½ teaspoons fine sea salt

¼ cup chopped dried cherries, cranberries, currants, or barberries*

Yogurt, pomegranate seeds, orange segments, and/or pure tahini, for serving

Makes
5½ cups

Active Time:
10 minutes

Total Time:
1 hour
(includes cooling time)

Preheat the oven to 350°F.

In a large bowl, combine the oats, pecans, coconut, pumpkin seeds, sunflower seeds, and sesame seeds. In a medium bowl, whisk together the tahini, olive oil, brown sugar, maple syrup, silan, vanilla, and salt, then pour over the oat mixture and toss to coat.

Spread the granola in a single even layer on a large rimmed baking sheet. Bake, stirring the outer edges toward the center every 5 minutes (this prevents burning), until golden brown, 20 to 25 minutes, or 5 minutes more for darker, crispier granola. Remove from the oven, let cool completely, break any clumps into smaller pieces, then stir in the dried cherries. Serve in bowls with yogurt, pomegranate seeds, orange segments, and tahini. The granola can be stored in an airtight container for up to 2 weeks.

*If you like your dried fruit softer, leave it out of the recipe and stir it in as you serve the granola. Or bake the dried fruit with the granola; it will caramelize and darken, and if you're anything like me, you will like that.

Shuk Family: The Amranis

So attached am I to the daily routine of visiting Noni and Nachliel (known as Nachli) Amrani at their spices and dry-goods store in the shuk that Jay and I paid them a visit in our wedding-day finery to receive a blessing and a ceremonial sprig of reichan, a type of flowering basil. Two of a brood of eight children who were raised nearby in the Yemenite Quarter, the boys grew up helping their grandfather, Yosef, who built the shop in 1935, and then their father, Yitzchak, make pickles, cure olives, and dry sweet peppers to grind into paprika and sell at the shop. "We were raised here," Nachli told me as he refilled a box of dried lemon verbena. The brothers took over thirty years ago when their father died, but this may be the last hurrah for the family business. Even if their children were interested in taking over, Noni and Nachli are opposed. "In a few years this place may be a boutique more than a shuk," said Nachli, referencing the planned renovations that could change the face of the market. But for now they still do a brisk business. I swing by most days for silan, tahini, rice, or spices, but I really come for the gentle ribbing that makes me feel so welcome. "If an Israeli makes fun of you, it means he likes you," Noni once told me after a particularly blush-inducing teasing. Relics from the past dot the hidden courtyard in the back: Oversized sifters used to sort beans, grains, and nuts line a wall out of sight, as do rusting enamel washbowls. Nearby, an old scoop sits near a pomegranate tree just beginning to blossom with this year's fruit. At this point, they tell me, they're here for their customers, some of whom they've known for sixty years. "This is our life," said Noni. "Besides," he said with a wink, "what else would two guys like us do?"

Everything Beigele

Jerusalem beigele aren't anything like the American bagels I grew up with; they are more bready, sold by Palestinians and Arabs from street carts all over Jerusalem's Old City, sweet and spongy and meant to be eaten very soon after they're made. I adapted the recipe into an American bagel-shaped bread topped with an "everything" spice mixture filled with Israeli twists: dried lemon peel, za'atar, spice, and lots and lots of seeds.

DOUGH

3¾ cups all-purpose flour, plus more as needed

1 cup warm water, plus more as needed

3 tablespoons honey

2 tablespoons extra-virgin olive oil

2¼ teaspoons instant (rapid-rise) yeast

2 teaspoons fine sea salt

EGG WASH AND TOPPING

1 large egg

Pinch of kosher salt

⅓ cup Israeli Everything Spice (page 26)

Makes
6 beigele

Active Time:
30 minutes

Total Time:
2 hours

Line a baking sheet with parchment paper.

Make the dough: In the bowl of a stand mixer fitted with the dough hook, combine the flour, water, honey, olive oil, and yeast and mix on low speed for 3 minutes. Add the salt and continue to mix, adding extra flour or water by the tablespoonful if necessary, until the dough is smooth and pulls away from the bowl (the dough can be slightly sticky), 4 to 5 minutes. Transfer to a floured bowl, cover with plastic wrap, and let rise in a warm place until doubled in size, 45 minutes to 1 hour. Line a baking sheet with parchment. Transfer the dough to a floured surface, use a sharp knife to cut the dough into 6 equal pieces, then form each piece of dough into a ball, tucking the ends underneath and pinching them together gently to help encourage a nice round shape. Place them, evenly spaced, on the prepared baking sheet, cover them with a clean kitchen towel, and let them rest for 30 minutes.

In a small bowl, lightly whisk the egg with a drop of water and the salt.

Bake the beigele: Preheat the oven to 350°F.

Uncover the dough. Using a lightly floured finger, poke a hole in the center of each piece of dough and stretch it into a circle that has a 3-inch hole in the center. Arrange the beigele back on the parchment paper–lined baking sheet, brush the top and sides with egg wash, and sprinkle generously with the spice mix, tilting the sheet to cover as much of the beigele with the spice mix as you can. Place the baking sheet in the oven. Rotate it after 10 minutes of baking. Bake until the beigele are golden, another 9 to 10 minutes. Cool on the baking sheet, and serve immediately. Beigele individually wrapped in plastic can be frozen for up to 3 months, then defrosted and toasted in a toaster oven.

RECIPE CONTINUES

Everything Beigele Breakfast Sandwiches

1 recipe Everything Beigele
(page 82)

Scrambled eggs, for serving

Roasted Sheet Pan Cherry
Tomatoes (page 42) or sliced
fresh tomatoes, for serving

Sliced avocados, for serving

Honey Harissa (page 37
or store-bought), for serving

Chopped fresh chives,
for serving

Slice the beigele horizontally and layer with your favorite scrambled egg recipe, roasted
tomatoes, sliced avocado, harissa, and chopped chives.

Dates and Silan

Date palms and their fruit are almost as ubiquitous in Israel as chickpeas and olive oil, but it wasn't always that way. The Old Testament refers to dates as one of the original seven species grown in the Holy Land, but they disappeared from Israeli soil for centuries until an early kibbutz settler, Ben-Zion Israeli, smuggled date palms into Israel to plant on his property about fifteen years before the War of Independence in 1948. The most treasured variety—fudgy, dense Medjools—were only brought to Israel for planting in the 1970s, in the form of saplings imported from California. Medjools—and even the drier, lighter-colored Deglet Noors—are fresh, chewy, and tender, great for eating out of hand or chopping into salads and even mixing into stews. Most Medjools are grown in the Jordan Valley and the Arava, two hot, southern regions where thousands of acres of land are covered with the majestic trees. In fact, this region has become the center of Medjool cultivation in the world: three out of every four such dates eaten globally are grown in Israel. A third type of dates commonly available here, the Chalawi, hails from Iraq and has the rich flavor of the Medjool with much less moisture, a sort of compromise between a Deglet Noor and a Medjool.

Silan, a deep-mahogany syrup with a pleasing sweetness, is made by boiling Medjool dates with water for a prolonged period of time. The thick, mushy pulp is then strained to yield a viscous liquid that tastes like honey cut with a drop of molasses. If kept sealed in a cool location, silan lasts for a very long time. Experiment with it in place of honey. Just keep in mind that its deep hue will shade your dishes a deeper brown. It also burns a little faster than honey, so make sure to watch it, for instance, when baking Tahini and Olive Oil Granola (page 78).

Tahini Smoothies

With so many incredible juice bars around, it's no wonder you'll find Israelis, cup in hand, sipping on a cool juice or shake at any given hour. This is a riff on the rich, milk- or yogurt-based shakes you'll find on offer for breakfast, lunch, or even dinner in a pinch. If you're a planner, freeze the bananas. Pit the dates and freeze those, too. Swap in any nuts you like, use regular (or any other faux) milk, or yogurt, instead of the almond milk. Other than the frozen banana and the ice, you can load the whole thing into your blender pitcher the night before and refrigerate it. Just don't skimp on the tahini; it's the glue, literally and flavorwise, that holds the whole thing together.

2 cups Date-Sweetened Almond Milk (page 302) or any milk of your choice

1 banana, sliced, frozen if you have time

4 pitted Medjool dates, frozen if you have time

¼ cup pure tahini paste

1 teaspoon pure vanilla extract

Dash of sea salt

Ice

Strawberries, other berries, chopped mango (optional)

Walnuts, cashews, or other nuts (optional)

ooooooooooo

Makes
2 smoothies

Active Time:
5 minutes

Total Time:
5 minutes

ooooooooooo

Combine the almond milk, banana, dates, tahini, vanilla, salt, and as much ice as you like in a blender and blend until smooth; if desired, blend in some optional fruit or nuts for extra richness, sweetness, and color.

BREAD AND SAVORY SNACKS

One of the things I love about Israelis is that Israelis love bread. Far from shunning carbohydrates, this is a nation that makes eating it a part of everyday life. You'll be hard-pressed to find a home without a bag of pitas during the week and a challah bread come the Sabbath, often used as vehicles for transporting Israeli classics like falafel and *salatim* from the plate to the palate. Just a word of warning: Once you make your own challah and pita, you may never go back to store-bought, though rest assured that the act of making bread is almost as much of a pleasure as eating it.

Cast-Iron Skillet Pita

Pita is the stuff of life in Israel. For swiping hummus, stuffing sandwiches, or making a grilled-cheese sandwich in a pinch—nothing beats a fresh round of this gluten-bound cornerstone of Israeli cuisine. You can buy them at every bakery and corner shop, but there's something about watching a pita puff up in your oven that is incredibly satisfying. My stepdaughter Shani's Iraqi father-in-law, Ezra Ovadia, took up bread baking when he retired a few years ago. In addition to delicious challahs and rolls, he makes pita every Friday for his family's rather unconventional Sabbath eve sabich dinner (sabich is typically eaten on Shabbat morning by Iraqi Jews). "His pitas always puff up," Shani told me. "I wonder how." One Friday when we were invited over to Ezra and his wife Carmela's for dinner, he invited me to come early to participate in the pita-making process. After a dough of both all-purpose and whole-wheat flours was risen, separated into balls, rolled out into rounds, and risen again, Ezra plugged in a plastic-handled aluminum contraption I'd never seen before. He placed a disc of dough on one side, and on the other an electric coil glowed. When closed and placed on the stovetop, the pita was heated from both sides, creating the blast of high heat that forced the dough into its signature pocket shape. I wanted to approximate this experience at home without such a machine, or even a pizza stone. Enter the underside of a cast-iron skillet. If you keep it clean, without any oil or burned bits on it, it's the perfect pita-baking surface (as is the flat side of a cast-iron griddle). I have one that I keep separate, expressly for this purpose. And since a good Lodge cast-iron skillet can be purchased for less than $15, you might consider doing the same; you can even do two pitas at a time if you have a 12-inch pan.

---

3 cups all-purpose flour, plus more for shaping

1 cup whole-wheat flour

2 cups warm water

4 teaspoons instant (rapid-rise) yeast

1½ tablespoons sugar

2 tablespoons olive oil

1 tablespoon fine sea salt

Makes
8 pitas

Active Time:
30 minutes

Total Time:
3½ hours

In the bowl of a stand mixer, use a wooden spoon to mix 1 cup of the all-purpose flour, ½ cup of the whole-wheat flour, 1½ cups warm water, the yeast, and ½ tablespoon of sugar. Rest, uncovered, until puffed and foamy, 20 to 25 minutes.

Add the rest of the all-purpose and whole-wheat flours, the remaining ½ cup water, the remaining 1 tablespoon sugar, the olive oil, and the salt. Attach the dough hook and bring the dough together over low speed, then raise the speed to medium and knead the dough until slightly springy but still slightly soft and sticky and pulling away from the side of the bowl, 5 to 6 minutes (add flour by the tablespoonful if needed, but try not to add too much). Remove the dough hook, cover the dough with a clean kitchen towel, and let it rest in a warm place until doubled in size, 45 minutes to 1 hour. Refrigerate the covered bowl for another 45 minutes to 1 hour (this helps develop the flavor and texture of the dough).

RECIPE CONTINUES

Flour a work surface, uncover the dough, gently transfer it to the board, and shape it into a rectangle about 1 inch thick. Use a sharp knife to cut the dough into 8 equal pieces, then form each piece of dough into a ball, tucking the ends underneath and pinching them together gently to help encourage a nice round shape. Cover the dough balls with a clean kitchen towel and let them rise for 30 minutes.

While the dough is rising, take a clean cast-iron skillet or griddle and scrub off any bits stuck to it (these can burn). Arrange a rack about 8 inches from the broiler, invert the skillet, and place it on the rack. Preheat the oven to the highest it will go (500° or 525°, or even 550°F).

Uncover the dough, gently flour each ball, and use a rolling pin to roll the dough into a circle by rolling up and down to form a 6-inch oval. Rotate the oval 90 degrees, then roll the dough again; it should roll into a beautiful 5-inch round. As you roll the dough into rounds, place them on the towel and cover them with another clean towel and let them sit for 10 to 15 minutes, until the pitas have fluffed up to about twice their original height.

Uncover the dough, open the oven, and place one of the rounds flat on the skillet, working quickly and closing the oven so it holds its high temperature. Bake the pita until it's puffed and golden, 2 to 2½ minutes. Using a spatula, remove the pita from the skillet and repeat with the remaining pitas, letting the oven and skillet preheat for a minute or two between pitas (if you have a really large skillet or a long cast-iron griddle, you can do two pitas at a time). Let the pitas cool, then ideally eat while still warm. Once cooled, wrap individual pitas tightly in plastic wrap and freeze for up to 3 months. To serve, defrost, then toast in a toaster oven; heat in a 400°F oven for 3 to 4 minutes; or warm directly over a flame on your stovetop.

Ezra Ovadia's magical pita contraption

Honey and Olive Oil Challah

Sabbath eve dinner is a special time in Israel, one where families get together whether they're religiously observant or not. On a typical Shabbat table two challahs are covered with a cloth, hands are ritually washed and blessed, and then the bread is blessed separately before being cut and shared. This ritual kicks off Shabbat in homes all over the world, and in Israel the whole country exhales a collective sigh as loaves are sliced and eaten and a day of rest commences. There are a thousand challah recipes under the sun, but this is the only one you'll need. It comes courtesy of my friend Uri Scheft, founder of Lehamim and Breads bakeries in Tel Aviv and New York, respectively. Making challah on Friday is one of the purest pleasures of my week, and even more so now that I use Uri's recipe.

He visited my kitchen one day to share his secrets for perfect challah. If you follow the instructions, the recipe is foolproof and solves a lot of the problems challah bakers have. Among many master bakers' tricks, one step—developing the gluten in the flour by tearing it and folding it over for about a minute—sets this dough apart. But even if you let the dough rise a drop too little or too much or your braids are uneven, you will have some of the best challah you've ever tasted: moist and springy, with perfect crumb. The recipe makes three loaves; I like to make two challahs, then use the third piece of dough to create Uri's Za'atar Chili Feta Bread (page 98). You can use any filling you want; use my ingredients as a guideline.

5 teaspoons instant (rapid-rise) yeast

7 cups all-purpose flour, plus more as needed and for shaping

3 large eggs

½ cup sugar

⅓ cup honey

1 tablespoon fine sea salt, plus more for egg wash

⅓ cup extra-virgin olive oil

⅔ cup sesame or poppy seeds, or a combination

Makes
3 challahs
(or 2 challahs
and a
za'atar-feta
twist bread)

Active Time:
25 minutes

Total Time:
2 hours
40 minutes
(including
rising and
cooling)

Make the dough: In the bowl of a stand mixer, whisk the yeast and 1¾ cups room-temperature water together. Attach the dough hook, then add the flour, 2 eggs, the sugar, honey, salt, and olive oil. Mix the dough on low speed to combine the ingredients, then increase the speed to medium and knead until a smooth dough forms, scraping down the sides of the bowl as needed and adding flour by the tablespoonful if the dough feels overly tacky, or water by the tablespoonful if the dough feels overly dry, 4 minutes. Very lightly flour a work surface, transfer the dough from the mixing bowl to the work surface, and use your palms to push and tear the top of the dough away from you in one stroke, then fold that section onto the middle of the dough. Give the dough a quarter turn and repeat the process 15 times. Tuck the ends of the dough underneath to form a ball.

Lightly dust a bowl with flour, add the dough, sprinkle the top with a drop of flour, cover, and rest in a warm place until the dough has almost doubled in size, 45 minutes to 1 hour depending on how hot the room is. Gently lift the dough out of the bowl and transfer it to a very lightly floured work surface, being careful not to deflate it. Pull the dough into a rectangular shape, then use a sharp chef's knife to divide the dough into 3 long pieces.

RECIPE CONTINUES

Take 1 piece of dough, cover it with a kitchen towel, and refrigerate it for another use, like the Za'atar Chili Feta Bread (page 98), while you deal with the challahs.

Cut each of the remaining 2 pieces of dough into 3 smaller equal parts crosswise so you end up with a total of 6 rectangular pieces. Use the palm of your hand to flatten 1 piece of dough into a rectangle. Fold the top portion over and use your palm to press the edge into the flat part of the dough. Fold and press 3 more times until you have a 7-inch-long cylinder. Set this piece aside and repeat with the other 5 pieces so you have 6 cylinders. Roll each cylinder into a 14-inch rope with tapered ends and very lightly flour the long ropes (this helps them look defined during baking). Pinch the ends of 3 ropes together at the top (weigh them down with a can or chef's knife if you like). Braid the dough, lifting each piece up and over so the braid is more stacked than it is long and is fatter and taller at the middle than at the ends. Press and seal the ends together on each. Repeat with the remaining 3 ropes, creating 2 braided challahs.

Place the challahs on parchment paper–lined rimmed sheet pans, cover them with a kitchen towel or loosely with a small plastic bag, and let them rise in a warm spot until doubled in volume, 40 to 45 minutes depending on how warm the room is.

Fit the racks in the top and bottom thirds of the oven. Preheat the oven to 425°F.

Once the challah loaves have roughly doubled in size, do the press test: Press your finger lightly into the dough, remove it, and see if the depression fills in by half. If the depression fills back in quickly and completely, the dough needs more time to rise; if you press the dough and it slightly deflates, the dough has over-proofed and will be heavier and less airy after baking.

Bake the loaves: Make the egg wash by mixing the remaining egg with 1 tablespoon of water and a pinch of salt together in a small bowl. Gently brush the entire surface of the loaves with a thin layer of egg wash (try to avoid extra egg wash in the folds of the braids). Generously sprinkle the loaves with the seeds, trying to adhere seeds to the sides of the loaves as well as the top.

Bake for 15 minutes. Transfer the bottom sheet pan to the top and the top sheet pan to the bottom, turning each sheet around as you go, and bake until the loaves are golden brown, about 10 minutes longer. Remove the loaves from the oven and set them aside to cool completely on the sheet pans.

Za'atar Chili Feta Bread

The unique cutting technique for this bread makes it extra fun to pull apart and eat. Obviously, if you want to make more of these, by all means use all three pieces of the Honey and Olive Oil Challah dough (page 95) that the recipe yields.

BREAD

⅓ recipe Honey and Olive Oil Challah dough (page 95)

All-purpose flour, for your work surface

2 tablespoons extra-virgin olive oil

1½ cups (6 ounces) crumbled feta cheese, gently patted dry

2 tablespoons Za'atar Spice Blend (page 28) or 1 tablespoon fresh chopped za'atar or oregano leaves

1 medium jalapeño, seeded and very finely diced, or ½ teaspoon dried red pepper flakes

Salt and freshly ground black pepper

EGG WASH AND TOPPING

1 large egg

Pinch of fine sea salt

○○○○○○○○○○

Makes
1 loaf

Active Time:
30 minutes

Total Time:
1 hour
40 minutes

○○○○○○○○○○

Make the bread: Preheat the oven to 350°F.

If you've chilled the challah dough you reserved for this recipe, remove it from the refrigerator and let it come to room temperature, about 30 minutes. Lightly flour a work surface and roll the dough out into a 12 x 16-inch rectangle. Brush the dough with 1 tablespoon of the olive oil, then sprinkle the feta, za'atar, and jalapeño over the dough, leaving a 1-inch border around the edge. Drizzle with the remaining 1 tablespoon oil and season with salt and black pepper to taste. Working from the short end of the dough, roll the dough into a log, pulling and tightening as you go along (if the dough sticks slightly to the surface, gently release it from the counter using a pastry scraper or just gently tug; once you get it going it will be fine). Arrange the dough on a large parchment-lined rimmed baking sheet with one of the ends facing you. Hold a pair of long, sharp scissors at a 45-degree angle with the point facing the top of the log and cut into the dough in 1-inch intervals, cutting almost to the bottom of the log but not all the way through to the bottom (you should have about 8 or 9 cuts that look sort of like a bird's beak). Use your hands to pull the snipped pieces away from the center, alternating one to the left and one to the right. Cover the dough with a kitchen towel and let it rise until fluffy and doubled in thickness, 45 to 50 minutes.

Bake the loaf: Make the egg wash by mixing the egg, 1 tablespoon of water, and the salt together in a small bowl. Gently brush the entire surface of the bread. Bake until golden, 25 minutes. Remove from the oven, cool slightly, and let people pull pieces from the hot bread.

Erez's Wedding Lamb Focaccia

○○○○○○○○○○

Makes
8 focaccias

Active Time:
1 hour

Total Time:
4 hours
(including
rising)

○○○○○○○○○○

Sometimes the things we eat are indelibly mapped into our memories, minds, and palates. Deciding to get married to Jay in Tel Aviv was easy since our relationship was cemented here and we lived here. Once our friends and family said they'd happily make the trip to celebrate with us, that sealed the deal. The obvious next question was: *What to do about the food?* Then someone reminded me that Erez Komarovsky, a legendary baker and cook who lives near the Lebanese border on eleven dunams of land where he gardens and cooks and tends to his chickens, might be able to do our wedding. We whooped with glee when it sunk in that he would be the person feeding our guests. On that night, there were figs split open to reveal jewel-like tuna crudo. There was meltingly tender roasted kohlrabi so delicious my friends gave it its own hashtag on Instagram. And then there was the lamb focaccia, which emerged from a wood-burning bread oven with an aroma so alluring it seduced people off the dance floor. I can still taste that crispy, olive oil–rich dough topped with spiced ground lamb, toasted pine nuts, mint, and a hint of fennel seed, which Erez referred to by its Arabic name, *yansoon.*

The bread served as a sponge for the lamb fat, which infused it with an extra layer of wow. So many people who were there that night have asked me for the recipe that I called up Erez and asked him if he would share it. Before I even had time to pull out a pen and notepad he began reciting it to me from memory. The multiple kneadings and resting times initially intimidated me, but Erez reassured me that all would be OK when I tried it at home. Yes, the dough is sticky, but if you make sure not to skimp on the olive oil, you'll be rewarded with a pliant dough that stretches over your palms with ease. The joy is in the imperfect shapes here. Make sure to ask for lamb with a good amount of fat, get your oven as hot as possible, and don't worry if it takes a few minutes before you slice and eat your creation; the flavors are even more pronounced after a little resting time.

FOCACCIA DOUGH

7 cups all-purpose flour, plus more for shaping

1 tablespoon instant (rapid-rise) yeast

3 cups cold water

1 tablespoon crushed fennel seeds

2½ teaspoons fine sea salt

3 tablespoons extra-virgin olive oil, plus more for drizzling and oiling the bowl

LAMB TOPPING

1½ pounds ground lamb (ask your butcher to give you a blend of 70% meat, 30% fat—you want the meat to be the opposite of lean here)

½ cup lightly toasted pine nuts

2 medium onions, finely chopped

3 garlic cloves, finely minced

½ cup finely chopped fresh mint, plus plenty more for garnish

1 tablespoon freshly ground black pepper

2 teaspoons kosher salt

1½ teaspoons ground coriander

¼ teaspoon ground nutmeg

¼ teaspoon ground cinnamon

¼ teaspoon ground cardamom

½ cup extra-virgin olive oil

Tahini, for drizzling

RECIPE CONTINUES

Make the focaccia: Sift the flour and yeast into a very large bowl (use your biggest salad bowl or even a large soup pot, if that's the biggest you've got), then pour the cold water on top of the flour and stir with a wooden spoon until the mixture starts to come together in a shaggy dough. Let the mixture rest for 8 minutes, then add the fennel seeds and salt and knead to incorporate, 1 minute. Let the dough rest for 3 more minutes, then drizzle in the olive oil and knead until the dough becomes very soft and silky (it will still be loose and a bit sticky, not like conventional bread dough). Place the dough in a large oiled bowl, cover loosely with a plastic bag, and let stand in a warm place until the dough loosens and puffs very slightly, 30 minutes.

Gently fold the dough in half over itself, rotate it 90 degrees, fold it in half again, rotate another 90 degrees, and fold in half one more time for a total of three folds. Cover the dough again with the plastic bag and let it rise for another 30 minutes and repeat the folding procedure. Cover one more time, let rest for a third 30-minute period, and repeat the folding procedure one more time. An hour and a half will have passed by the time this process is over. The dough will be fluffy, risen, and jiggly.

Generously flour a work surface, then turn the bowl over onto the floured surface. Using a sharp kitchen knife or pastry scraper, cut the dough into 8 equal pieces (it's OK if they're not perfectly even). Generously flour the tops of the pieces, then cover with a garbage bag or several plastic bags and let rise for another hour. While the dough is rising, set a rack in the center of the oven and preheat a pizza stone on the highest temperature for 1 hour (if you don't have a pizza stone, you can also preheat an inverted large, clean cast-iron skillet for 30 minutes or a heavy baking sheet for 15 minutes).

Make the topping: Gently combine the lamb, pine nuts, onions, garlic, mint, pepper, salt, coriander, nutmeg, cinnamon, and cardamom in a large bowl. Pour the olive oil into a small bowl and set up a stack of 8 pieces of parchment paper cut to around the size of a standard 8 x 11-inch piece of paper. Using the oil in the bowl, oil up your hands, then stretch 1 piece of the dough, trying not to force the gas out of the focaccia, and into either a 9-inch circle or an oval or whatever you want, really. Gently move the dough onto a piece of the parchment, then top with one eighth of the lamb filling, leaving a 1-inch border around the edges. Slide the pizza-topped parchment sheet onto an unrimmed plate or a pizza peel, open the oven, then slip the pizza onto the pizza stone and bake until the focaccia is puffed and the lamb is fully cooked, 8 to 11 minutes, depending on how hot your oven gets. (Depending on the size of the oven and your baking surface, you may be able to bake 2 focaccias at a time.) Remove from the oven, top with lots of chopped mint, and drizzle with tahini. Repeat with the other 7 pieces of dough.

Hot Date, Kumquat, and Kashkaval Focaccia Pizzas

Even after all these years it's hard for my brain and taste buds to cooperate long enough to reconcile the fact that the rind of a kumquat is sweet and the flesh is tart. Other than eating them by the bushel, I try to keep the party going by using them in as many ways as possible. Putting them on Erez's focaccia dough (see Erez's Wedding Lamb Focaccia, page 100) with chewy charred dates, sharp kashkaval cheese, and fiery chilies is a combination I turn to again and again. If you don't feel like making focaccia, use your favorite pizza dough for this recipe.

Makes 4 focaccias
Active Time: 45 minutes
Total Time: 4 hours

½ recipe Focaccia Dough (page 100)

¼ cup extra-virgin olive oil

1 cup (4 ounces) grated kashkaval cheese

8 kumquats, thinly sliced, or ½ orange, thinly sliced, seeds removed

8 Medjool dates, pitted and sliced or torn into pieces

1 red hot chili pepper, seeded and thinly sliced

Fresh oregano or za'atar leaves

Kosher salt and freshly ground black pepper to taste

Make a half recipe of Erez's Wedding Lamb Focaccia (page 100) and follow all instructions for shaping. Instead of making the lamb topping, sprinkle each of the pizzas with ¼ cup of the kashkaval cheese, 2 sliced kumquats, 2 torn dates, some chilies, and some oregano. Season with salt and pepper and bake using the same instructions as for the lamb pizzas. Remove from the oven and garnish with more oregano leaves.

Seeded Za'atar Crackers
(Za'atar Malatit)

On a chilly January afternoon a few years back, I took a drive up north with my friend, photographer Haim Yosef, to bake with Nabila Doha in the Christian Arab city of Rameh. Upon arrival, we were surprised to be greeted not only by Nabila, but forty other women chatting and rolling out cookies from pliant dough, shaping them with molds and crimping them with decorative pincers into tiny works of art. They were part of a women's collective that Nabila founded years ago to raise money for her church. Twice a year they plan for weeks, then bake to raise tens of thousands of dollars, which they dutifully hand over to the priest. Nabila's friend Soraya showed me how to make an oil-rich dough studded with multicolored seeds and za'atar, which we rolled out on parchment paper, scored with a pastry wheel, and slid into the oven. Soon we had fragrant, crispy crackers that have spoiled boxed ones for me ever since.

1½ cups all-purpose flour, plus more as needed

½ cup extra-virgin olive oil

⅓ cup raw sesame seeds

3 tablespoons Za'atar Spice Blend (page 28 or store-bought)

3 tablespoons nigella seeds

2 teaspoons kosher salt

2 teaspoons baking powder

¼ teaspoon dried red pepper flakes

Makes
80 crackers (or more depending on how thin you roll the dough)

Active Time:
25 minutes

Total Time:
1 hour (including cooling)

Arrange the oven racks in the top third and lower third of the oven and preheat the oven to 350°F.

In a large bowl, combine the flour, olive oil, sesame seeds, za'atar, nigella seeds, salt, baking powder, and red pepper flakes and mix well to incorporate. Add ½ cup water, mixing until the dough is pliable, a bit spongy even, but no longer sticky (give the dough a minute to absorb the water and oil; it will become less sticky with a very short rest), adding more flour by the tablespoonful if necessary. Divide the dough into 2 equal pieces. Roll out each piece of dough between 2 large sheets of parchment paper to ⅛ inch thickness (or even a bit thinner if you like wispier crackers). While still between the 2 sheets of parchment, transfer the dough to a large, preferably unrimmed baking sheet and peel off the top layer of parchment. Using a pastry wheel, pizza cutter, or sharp chef's knife, cut the dough into 2-inch squares, then cut them on the diagonal into triangles. Repeat the same procedure with the remaining dough.

Bake, rotating the baking sheets midway through, until the crackers have separated themselves and are golden and fragrant, 15 to 16 minutes total. Remove the crackers from the oven and cool completely on the baking sheets (if any have stuck together, gently separate them with your hands once they're cool enough to touch). The crackers will keep stored in an airtight container at room temperature for up to 1 week, or can be frozen for up to 6 months.

Sweet Potato Frico Burekas

Here, delicious handmade burekas come wrapped in a variety of doughs: puff pastry, Turkish-style (which is slightly thicker and denser), even a short crust used to encase salty Bulgarian cheese. For the sake of simplicity, I start with frozen store-bought phyllo, the kind that comes in a roll. My filling is pretty untraditional, too, pairing sweet, oven-roasted mashed sweet potatoes with sharp kashkaval cheese. I top the burekas with a drift of Parmigiano-Reggiano cheese. When baked, it forms crunchy frico on top of the phyllo and pulls up along with your bureka.

12 sheets phyllo dough, defrosted if frozen

2 large sweet potatoes (2 pounds), scrubbed

1 cup (4 ounces) shredded kashkaval or sharp white Cheddar cheese

1 teaspoon kosher salt

½ teaspoon freshly ground black pepper

½ cup (¼ stick) melted butter or olive oil

1 cup (1½ ounces) finely grated Parmigiano-Reggiano cheese*

Makes
12 burekas

Active Time:
40 minutes

Total Time:
2½ hours

Remove the phyllo from the freezer 2 hours before you start making the burekas (about 30 minutes before you roast the sweet potatoes, if you're doing everything at once; you can also defrost the phyllo in the refrigerator overnight). Preheat the oven to 400°F. Prick the sweet potatoes, wrap each one individually in foil, arrange on a rimmed baking sheet, and bake until tender, 1 hour. Cool for 30 minutes, then unwrap them and scoop the flesh out of the skins into a medium bowl. Add the kashkaval, salt, and pepper and mash until incorporated (you should have about 2¼ cups filling). Reduce the oven to 350°F. Clear and clean a work surface.

Unroll the phyllo (it usually comes in a log), remove 12 sheets, then reroll the rest and return to its packaging. Cover the 12 unfurled sheets with a damp towel to keep them from drying out. Brush one sheet with butter, layer another sheet on top, butter the top, then cut the phyllo into long strips about 3½ to 4 inches wide and 12 to 14 inches long; you may have to trim your phyllo a bit. You should be able to get 2 bureka-ready double-strips from each double layer. Center 2½ to 3 tablespoons of the filling about ½ inch from the bottom of the strip, then fold the bottom right corner over the filling to meet the left edge and form a triangle. Fold the triangle upward to create another layer of phyllo over the triangle, then continue folding until you have a multilayered triangle. Tuck any edges under, arrange on a large baking sheet, and repeat with the remaining phyllo and filling until you have 12 burekas. Space them out evenly on the baking sheet, brush with butter, then scatter the Parmigiano-Reggiano all over the top and bake until golden brown and crisp, 20 to 22 minutes.

Remove from the oven, cool slightly on the baking sheets, and serve warm. Burekas will keep, refrigerated, for up to 3 days, or tightly wrapped and frozen for up to 3 months. Rewarm (defrost first, if frozen) in a 325°F oven for 8 to 10 minutes.

*My favorite Parm and lemon zest grater is a Microplane citrus/cheese grater hybrid—the long-handled wand with a grating blade that's about 1½ inches wide (see Shopping Guide). It gives you a fluffy drift of cheese that enhances every recipe.

Toast

Some of my earliest memories of eating in Israel came from the monthlong trip my family took in 1979, when we toured the country from top to bottom, bunked on friends' living room couches and in cheap hotels, and ate a lot of *tostim*, pressed sandwiches that can be made either on Jerusalem bagels (round, mildly sweet, squishy rolls; try my interpretation on page 82) or on *kasten*, a German word for the Israeli equivalent of Wonder Bread, which is my preference. It squishes down and crisps to perfectly encase gooey cheese, tomatoes, and olives. As long as there's a cheese with stretch inside, you're golden (as is the outside of a well-made toast, thanks to a generous lashing of butter). I'd call a toast machine, a simple electric sandwich maker found at every hardware store in Israel, an Israeli kitchen's ace in the hole.

Here are a few fillings I recommend for your eating pleasure. Simply layer the ingredients, butter the outside of each bread slice, and toast in a sandwich maker or cast-iron skillet until golden brown.

Cheeses: White Cheddar, feta, Gouda, mozzarella

Vegetables and Herbs: Sliced tomatoes, sliced red onion, pitted olives, basil leaves, cilantro leaves

Spreads: Pistachio-Cilantro Pesto (page 218), Preserved Lemon Paste (page 40), Honey Harissa (page 37), Amba Mayo (page 36)

Za'atar Flatbreads

When you just want some hot, fresh bread fast, these rounds can't be beat. Palestinian, Arab, and Jewish bakeries sell these like hotcakes and they're best served very fresh. They're perfect for soaking up sauce from a chicken dish; scooping up labaneh; or, when they've gone a bit stale (which happens pretty fast with this type of bread), slicing into strips for my Israeli-style Pitaquiles (page 70).

3½ cups bread flour, plus more if necessary

1½ teaspoons fine sea salt

1¼ teaspoons instant (rapid-rise) yeast

2 tablespoons plus ½ cup extra-virgin olive oil, plus more for oiling the bowl

2 teaspoons honey

1 cup warm water

½ cup Za'atar Spice Blend (page 28 or store-bought)

⚬⚬⚬⚬⚬⚬⚬⚬⚬⚬

Makes
6 flatbreads

Active Time:
20 minutes

Total Time:
1 hour
45 minutes

⚬⚬⚬⚬⚬⚬⚬⚬⚬⚬

Combine the flour, salt, yeast, 2 tablespoons of the olive oil, honey, and water in the bowl of a stand mixer fitted with the dough hook. Mix on medium-low speed for 1 minute, then increase the speed to medium-high and knead until smooth and very slightly tacky but not sticky, adding flour by the tablespoonful if necessary, 4 to 5 minutes. Transfer the dough to a lightly oiled bowl, cover with a clean kitchen towel, and keep in a warm place until doubled in size, about 1 hour.

Preheat the oven as high as it can go, anywhere between 500° and 550°F. Place a pizza stone, inverted heavy baking sheet, or clean cast-iron skillet in the oven. Precut six 10 x 10-inch pieces of parchment paper. Meanwhile, whisk together the remaining ½ cup olive oil and the za'atar in a small bowl.

Once the dough has doubled in size, uncover it and gently transfer to a lightly floured work surface. Use a knife to cut the dough into 6 equal pieces. Using lightly oiled hands, form each piece into a ball, tucking the ends underneath and pinching them together gently to encourage a nice round shape. Lightly flour the work surface again and roll the balls into 6-inch rounds, letting them rest for 5 minutes, then rolling them again and keeping them covered with a towel. Transfer a round to one piece of parchment paper, spoon 1½ to 2 tablespoons of the za'atar mixture onto the center of the round and use the back of the spoon to spread it, leaving a ½-inch border around the edges.

Transfer the bread with the parchment paper underneath it onto the heated baking sheet and bake until golden and puffed (some bubbles may form in the dough; that's great!), 6 to 7 minutes. Repeat with the remaining dough and za'atar. Serve warm or on the same day. If you're serving the next day, reheat in a 300°F oven for 6 to 7 minutes (I don't recommend a regular toaster, since the za'atar topping will fall off and burn). Right after baking, za'atar breads can be cooled completely then wrapped tightly and individually in plastic wrap and frozen for up to 3 months.

SALATIM AND OTHER SMALL PLATES

Typically served as a first course, salatim are so much more than that. These are the spreads, salads, and other small plates that mark the opening of a meal—or can be made into a meal in and of themselves. At a restaurant, salatim can cover an entire table, with proprietors taking great pride in the freshness and variety of their offerings. And the refrigerated salatim case at an Israeli supermarket or prepared foods store is an exercise in optimism: It seems that in a nation of eight and a half million people, the hunger for almost as many varieties of spreadable, dippable, edible salads never abates. You could eat one a day for a year and never work your way through every variety, but here is a small selection of favorites.

Magical Hummus

∘∘∘∘∘∘∘∘∘∘

Makes
3½ cups

Active time:
15 minutes

Total Time:
about
30 hours
(including
soaking and
chilling)

∘∘∘∘∘∘∘∘∘∘

"Either the food sends you to heaven or it doesn't," Ariel Rosenthal told me one afternoon as we re-created the hummus (see photo, page 115) from his Tel Aviv restaurant, Hakosem, in my kitchen. Around the time I moved to Tel Aviv, Hakosem (Hebrew for "the magician") went from local favorite to international phenomenon, complete with celebrity sightings and round-the-block lines. But if you think Hakosem would ever just rest on its laurels, you haven't met Ariel. I have watched him personally check that each member of his multicultural staff has eaten lunch. I have listened to him validate the pithy micro critiques of a million regular customers, killing them with kindness and gin-and-tonics. I have watched him hand out falafel balls to patrons waiting patiently to order from a menu of elevated street food of staggeringly high quality. And that hummus! Almost criminally creamy, rich, and simultaneously light, it's a miracle every time. Thankfully re-creating it isn't that hard. First, soak the chickpeas for a full 24 hours. Next, cook them with baking soda and *lots* of liquid until very soft and almost soupy (you'll come out of this recipe with extra cooked chickpeas, which you will portion out and save for future hummus batches). Third, use more tahini than you think it socially acceptable. Fourth, it is Ariel's belief that fresh lemon juice curdles the hummus so he uses citric acid (often found in the supermarket's canning aisle). Finally, let the hummus chill until it achieves the texture of buttercream frosting. I was skeptical, but six hours later I was eating the best hummus of my life. Magical, indeed.

COOKED CHICKPEAS
(Makes just over 4 liquidy cups,
enough for 3 portions of hummus)
1⅓ cups dried chickpeas
1 teaspoon baking soda

HUMMUS
(Enough for one 2-cup serving)
1½ teaspoons kosher salt
1½ teaspoons citric acid

1 garlic clove (optional)
1¾ cups pure tahini paste
1 cup ice water
Extra-virgin olive oil, for serving

TATBILA*
¼ cup fresh lemon juice
Pinch kosher salt

½ teaspoon seeded minced jalapeño
1 small garlic clove, finely minced

FOR SERVING
Raw onion wedges
Tomato wedges
Salt-Brined Dill Pickles (page 32)
Cardamom-Kissed Schug (page 35)

Soak and cook the chickpeas: Place the chickpeas in a bowl, cover with 4 inches of water (the chickpeas absorb at least their own weight in water) and soak in the refrigerator for 24 hours.

Drain the chickpeas well, place them in a medium saucepan, cover them with about 2 inches (6 cups) of water and the baking soda, and bring to a boil. Reduce the heat to a simmer, skimming off the foam and making sure the water is always in motion.

After about 20 minutes, test a chickpea—if it's cooked through but not mushy, remove about ¼ cup of the chickpeas to save for your finished hummus. Then keep cooking the rest of the chickpeas until the water is very cloudy and gelatinous and the chickpeas look

RECIPE CONTINUES

like they're sort of disintegrated, another 45 to 55 minutes (this timing can vary; you'll have to use your intuition a bit).

Cool the chickpeas in their liquid; you will end up with about 4 cups total. At this point, you can individually portion out three 1⅓-cup portions of the cooked chickpeas (about 1 cup chickpeas and ⅓ cup liquid), in sandwich-sized plastic bags, lay flat, and freeze, so you have little packets of cooked chickpeas whenever you're ready for hummus.

Make the hummus: Place one of the 1⅓-cup portions of cooked chickpeas in the bowl of a food processor with the salt and citric acid (and garlic if using). Process until very smooth, about 2 minutes, stopping to scrape down the sides and bottom of the bowl if necessary. With the processor still running, drizzle in half the tahini and water and process until very smooth, 1 more minute. Drizzle in the remaining tahini and water until very smooth and creamy (it should be the texture of warm buttercream frosting), 1 minute. Transfer to an airtight container and let it firm up for at least 4 hours and up to 8 hours.

Make the tatbila: In a small bowl combine the lemon juice, salt, jalapeño, and garlic.

To serve, spread the hummus on a plate and garnish with some cooked chickpeas and olive oil. Serve with onion and tomato wedges, pickles, schug, and tatbila. Hummus will keep, stored in an airtight container in the fridge, for up to 2 days.

Quick and Easy Hummus

When you don't have the time to soak and cook, hummus made with canned chickpeas does the trick. This one is garlicky and lemony to the max. There's no shame in this super creamy version, which you can get on the table in 15 minutes flat.

Makes about 3 cups
Active Time: 10 minutes
Total Time: 15 minutes

HUMMUS
Two 15-ounce cans chickpeas, drained, ¾ cup liquid reserved

3 garlic cloves, minced

½ cup pure tahini paste

⅓ cup freshly squeezed lemon juice, plus more if you like very lemony hummus

2 teaspoons kosher salt, plus more to taste

Extra-virgin olive oil and smoked paprika, for serving

In the bowl of a food processor, combine the chickpeas with ½ cup of the reserved chickpea liquid, the garlic, tahini, lemon juice, and salt and process until smooth and creamy, 2 to 3 minutes depending on the strength of your processor and how creamy you want the hummus to be. Add more of the reserved chickpea liquid as needed to reach the consistency you want, and season with more salt to taste.

*Tatbila is a traditional Arabic condiment, laced with lemon, garlic, and chilies, that cuts the richness of the hummus.

A Tale of Two Chickpeas

Like the sesame seed and the eggplant, the chickpea holds pride of place among Israeli staple ingredients. Not only does it power hummus, that most central staple of local cuisine, but it adds heft and substance (not to mention protein) to soups like Harira (for my interpretation, see Chickpea and Spinach Harira, page 174) and as a filling in a hearty eggplant salad (Sabich Fattoush, page 182). The best *hummusiyot* (hummus joints) seek out the smallest varieties (above, left). The tiniest and most popular chickpeas for hummus are imported from Bulgaria, but there is also another small variety, called Hadas, grown locally in smaller quantities. Their thinner skins melt away when cooking, resulting in a creamier finished product. Though Hadas and other tiny chickpeas generally aren't available abroad, the next time you're in Israel (or Bulgaria, for that matter), pick up a bag to up your hummus game. That being said, the more common Mexican garbanzo bean you'll likely be using makes great hummus, too. Using baking soda and cooking the chickpeas for a long time, like Ariel Rosenthal from Hakosem recommends, becomes extra important.

Tahini Sauce

This is the one thing your fridge should never be without. Served with many dishes as a dressing or condiment, it's the ideal snack with a warm pita or cut-up vegetables. Called *salat techina* (tahini salad) in Hebrew, this recipe comes together in minutes. The ice water is really important here; it helps the tahini fluff up and remain that way, even after a day or two in the fridge. If the tahini thickens a little too much for your liking, just incorporate some water or lemon juice to return it to the texture you love. There are also variations below for making gorgeous colored tahinis and easy toppings that also happen to taste great. Make them all for a rainbow spread of salatim, or choose the one to suit your mood. The golden variety takes on the dusky, earthy notes of the turmeric; the pink tahini is mildly sweet thanks to cooked beets; the green tahini is a riot of herbs you can improvise based on what you've got in the house; and the charcoal-gray tahini, speckled with little bits of charred eggplant skin (waste not, want not), is positively addictive—rarely has something so gray tasted so great.

Basic Tahini Sauce

○○○○○○○○○○
Makes
2 cups

Active Time:
5 minutes

Total Time:
5 minutes
○○○○○○○○○○

1 cup pure tahini paste

3 garlic cloves, minced

¾ cup ice water, plus more if necessary

⅓ cup freshly squeezed lemon juice, plus more to taste

2 teaspoons kosher salt, plus more to taste

Place the tahini and garlic in the bowl of a food processor. With the processor running, add the water in a slow stream and process until the tahini is light and fluffy, about 1 minute. Add the lemon juice and the salt and process 30 more seconds. Stop the processor, taste the tahini, and add additional salt and lemon juice to taste. Stored in the fridge, tahini keeps for up to 1 week. When you take it out of the fridge, thin it with water or lemon juice and season with salt to brighten it up.

Charcoal-Gray Tahini

In the bowl of a food processor, add ¼ cup chopped charred eggplant skin (from charred eggplant, page 133) to the Basic Tahini Sauce and process until smooth. Chill until ready to use.

TOPPING: Pom and Cilantro *(Active/Total Time: 10 minutes)*
Spread 1 cup of the tahini on a plate. Toss ½ cup pomegranate seeds with ¼ cup chopped red onion, 2 tablespoons extra-virgin olive oil, 1 tablespoon freshly squeezed lemon juice, and 2 tablespoons chopped fresh cilantro. Spoon the mixture over the tahini.

RECIPE CONTINUES

Golden Tahini

Green Tahini

Charcoal-Gray Tahini

Pink Tahini

Basic Tahini Sauce

Green Tahini

In the bowl of a food processor, add ½ cup packed tender fresh green herbs (parsley, cilantro, basil) to the Basic Tahini Sauce and process until smooth; add more if needed to achieve desired color. Chill until ready to use.

TOPPING: Roasted Sweet Potatoes *(Active Time: 5 minutes/Total Time: 50 minutes)*
Preheat the oven to 450°F. Prick 2 baby sweet potatoes or 1 small sweet potato with a fork, rub with olive oil, and roast until soft and the skins are slightly blackened, 50 to 55 minutes. Spread 1 cup of the tahini on a plate, split the sweet potatoes, and arrange them on top. Drizzle with olive oil and garnish with sliced scallions.

Pink Tahini *(Active Time: 5 minutes/Total Time: 50 minutes)*

In the bowl of a food processor, add ¾ cup chopped cooked beets to the Basic Tahini Sauce and process until smooth; add a bit more if needed to achieve desired color. Chill until ready to use.

TOPPING: Shredded Radish and Nigella Salad *(Active/Total Time: 10 minutes)*
Toss ½ cup thinly sliced assorted radishes with 1 tablespoon each extra-virgin olive oil and freshly squeezed lime juice. Season with salt and pepper. Spread 1 cup of the tahini on a plate, top with the radishes, and sprinkle with nigella seeds. Drizzle with more oil.

Golden Tahini

In the bowl of a food processor, add 2 tablespoons Microplane-grated fresh turmeric or 1 teaspoon ground turmeric to the Basic Tahini Sauce and process until smooth; add more turmeric if desired to deepen the color. Chill until ready to use.

TOPPING: Crispy Smoky Brussels Sprouts *(Active/Total Time: 15 minutes)*
Trim and quarter 1½ cups (5 ounces) small Brussels sprouts. In a large skillet, heat 3 tablespoons extra-virgin olive oil over high heat. Add the Brussels sprouts and cook without stirring until the undersides begin to turn golden, 5 minutes. Shake the skillet and add ½ teaspoon smoked paprika, 1 teaspoon Honey Harissa (page 37), and salt and freshly ground pepper to taste. Cook, moving the sprouts as little as possible, until they crisp up and turn a deep golden brown, 4 to 5 more minutes. Spread 1 cup of the tahini on a plate and top with the cooked Brussels sprouts and more harissa, if desired.

Crispy Smoky Brussels Sprouts

Shredded Radish and Nigella Salad

Pom and Cilantro

Roasted Sweet Potatoes

Golden Onion, Chickpea, and Fava Spread

An innocuous-looking store-bought spread I tasted at a potluck party appeared on the surface to be nothing more than hummus or white bean dip, but one bite revealed something sweeter, softer, and altogether more surprising: caramelized onions! An hour later I had made my own version, which I now find myself topping with all kinds of goodies depending on the season. Fava beans, or *ful* as they're known here, require enough work as it is; you have to shell, boil, then shell again. So I do little more than warm them with olive oil and thyme. If you can't find favas, then frozen, defrosted peas work really well, too. Either way, it's spring on a plate.

¼ cup plus 2 tablespoons extra-virgin olive oil, plus more for serving

¼ cup vegetable oil

3 jumbo or 4 large onions, finely diced (6 cups)

1 teaspoon fresh thyme leaves, plus a sprig for the favas

1 teaspoon kosher salt, plus more to taste

¼ teaspoon freshly ground black pepper, plus more to taste

½ cup cooked chickpeas (page 116), or ½ cup canned and drained chickpeas

1 pound fresh fava beans in their pods*

Lemon wedges, for serving

○○○○○○○○○○○

Serves 4

Active Time:
30 minutes

Total Time:
1 hour
20 minutes
(including
shelling
favas)

○○○○○○○○○○○

In a large, high-sided skillet or a soup pot, heat ¼ cup of the olive oil and the vegetable oil over medium-high heat. Add the onions, thyme leaves, salt, and pepper and cook, stirring, until the onions begin to soften and glisten, 5 minutes. Reduce the heat to medium and cook, stirring often, until the onions are evenly golden but not charred and have reduced to about 1½ cups, 35 to 40 minutes. Cool slightly, then transfer all but 2 tablespoons of the onions to the bowl of a food processor and add the chickpeas. Process until smooth.

During the last 30 minutes of the onions caramelizing, bring a medium pot of salted water to a boil and set up an ice-water bath with lots of ice.

While the water is coming to a boil, shell the favas and discard the pods. Drop the shelled beans into the boiling water and cook until they float to the surface, 2 to 3 minutes (you can also cook the fresh peas or frozen peas at this point using the same timing and instructions). Drain well, drop into the ice water for 1 minute, drain again, then pop the favas out of their skins (if this is hard, make a tiny slit in each fava shell to help it pop out of its skin; you should have about 1 cup shelled favas).

Add the remaining 2 tablespoons olive oil to the onions in the skillet with the favas and the thyme sprig and just warm through over medium-low heat, 2 to 3 minutes. Season with salt and pepper to taste. Spread the onion mixture on a plate and top with the warmed fava beans. Drizzle with olive oil and squeeze lemon wedges on top.

*If you can't find fresh fava beans, substitute ⅔ cup frozen fava beans, defrosted, or ⅔ cup fresh shelled peas.

Lemony Cauliflower over Labaneh

At restaurants all over Israel, you'll find a plate of simply fried (well, deep-fried) cauliflower, or *cruvit*, its edges crisp, its sweetness intensified by the high heat. I oven-roast the cauliflower instead and add a generous lashing of freshly squeezed lemon juice before roasting, which helps that lemony punch permeate every bite. I like to have a lot of cauliflower "crumbs," little pieces that turn dark and golden upon contact with high heat and oil. Serving the warm cauliflower over the cool, creamy labaneh allows you to multiply exponentially the number of textures and flavors you get in one bite.

1 medium head cauliflower, leaves trimmed

¼ cup extra-virgin olive oil, plus more for drizzling

Finely grated zest and juice of 1 lemon

1½ teaspoons kosher salt, plus more to taste

½ teaspoon freshly ground black pepper, plus more to taste

1 teaspoon chopped fresh jalapeños, or ¼ teaspoon dried red pepper flakes

¼ cup dried barberries, chopped dried cranberries, or pomegranate seeds

¼ cup toasted pine nuts

1 small garlic clove, very finely minced

¾ cup 4-Hour Labaneh (page 44 or store-bought) or Greek yogurt, for serving

Chopped fresh chives, cilantro, or parsley, for serving

Serves 4

Active Time:
10 minutes

Total Time:
40 minutes

Preheat the oven to 450°F.

Halve the cauliflower through the core and stem. Using a sharp knife, cut the florets into varying sizes, making sure there are some really small pieces. Slice any tender stem parts into tiny pieces, too. In a medium bowl toss the cauliflower with the olive oil, half the lemon juice and zest, the salt, black pepper, and jalapeños. Spread evenly on a large rimmed baking sheet and roast until the edges begin to char, 20 minutes. Using a spatula, scrape the cauliflower to move it around, then roast until the cauliflower is crispy and dark golden, another 10 minutes (it's OK if some of the smaller pieces are really charred—that's kind of the point!). Remove from the oven, sprinkle the remaining lemon juice and zest all over the cauliflower right on the pan, add the barberries and pine nuts, toss, and season with salt and black pepper to taste.

To serve, stir the garlic and labaneh in a medium bowl until incorporated, spread on a medium plate, and top with the cauliflower. Season with additional salt and pepper, drizzle generously with olive oil, and garnish with chives.

Matbucha

On the surface, store-bought matbucha (which means, simply, "cooked" in Arabic) seems like not much, a ho-hum side dish of long-cooked tomatoes. But when you start talking about homemade matbucha, people's eyes light up. They fantasize about trailing a shred of still-warm challah through the deeply reduced, slightly tart, salty-sweet tomato sauce laced with a bit of heat. It's something to make in Israel all year but especially in the summer, when riper tomatoes are abundant (I like to use Maggie tomatoes, which are very red, juicy, and a little acidic, the platonic ideal of a peak-season vine tomato). The secret, like a good Italian sauce, is to blanch and shock the tomatoes before cooking and slip them out of their skins, then let the tomatoes simmer for a few hours at a low temperature, with very little interruption and very few flavor enhancements other than the slight char of bell peppers and the spice from roasted jalapeños. I know, I know—you don't love green peppers. But here, their lack of sweetness and vegetal qualities lend some green earth to this tomato party. Be warned—four pounds of tomatoes reduces down to about three cups, and that will be gone long before you learn how to pronounce "matbucha" (for the record, it's "mat-BOO-cha").

11 to 12 medium ripe tomatoes (about 4¼ pounds), or three 28-ounce cans diced tomatoes in juice

1 large red bell pepper
1 large green bell pepper
2 medium jalapeños
6 tablespoons extra-virgin olive oil

5 garlic cloves, halved lengthwise
2 tablespoons kosher salt
1 tablespoon sugar
1 teaspoon sweet paprika

Makes
2½ to 3 cups

Active Time:
15 minutes

Total Time:
2½ hours

If using whole tomatoes, bring a large pot of water to a boil. Set up an ice-water bath. Using a paring knife, cut out and discard only the green stem circle from the top of each tomato and then cut an *X* into the bottom of each tomato. Use a spider or a slotted spoon to lower the tomatoes into the boiling water, 6 or 8 at a time, for 30 to 45 seconds. Lift them out and drop them into the ice-water bath for 30 seconds (refresh the ice-water bath with more ice as needed). Slip the tomatoes out of their skins, dice them, and transfer them to a large bowl.

Char, cool, skin, and seed the bell peppers and jalapeños using the method on page 135. Chop the peppers and dice the jalapeños and add them to the tomatoes.

Heat ¼ cup of the olive oil in a large (at least 10-inch) high-sided skillet or soup pot over medium-low heat. Add the garlic and cook, stirring, until softened and golden but not deeply browned or crisped, 5 minutes. Add the tomatoes, chopped peppers and jalapeños, salt, and sugar. Bring to a boil over medium-high heat, reduce to a low simmer, and cook, stirring and scraping the bottom of the pan every 5 to 10 minutes so it doesn't burn, until the liquid has evaporated, the matbucha is concentrated, and the tomatoes are very soft, 1½ hours. Reduce the heat to the lowest simmer, stir in the remaining 2 tablespoons oil with the paprika and cook, stirring often, until the matbucha darkens in color, looks shiny, and is reduced to about 3 cups, another 1 to 1½ hours. Cool and serve at room temperature.

Store in the refrigerator for up to 4 days.

Lachmajun Spiced Meat Hummus

At Lachmajun Turek, a shawarma joint near my house in Tel Aviv, I always order the namesake dish (translated as "meat and dough" in Arabic), a stretchy sheet of dough blanketed with a thin layer of umami-packed ground meat. If you've traveled in Turkey, Syria, or Lebanon, you'd be familiar with the dish, which often is delivered in tiny, individual rounds or in a larger pizza-like format. I can never get enough of that addictive flavor, so I infused it into a topping for meat hummus (hummus basar), a favorite way to transform this into even more of a main course. The meat is browned and simmered with tomatoes and tamarind paste, which helps this dish tartly go where no meat hummus has gone before: into the territory where you actually finish it all in one sitting. Tamarind paste can vary in intensity, so by all means adjust to your liking.

2 tablespoons extra-virgin olive oil

1 pound 80/20 ground beef

1 medium onion, finely chopped

3 garlic cloves, chopped

1 teaspoon kosher salt

1 teaspoon cayenne pepper

1 teaspoon ground cumin

½ teaspoon ground sumac

⅓ cup beef or chicken broth or water

2 tablespoons pure tamarind paste, plus more to taste

2 tablespoons tomato paste

1 tablespoon freshly squeezed lemon juice

1 medium tomato (6 ounces), diced, or 1 cup canned diced tomatoes in juice

½ cup chopped fresh flat-leaf parsley, plus more for garnish

1½ cups hummus (page 116 or 118), for serving

¼ cup lightly toasted pine nuts, for serving

○○○○○○○○○○

Serves 4

Active Time: 15 minutes

Total Time: 30 minutes (assuming hummus is premade)

○○○○○○○○○○

In a large skillet, heat the olive oil over medium-high heat. Add the ground beef and cook, stirring, until the meat is cooked through and has released its liquid, 5 to 6 minutes. Transfer the meat to a bowl, leaving 2 to 3 tablespoons of liquid in the skillet. Add the onion, reduce the heat to medium, and cook until lightly golden and slightly softened, 8 to 9 minutes. Add the garlic and cook for 1 minute more. Return the meat to the pan and stir in the salt, cayenne, cumin, and sumac and cook, stirring, for 1 minute.

In a small bowl, whisk together the broth, tamarind paste, tomato paste, and lemon juice. Pour over the meat, add the tomatoes, and stir to combine. Reduce the heat to medium-low and simmer until the meat has absorbed most of the liquid, 6 to 7 minutes. Stir in the parsley.

Mound the hummus into a large bowl and top with the meat mixture. Garnish with pine nuts and parsley.

Charring Eggplants, Tomatoes, and Peppers over Fire or in the Oven

Though you may not have a giant coal-fired grill like many restaurants do here, you can still char vegetables over an open flame at home. That little bit of time over fire brings new dimension to the finished product. The extra time and mess are worth it, but if you prefer to keep your stovetop pristine, the alternative oven methods listed below work beautifully as well. (If you have an electric stove, the oven method is going to be the way to go for you.)

To char eggplant, set a cooling rack over a rimmed baking sheet and set aside. Turn a large flame on to its highest power and lay the eggplant directly on the flame, or set a heatproof grid over the flame.

Char the eggplant, using tongs to turn it every 5 minutes or so, until it is slumped and the skin is papery, blackened, and cracking all over, 20 to 25 minutes depending on the size of the eggplant.

To charbroil the eggplant, arrange a rack 4 to 6 inches from the broiler, depending on your oven and the size of the eggplant. Preheat the broiler, and arrange the eggplant on a foil-lined baking sheet. Broil, turning every 5 minutes, until charred and blackened, 20 minutes total.

Transfer the eggplant to the rack set above a rimmed baking sheet and cool until easy to handle, about 30 minutes. Discard the liquid drained onto the rack, peel off the skin (if desired, save it for the Charcoal-Gray Tahini, page 120), split open the eggplant, and discard the seeds.

To char jalapeño and bell peppers, place them over the fire, turning every 5 minutes, until the peppers puff up and are blackened and blistered in parts, 5 to 6 minutes for the jalapeños and 15 to 20 minutes for the bell peppers (the timing may vary depending on how sturdy your peppers are; some are thinner-skinned and require less time).

To oven-char jalapeño and bell peppers, preheat the oven to 450°F. Place the jalapeños and bell peppers on a foil-lined rimmed baking sheet and roast, turning occasionally, until they are puffed and the skins are partially blackened, 10 to 15 minutes for the jalapeños and 20 to 25 minutes for the bell peppers. As they are done, place them in a medium bowl and seal tightly with plastic wrap. Cool until easy to handle, 20 to 30 minutes. Open the bag, drain off and discard all the liquid, and remove and discard the stems, seeds, and skin.

To char tomatoes, place them over the fire, turning occasionally, until the outsides are blackened in spots but the tomato has not completely slumped, 10 to 12 minutes.

To oven-char tomatoes, preheat the oven to 450°F, place the tomatoes on a rimmed baking sheet, and roast, turning occasionally, until they are puffed and the skin is partially blackened, 20 to 25 minutes.

The Best Baba Ghanoush

In Israel, there are two classic ways to make baba. One is with tahini, which yields a creamy, perfectly balanced eggplant salad. But if you go rogue and opt for the mayonnaise version, you may be converted for life. Mayo's lemony, slightly sweet flavor tames the eggplant's smokiness, turning it into a party dip that might just replace French onion soup dip forever.

2 medium eggplants (2 pounds), charred and cooled (page 133)

TAHINI BABA

3 tablespoons pure tahini paste

2 tablespoons freshly squeezed lemon juice

2 tablespoons extra-virgin olive oil

2 teaspoons kosher salt, plus more to taste

¼ teaspoon freshly ground black pepper

1 small garlic clove, very finely minced

MAYO BABA

3 tablespoons mayonnaise

1 tablespoon freshly squeezed lemon juice

1 tablespoon extra-virgin olive oil

2 teaspoons kosher salt, plus more to taste

¼ teaspoon freshly ground black pepper

1 small garlic clove, very finely minced

ᘓᘓᘓᘓᘓᘓᘓᘓᘓᘓ

Makes
2 cups

Active Time:
10 minutes

Total Time:
2 hours
(including charring eggplants and chilling)

ᘓᘓᘓᘓᘓᘓᘓᘓᘓᘓ

Scoop the charred eggplants out of their skins. Discard the skins (or reserve for Charcoal-Gray Tahini, page 120).

To make the tahini baba: In a medium bowl, whisk together the tahini, lemon juice, olive oil, salt, pepper, and garlic. Finely chop the eggplant, stir it into the tahini mixture, and season with more salt to taste. Chill for at least 1 hour to let the flavors meld.

To make the mayo baba: In a medium bowl, whisk together the mayonnaise, lemon juice, olive oil, salt, pepper, and garlic. Finely chop the eggplant, stir it into the mayo mixture, and season with more salt to taste. Chill for at least 1 hour to let the flavors meld.

The Best Baba Ghanoush (left) and Pecan–Lime Muhamarra (right)

Pecan-Lime Muhamarra Dip

With its combination of nuts, roasted peppers, and olive oil, I like to think of this as a Middle Eastern version of romesco, the Spanish spread made with almonds and stale bread. Muhamarra usually calls for walnuts, but I love the way the sweetness of pecans and the tart lime juice and pomegranate molasses bring the mix alive. Serve this with crudités, toasted pita, or swirled into labaneh.

3 large bell peppers, charred (page 135), or one 16-ounce jar fire-roasted peppers, drained, well rinsed, and patted dry

⅔ cup toasted pecans*

½ small pita, torn into small pieces, or ½ cup fresh bread crumbs

2 tablespoons Pomegranate Molasses (page 48), plus more to taste

1 tablespoon freshly squeezed lime juice, plus more to taste

1 garlic clove, smashed

1 teaspoon ground cumin

1 teaspoon kosher salt, plus more to taste

¼ teaspoon dried red pepper flakes, or more to taste

⅓ cup extra-virgin olive oil

Makes
2 cups

Active Time:
15 minutes

Total Time:
15 minutes

In the bowl of a food processor, combine the bell peppers, pecans, pita, pomegranate molasses, lime juice, garlic, cumin, salt, and red pepper flakes and process until almost smooth, 30 seconds. With the motor running, drizzle in ¼ cup of the oil until incorporated. Season with more lime juice, pomegranate molasses, and salt, spread on a plate, and drizzle with the remaining olive oil.

*To toast pecans, bake in a preheated 350°F oven until fragrant, 5 to 6 minutes. Transfer to a plate to cool.

Spicy Lemony Carrot Salad

This salad (pictured on page 252 with the Kebaburgers) is inspired by a similar one I eat at Itzik Hagadol, a steak joint in Jaffa, as part of a giant table of salatim. It takes no time to put together and goes with a multitude of dishes that beg for spice, acid, or crunch. You can shred the carrots on the large holes of a box grater, or use a spiralizer or julienne peeler to make longer, wispier carrot ribbons.

2 very large carrots, shredded

1 jalapeño, seeded and thinly sliced into rings

5 tablespoons freshly squeezed lemon juice

Sprinkle of sumac (optional)

○○○○○○○○○○○

**Serves
4 to 6**

Active Time:
10 minutes

Total Time:
10 minutes

○○○○○○○○○○○

In a large bowl, toss the carrots, jalapeño, and lemon juice. Refrigerate for at least 30 minutes and up to 4 hours. Transfer to a serving bowl and sprinkle with sumac, if using.

VEGETABLES

Broccoli Cottage Cheese Pancakes

It's not uncommon in Israel to see all manner of savory *levivot*, or pancakes, and *ketzizot* (patties). This decidedly retro one, made with cottage cheese and broccoli, falls somewhere in the middle. Cottage cheese is so rich and creamy here—it really adds something to the finished pancakes—so don't skimp on the fat. Aim for a minimum of 4%, which is usually the highest you can find in American supermarkets. It's all about getting the proportions right for a lacy, cloudlike creation that's as good for dinner, lunch, or a snack as it is for breakfast.

1½ cups broccoli florets (from ½ small head), finely chopped

1 cup full-fat cottage cheese

2 large eggs

¼ cup all-purpose flour

2 tablespoons chopped fresh chives

2 tablespoons chopped fresh dill, plus more for serving

1 teaspoon baking powder

1 teaspoon kosher salt

½ teaspoon freshly ground black pepper

¼ cup extra-virgin olive oil, plus more if needed

Sour cream, for serving

Serves 4 to 6

Active Time: 10 minutes

Total Time: 30 minutes

In a medium bowl, stir the broccoli, cottage cheese, eggs, flour, chives, dill, baking powder, salt, and pepper until combined. Heat 1 tablespoon of the olive oil in a 10-inch skillet over medium heat. Make pancakes out of the batter, using 3 tablespoons per pancake. Fry until the edges are lacy and browned, 2 to 3 minutes per side, adding more oil to the skillet between batches as needed. Serve with sour cream and garnish with chopped dill.

Grape Leaves with Quince and Barberries

I met Gil Hovav somewhere around 1999, when I was a fledgling food writer with only a murky idea of what I wanted to be when I grew up. Gil, who comes from a long line of prolific writers—his great-grandfather, Eliezer Ben-Yehuda, modernized the Hebrew language for the new nation—has done everything from serving as a restaurant critic to publishing some of Israel's best cookbooks, not to mention starring on countless television shows. When my love of food and passion for Israel dovetailed into professional ambitions for the first time, Gil took me under his wing, and I'm still resting comfortably there nearly twenty years later. We've traveled to Berlin and New York together to cook Yemenite dinners and road-tripped while he regaled me with stories. His love for Israel, and the idea that we all learn from one another when we share plates, is his unifying principle. One morning over martinis (*always* martinis), he taught me the recipe for these delicious grape leaves, which he learned from Israeli Jews of Turkish descent. Tangy without being briny and just a touch sweet, they're as beautiful as they are delicious. Gil added his own flourishes to the traditional recipe in the form of fresh quince and zereshk, or barberries, a tart, dried fruit I was more familiar with as a staple of Persian and Afghani cooking. If you can't find them, you can use unsweetened currants or cranberries.

GRAPE LEAVES

One 12-ounce jar grape leaves (at least 40 leaves)

FILLING

½ cup (3 ounces) pine nuts

¼ cup extra-virgin olive oil

1 large onion, finely diced

1 cup uncooked round rice, such as Arborio, unrinsed

⅓ cup tomato paste

2½ cups loosely packed fresh parsley leaves, finely chopped

2½ cups loosely packed fresh dill fronds, finely chopped

2½ cups loosely packed fresh cilantro leaves, finely chopped

¾ cup barberries, currants, or chopped unsweetened dried cranberries

1½ teaspoons kosher salt

1 teaspoon freshly ground black pepper

1 small quince or tart apple, such as Honeycrisp, cored and cut into 12 wedges

12 whole pieces of dried fruit (prunes, apricots, or figs), pitted and halved

LIQUID

1 cup chicken broth

½ cup water

⅓ cup tomato paste

3 tablespoons freshly squeezed lemon juice

1 tablespoon silan (date syrup) or honey

½ teaspoon kosher salt

¼ teaspoon freshly ground black pepper

Makes
about
40 stuffed
grape leaves

Active Time:
1 hour

Total Time:
2 hours

Prepare the grape leaves: Rinse and drain the grape leaves, pat them dry, and trim off any tough stems from the base of each grape leaf.

Prepare the filling: In a very large, high-sided, heavy-bottomed skillet, toast the pine nuts over medium heat, stirring occasionally, until golden, 4 to 5 minutes. Transfer the pine nuts to a plate to cool. Add the olive oil to the pan, then add the onion and cook, stirring, until tender and lightly golden, 8 to 9 minutes. Stir in the rice, then the tomato paste. Remove from the heat and stir in the chopped herbs, barberries, salt, and pepper.

RECIPE CONTINUES

Clear a work surface before you get to rolling the grape leaves. Arrange a grape leaf, shiny side facing down, on the work surface, and spoon the filling (1½ teaspoons of the filling for larger leaves, 1 teaspoon for smaller leaves) centered and about 2 inches from the bottom of the leaf. Fold the bottom over the filling, then fold the sides over toward the center. Continue rolling, gathering and narrowing the sides with your hands as you roll so the finished, stuffed leaf is a neat log; leave a bit of room in the rolled log to give the rice room to expand. Continue with the remaining filling and grape leaves, arranging them inside the skillet in a circular pattern from the outside in as you go along. It's OK if there's a little space in the pan since the rolls will expand, but not too much room. Tuck the quince and dried fruit between the grape leaves, arranging a few pieces on top (like the dried figs pictured on the previous page) if they're particularly pretty.

Make the liquid: Whisk together the broth, water, tomato paste, lemon juice, silan, salt, and pepper in a medium bowl and pour evenly over the skillet, using a dull knife to move the rolls around so the liquid fills every gap and crevice. Bring to a low boil over medium heat, reduce the heat to a low simmer, cover with a tight-fitting lid, and cook until the leaves are tender, the filling is soft, and the fruit has plumped, 50 minutes to 1 hour. Remove from the heat, let cool for at least 15 minutes, and serve warm or at room temperature.

Beginning in March, fresh grape leaves begin showing up. If you can find them at a farmers' market (or friend's vineyard), trim the stems and use them in place of the jarred version.

Long-Cooked Romano Beans, Tomatoes, and Onions

One day on set my stylist, Nurit Kariv, turned me on to this dead-simple, dead-delicious recipe, which uses the flat, inch-wide romano beans that look like ribbons piled high in the shuk (plain green beans work really well, too). Everyone underestimates this dish! I knew I wanted to include a recipe for tomato-y stewed green beans that disproves the idea that vegetables need to be cooked al dente. All you do is layer onions, beans, and tomatoes in a pot with a little olive oil, salt, and pepper, cover, and cook, undisturbed, over a low flame for a couple of hours. When done, you are left with gorgeously slumped vegetables and a golden liquid that may very well be the best vegetable broth you've ever tasted. Serve that broth out of mugs like consommé, pour some over the vegetables when you spoon them onto plates or into bowls, or freeze for future use as stock.

¼ cup extra-virgin olive oil

4 medium onions, cut into ¼-inch-thick rounds

2 pounds green beans, preferably flat (romano), trimmed and cut into 2-inch lengths

8 small vine tomatoes, cut into ½-inch rounds

5 garlic cloves, halved

Kosher salt and freshly ground black pepper to taste

Lemon wedges (optional)

Serves 6 to 8

Active Time: 25 minutes

Total Time: 2 hours

In a large (at least 5-quart) high-sided skillet or stockpot with a tight-fitting lid, heat the olive oil over medium-low heat. Layer in half the onions, followed by half the green beans, half the tomatoes, and half the garlic cloves. Season generously with salt and pepper and repeat with the remaining onions, green beans, tomatoes, and garlic. Season again with salt and pepper, cover with a tight-fitting lid (you can seal it with foil for extra security), reduce heat to low, and cook until tender, 2 hours. Uncover, season with salt and pepper to taste, and serve with lemon wedges, if desired.

Israeli Street Corn

Israeli corn season is short but, as of late, sweet. Versions more like the summer corn I grew up eating—juicy, sugary-sweet, and almost bursting with juice—are slowly making inroads where varieties more commonly associated with animal feed used to be the norm. I've always loved the creamy, spicy, juicy, savory, and sweet contrasts in a bite of Mexican-style corn, and this adaptation—using labaneh, feta, and za'atar—is out of this world in both looks and taste; it's messy and hands-on, and I've had this as a light lunch on more than one occasion. It's so simple yet so packed with contrasting flavors, and people really do go bonkers when they try it.

4 ears corn, shucked

⅓ cup 4-Hour Labaneh (page 44 or store-bought), or plain Greek yogurt

1 tablespoon chopped fresh cilantro

1 tablespoon extra-virgin olive oil

¼ teaspoon fine sea salt

¼ teaspoon freshly ground black pepper

1 lime, cut in half

¾ cup (3 ounces) finely crumbled feta cheese

1 tablespoon Za'atar Spice Blend (page 28 or store-bought)

1 small jalapeño, seeded and finely diced

Serves 4

Active Time:
15 minutes

Total Time:
25 minutes

Preheat a grill or grill pan over high heat. Grill the corn, turning occasionally, until charred in sections, 6 or 7 minutes total. While the corn is grilling, whisk together the labaneh, cilantro, olive oil, salt, and black pepper. Zest half of the lime into the yogurt mixture. Pat the feta dry if it's on the wetter side and scatter it on a plate. Brush each grilled corn cob with about 1½ tablespoons of the yogurt mixture, then roll each cob in the feta, pressing so the cheese adheres. Sprinkle each cob with za'atar and a little bit of jalapeño and zest the remaining half of the lime right onto the corn. Serve zested lime halves with the corn.

Melted Green Cabbage

Proud recipe rip-off alert! This dish is my interpretation of the braised green cabbage you'll see on menus all over Tel Aviv. In my version I sear the wedges of cabbage like vegetable steaks, splash them with wine and stock, cover them, and cook them slow and low until the vegetables soften and deepen in color. If you want the wedges to hold their shape, stop at about 2 hours. But if you're OK with a messier, slightly mushier finished product that takes on more delicious flavor the longer you leave it in the oven, by all means cook it for an extra hour; just make sure the bottom of your pot doesn't begin to burn. Once the cabbage is done to your liking, finishing with butter and crème fraîche is highly recommended, but a glug of good olive oil adds its own kind of wonderful. Either way, this is a dish you could make a meal out of, paired with a glass of crisp, dry white wine and a piece of crusty bread, at least once a week.

⅓ cup extra-virgin olive oil

2 teaspoons kosher salt, plus more to taste

½ teaspoon coarsely cracked black pepper, plus more to taste

2 small heads of green cabbage (2 pounds), quartered (but *not* cored)

10 whole garlic cloves, peeled

4 shallots, peeled and halved

½ cup dry, acidic white wine, such as Albariño or Grüner Veltliner

½ cup chicken or vegetable broth, plus more if necessary

4 sprigs fresh thyme

3 tablespoons unsalted butter, cut into small pieces

¼ cup crème fraîche or sour cream

Lemon wedges, for serving (optional)

◇◇◇◇◇◇◇◇◇◇

Serves 4

Active Time:
20 minutes

Total Time:
2½ to
3 hours

◇◇◇◇◇◇◇◇◇◇

Preheat the oven to 300°F.

In a heavy, large, high-sided skillet or shallow Dutch oven, heat the olive oil over medium-high heat. Sprinkle 1 teaspoon of the salt and ¼ teaspoon of the pepper directly onto the oil, then arrange the cabbage wedges in the pot, making sure that each is lying on a flat side (you can cram them in; they'll relax into one another as they release liquid). Let the undersides get nice and brown, resisting the urge to move them too much but checking once to make sure they're not burning (reduce the heat slightly if they are), 6 to 7 minutes. Using tongs, flip the cabbage wedges, then tuck the garlic cloves and shallots into the pot, and brown the undersides of the cabbage, another 6 to 7 minutes. Add the wine and broth, bring to a boil, reduce the heat, and add the remaining 1 teaspoon salt and ¼ teaspoon pepper along with the thyme. Cover with a tight-fitting lid, transfer to the oven, and cook until soft, slumped, and mahogany brown, 2 hours, or 2½ hours for even softer cabbage. Uncover, cool slightly, and serve the cabbage with the liquid accumulated in the pot. Season with salt and pepper and top with butter and crème fraîche. Serve with lemon wedges, if desired.

Oven-Roasted Artichokes and Garlic

History tells us that Jews were among the first to consider artichokes as food rather than a weed. Confined to the ghetto in Rome nearly two thousand years ago, they had to get creative about procuring fresh vegetables, so they turned to the spiky, cone-like objects growing wild around them, which they smashed and fried into the delicacy known as Carciofi alla Giudia. I grew up eating artichokes prepared in the conventional way: steamed in a pot for a really long time, where they'd grow heavy with water. My updated method, where the artichokes are cleaned, halved, and roasted facedown, yields a firmer texture but still allows you to scrape the tender meat from each leaf. A whole head of garlic, which steam-roasts right in the pan with the artichokes, forms the basis for a garlicky dressing that replaces the drawn butter or mayo of my California childhood, updated for my grown-up life in Tel Aviv.

4 medium artichokes (about 1½ pounds total)

2 medium lemons, halved

⅓ cup plus ¼ cup extra-virgin olive oil

Kosher salt and freshly ground black pepper to taste

¼ cup dry white wine

¼ cup water

1 head garlic, plus extra unpeeled cloves, if desired

8 sprigs thyme

○○○○○○○○○○

Serves 4

Active Time:
20 minutes

Total Time:
1 hour
10 minutes

○○○○○○○○○○

Preheat the oven to 425°F.

Trim the bottoms of the artichokes and peel the stems (but leave the stems attached if they seem fresh—they are edible and delicious!). Split the artichokes lengthwise and lay them flat on a cutting board. Using a sharp paring knife, cut out and discard the chokes but leave the pale artichoke hearts (this is the best part after you roast the artichokes). Pull out the small, hard inner leaves (these are bitter and inedible after they are roasted). Place the artichokes faceup in a 9 x 13-inch nonreactive baking dish. Squeeze one of the lemon halves all over the exposed pale green choke and the peeled stems. Cut the other half of the lemon into 8 chunks and place one chunk inside the cavity of each artichoke. Drizzle ⅓ cup of the olive oil all over the cut sides of the artichokes, season generously with salt and pepper, and pour the wine and water into the pan. Flip the artichokes so the cut sides are facing down. Nestle the garlic head into the dish, arrange the thyme sprigs on top, scatter any additional garlic cloves around the pan, if using, seal tightly with foil, and roast in the oven until the artichokes and garlic are tender, 50 to 55 minutes. Remove the pan from the oven and uncover the pan. Let the garlic cool slightly. Squeeze the garlic into a small bowl. Mash in the remaining ¼ cup olive oil and the juice of half of the remaining lemon with a fork. Season with salt and pepper and serve with the artichoke halves. Cut the remaining lemon half into wedges and serve with the artichokes.

Mushroom Arayes with Yogurt Sauce

A night in the garden at M25 steakhouse, in the shuk, where our friend Jonathan Borowitz is co-owner and chef, always starts with their arayes, a Lebanese-inspired dish of raw ground meat stuffed into pitas and grilled. I was shocked at how well mushrooms worked in an arayes-style dish made in mini-pitas. Similar to the meat version, the filling cooks up juicy and flavorful, a perfect handheld snack that starts with the simplest white button mushrooms. I tried it with fancier versions, but I actually prefer these; they keep their shape and texture after cooking without trying to pretend like they're meat at all.

YOGURT SAUCE

1 cup full-fat yogurt

2 tablespoons freshly squeezed lemon juice

1 tablespoon extra-virgin olive oil

2 tablespoons chopped fresh herbs of your choice

¼ teaspoon kosher salt

ARAYES

2 pounds button mushrooms, trimmed

1 medium onion, finely minced

3 tablespoons finely minced garlic

¼ cup extra-virgin olive oil, plus more for brushing the pitas

3 tablespoons chopped fresh parsley or cilantro

1½ teaspoons ground cumin

1½ teaspoons kosher salt

Scant 1 teaspoon smoked paprika

½ teaspoon freshly ground black pepper

8 to 10 mini pitas, depending on the size of the pitas

24-Hour Salted Lemon Spread (page 34), tahini, and Honey Harissa (page 37), for serving

Makes
8 arayes

Active Time:
30 minutes

Total Time:
45 minutes

Make the yogurt sauce: In a medium bowl combine the yogurt, lemon juice, olive oil, herbs, and salt. Chill until ready to use.

Make the arayes: On the large holes of a box grater set over a bowl, or in the bowl of a food processor with the coarse grating blade (larger holes) attached, grate the mushrooms. Add the onion, garlic, olive oil, parsley, cumin, salt, paprika, and pepper. Split the pitas, leaving them connected at one end. Preheat a grill, grill pan, or cast-iron skillet over medium-high heat. Working four at a time, divide the filling evenly among the pitas, pressing down lightly so the pita adheres to the filling. Brush the outsides of the pitas with oil and grill the arayes until each side is charred and the filling is hot, 2 to 3 minutes per side.

Slice the arayes in half if desired and serve with the yogurt sauce, lemon condiment, tahini, and harissa.

Crispy Spicy Okra Fries

At one of the liveliest intersections of the shuk sits one of its most vibrant destinations. Kitty-corner from a fishmonger and next to a butcher is a produce shop where I can buy gourd melons, Scotch bonnet peppers, two kinds of plantains, lemongrass, green papayas, baby eggplants, limes, and much more. There's a reason for this recent abundance: In the past decade Israel has become home to thousands of foreign workers from the Philippines, Thailand, and other Asian and Southeast Asian countries, and upward of sixty thousand asylum seekers who slipped into Israel from Eritrea and Sudan looking for shelter from violence and repressive regimes. Though many have left their lives behind, they've brought with them a hunger for fruits and vegetables from home. So Israeli growers have begun cultivating crops rarely seen in Israel, serving this new population as well as curious Israelis seeking more variety. One newish import is so-called Thai okra, which is longer and snappier than the baby varieties prized for stews and other long-cooked dishes (though you can roast those in the same way, too). This new import cooks up crispy and golden, almost like a French fry but so much healthier.

¼ cup extra-virgin olive oil

1 teaspoon kosher salt

½ teaspoon freshly ground black pepper

¼ teaspoon cayenne pepper

¼ teaspoon ground cumin

1½ pounds very fresh okra

½ cup Preserved Lemon Paste (page 40)

¼ cup mayonnaise

Serves 4 to 6

Active Time: 15 minutes

Total Time: 40 minutes

Arrange two baking racks in the top third and bottom third of the oven and preheat the oven to 425°F. In a large bowl whisk together the olive oil, salt, black pepper, cayenne, and cumin. Using a sharp knife, trim the tips of the okra but leave the stems on if they feel tender and easy to cut (this means they'll be edible when roasted); slice each okra in half lengthwise, add to the oil, and toss to coat. Place the okra on two rimmed baking sheets. Roast until crisped and the edges are a deep brown, switching the pans midway through roasting, 20 to 25 minutes total. While the okra is roasting, in a medium bowl whisk together the preserved lemon paste and mayonnaise. Serve the okra with the preserved lemon mayo.

Tahini-Glazed Carrots

More than any other veggie dish in my repertoire, this is the one people request again and again. This recipe originally appeared in my mini-but-mighty *Tahini* cookbook in 2016, but once I moved to Israel, I made a few changes, like eliminating butter and swapping in olive oil, that reflect the way I cook here. If you can find multicolored carrots, great, and if you can find thinner farmers' market–style ones, even better. If your carrots are on the larger side, cut them lengthwise so no piece is more than half an inch thick; this softens them up in preparation for their deliciously sweet, lemony tahini glaze. The recipe purposely makes a generous amount of dressing, because you'll want to put it on everything, from cold noodles to fish and any roasted veggie under the sun. I recommend doubling or even tripling this recipe; the carrots shrink, but people's appetite for them never does. If you do multiply, make sure to use more baking sheets so the carrots roast, not steam. The carrots are just as good, if not better, at room temperature, making them perfect sit-around buffet food.

CARROTS

14 to 16 (1½ pounds total) thin carrots, peeled and trimmed

2 tablespoons extra-virgin olive oil

½ teaspoon kosher salt, plus more to taste

½ teaspoon ground cumin

TAHINI GLAZE
(Makes 1 cup)

⅓ cup extra-virgin olive oil

¼ cup pure tahini paste

¼ cup freshly squeezed lemon juice

3 tablespoons silan

2 tablespoons water, or more as needed

½ teaspoon fine sea salt

¼ teaspoon cayenne pepper

○○○○○○○○○○

Serves 4

Active Time:
10 minutes

Total Time:
35 minutes

○○○○○○○○○○

Roast the carrots: Preheat the oven to 425°F. Arrange the carrots on a large rimmed baking sheet and drizzle with the olive oil. Sprinkle with the salt and cumin, shake the pan to coat the carrots, and roast them, turning once midway through, until they have softened and their edges are golden, 25 to 27 minutes.

Make the tahini glaze: While the carrots are roasting, whisk the olive oil, tahini, lemon juice, silan, water, salt, and cayenne in a medium bowl until smooth and pourable, adding an additional tablespoon of water if necessary.

Remove the carrots from the oven, transfer them to a serving platter, and drizzle them with the tahini glaze. Using tongs, gently toss to coat.

SOUPS

Chilled Beet and Cherry Borscht

A far cry from the jarred kosher borscht of my childhood, this one is almost as much a color story as it is a flavor play. The cherries intensify the shade of the glistening liquid to a sort of purple midnight, at the same time adding playful sweetness to borscht's earthy pull. Though I leave the cherries raw, I precook the beets using a method I learned from Elena Koros, a talented Russian-Israeli cook who lives in Holon, a suburb of Tel Aviv. By boiling, then cooling, the beets in their skins, they retain their color and texture when shredded.

2 medium beets (8 ounces each), scrubbed

1 cinnamon stick

2½ cups unsweetened sour cherry juice or natural (unsweetened) pomegranate juice

4 ounces (⅔ cup) fresh cherries (or frozen, defrosted), stemmed, pitted, and halved

2½ tablespoons freshly squeezed lemon juice, plus more to taste

1½ teaspoons honey

¼ cup sour cream or labaneh (page 44 or store-bought)

Lemon zest, for serving

Serves 4

Active Time:
15 minutes

Total Time:
3 hours (including minimum chilling time)

Cover the beets with water in a medium pot, add the cinnamon stick, bring to a boil over high heat, reduce the heat to low, and simmer until the beets can be pierced with a skewer but aren't mushy, 20 to 25 minutes. Drain, discard the cinnamon stick, cool the beets for 5 minutes, place them in a plastic bag, and freeze for 20 minutes. Remove the beets from the freezer, slide the skins off with a paper towel and discard, and grate on the large side of a box grater into a medium bowl (you should have about 1 cup grated beets). Stir in the sour cherry juice, cherries, lemon juice, and honey; cover and chill to let the flavors meld for at least 2 hours and up to 24. Taste the soup, and if it's too sweet for you, add a little more lemon juice until you've got the sweet-tart combination you love. Divide among bowls, and top each bowl with a dollop of sour cream and a grating of lemon zest.

Freekeh Vegetable Soup

It's not all palm trees and hot beaches; Tel Aviv has a winter, too, bringing hard rain and strong winds that practically make you beg for a bowl of soup. Freekeh (smoked, cracked wheat; see The Freekeh Connection, page 166) adds both body and flavor to this one. Though most wheat in Israel is imported, a small amount is harvested locally every spring. In Arab communities, prized young green wheat is picked and dried in the field over wood to create freekeh (pronounced "freaky" in Israel), a beguiling grain that can be used a million ways (though some of the freekeh I buy here is local, much of it is imported from Turkey). If you throw in a little extra, its starch makes the soup grow thick, so that one minute you have a normal broth and the next you're looking at almost-porridge . . . but in the best possible way. The freekeh adds just a wisp of smoky flavor, as though a blown-out match had passed through each spoonful for a second.

1 cup freekeh (cracked or whole)

3 tablespoons extra-virgin olive oil, plus more for drizzling

1 large onion, diced

1 medium kohlrabi, rind and tough outer membranes peeled off, diced

2 medium carrots, diced

1 teaspoon kosher salt, plus more for seasoning

½ teaspoon freshly ground black pepper, plus more for seasoning

3 garlic cloves, minced

8 cups vegetable or chicken broth, plus more if needed

2 medium zucchini, diced

1 Parmesan rind or 1 tablespoon nutritional yeast (optional)

2 teaspoons chopped fresh za'atar or oregano

¼ teaspoon cayenne pepper, or more to taste

Chopped fresh herbs (za'atar, parsley, chives, or scallions), for garnish

Serves 6 to 8

Active Time: 15 minutes

Total Time: 55 minutes

Place the freekeh in a medium bowl, cover with cold water, and set aside. Heat the olive oil in a large (4- or 5-quart) saucepan over medium heat. Add the onion and cook, stirring, until softened, 8 minutes. Add the kohlrabi and carrots and cook, stirring, until the vegetables begin to soften, 5 minutes; season generously with salt and black pepper. Add the garlic and cook 1 more minute. Drain the freekeh, rinse it with cold water, and add it to the pot. Add the broth, zucchini, Parmesan rind if using, za'atar, salt, and the cayenne. Bring to a boil, then reduce the heat and simmer, uncovered, until the soup is thickened, 25 to 30 minutes (or a few minutes longer if you're using whole freekeh instead of cracked freekeh). Remove the Parmesan rind, season with more salt and black pepper to taste, divide among bowls, garnish with herbs, and drizzle with olive oil.

The Freekeh Connection

I may not go to the supermarket much, but I do frequent a makolet, or minimarket, around the corner from both our house and the shuk. It's where I get my packaged cookies and pasta and tubs of rich sour cream. More often than not I end up spending time talking to Khalifa Zeadat, who lives near the shuk but originally hails from East Jerusalem. With perfect Hebrew, Russian, English, and Arabic, he's a quadruple threat, capable of communicating with more Israelis than possibly anyone else I know. And communicate he does—he's friendly, funny, and wise, always knowing how to extend a kind word if I seem tired from shuttling my packages or to show me photos of a Russian meal he made in his apartment for friends. One day, realizing I'd walked out of the shuk without buying freekeh, I mentioned it to him. "How do you even know what that is?" he asked me, since, surprisingly, many Israelis still don't. I explained that it was quite popular in the United States and that I loved it. He made me an offer I couldn't refuse. "I get the best freekeh in East Jerusalem, where I'm from, the kind my mother buys," he told me. "Want me to bring you some?" Ever since, I put in my order and Khalifa brings me the real deal: local wheat harvested and smoked in the field. It's greener and smokier than the freekeh I can usually get and, more important, it comes courtesy of one of the friendliest guys in the vicinity of Shuk HaCarmel.

Medjool Date Gondi
(Chickpea and Chicken Meatball Soup)

Rottem Lieberson's entire house in north Tel Aviv smells like turmeric and rose petals, only one of the reasons I love going there to cook with her. A prolific, highly intelligent, and deeply talented cook and writer who trained and worked in New York restaurants for years, Rottem brings vibrant, traditional Persian cooking alive from her gorgeous marble-countered kitchen. Everything I've made from her Hebrew-language Persian cookbook has been stellar, and one day she showed me how to make these oversized chicken and chickpea meatballs from scratch. Gondi were a staple in her house growing up, where they would sit on the stove on Fridays waiting for hungry children eager for a pre-Shabbat snack of one meatball and some broth. The Medjool date she tucks inside each gondi softens while cooking, breaking apart easily so you can get a little sweetness with every savory bite. Of course, feel free to leave out the dates if you prefer.

GONDI

1¼ cups dried chickpeas*

1 medium onion (just over 1 cup), coarsely chopped

2 teaspoons ground turmeric

1½ teaspoons kosher salt

¾ teaspoon ground cumin

¾ teaspoon ground cardamom

12 ounces ground chicken, preferably dark meat

3 tablespoons chickpea flour

1 tablespoon vegetable oil, olive oil, or schmaltz

4 medium pitted Medjool dates, halved

BROTH

7 cups low-sodium chicken broth

1 small onion, quartered

1¼ teaspoons ground turmeric

1¼ teaspoons kosher salt

¼ teaspoon freshly ground black pepper

1 jalapeño, halved, seeded, and thinly sliced

Chopped fresh cilantro, for serving

Serves 4

Active Time:
35 minutes

Total Time:
1 hour
45 minutes
(if using canned chickpeas:
12 hours
45 minutes
with
minimum
soaking time)

Make the gondi: In a large bowl, cover the chickpeas with at least 4 inches of water, cover the bowl, and soak for 10 to 12 hours at room temperature or for 24 hours in the refrigerator. Check in on the chickpeas every few hours, and replenish the water if it seems like it's all getting soaked up by the chickpeas. Drain the chickpeas, transfer to a medium saucepan, cover with 2 inches of water, bring to a boil, reduce the heat to medium, and keep the chickpeas on a vigorous simmer, skimming off and discarding any foam and scum, until a chickpea collapses between your fingers when pressure is applied but isn't totally mushy, anywhere from 45 to 55 minutes. Drain and slightly cool the chickpeas and transfer 2 cups of them to the bowl of a food processor; reserve the remaining chickpeas for the broth. Add the onions to the food processor along with the turmeric, salt, cumin, and cardamom and process, scraping down the bowl once if necessary, until almost totally

RECIPE CONTINUES

smooth, 20 to 30 long pulses; transfer to a large bowl. Add the chicken, chickpea flour, and oil and mix gently with your hands until evenly incorporated. Wash and moisten your hands, then form the mixture into 8 large, equal-sized balls; each ball will use a scant ½ cup of the mixture. Poke a date into the center of each ball, then make sure it's well sealed around the date. Chill on a plate, covered, for 30 minutes.

Make the broth: In a large, high-sided 10-inch skillet or stockpot, bring the broth, onion, turmeric, salt, black pepper, jalapeño, and reserved chickpeas to a simmer over medium-high heat and gently lower the gondi balls into the soup. Return the pot to a simmer, then reduce the heat to low, cover with a tight-fitting lid, and simmer gently until the gondi are cooked through and have expanded and look like gorgeous, perfectly cooked, oversized matzo balls, 40 to 45 minutes. Uncover, place 2 gondi in a bowl, and cover with some of the broth. Garnish with cilantro.

*To quick-soak chickpeas, cover them with 3 inches cold water and bring the water to a boil over medium-high heat. Boil for 5 minutes, remove from the heat, and let the chickpeas sit in their hot water for 1 hour. Drain and proceed! Dried chickpeas can be replaced with two 15-ounce cans cooked chickpeas, drained and rinsed (about 3 cups drained chickpeas).

Marak Katom (Orange Soup) with Crunchy Seeds and Harissa

Back when this root-vegetable soup was having its first "moment," you'd find a version in nearly every Tel Aviv restaurant, the only problem being that they often weren't that great. The idea is a good one: Take all the delicious orange vegetables of the season, combine them to your liking, and blend to create a soup that's good hot or cold, plain or accessorized with nuts and other goodies. But too many start with the idea of hiding old vegetables past their prime, and you can really taste the difference in the finished product. Use the freshest vegetables you can find, and don't hold back on the nutty multiseed topping and harissa.

SOUP

3 tablespoons canola oil

1 large onion, diced

3 garlic cloves

6 cups peeled, chopped orange vegetables—any combination of carrot, sweet potatoes, pumpkin, butternut squash you like (about 2½ pounds total chopped)

One 13.5-ounce can coconut milk, preferably full-fat

1 tablespoon honey

1 teaspoon kosher salt

½ teaspoon ground turmeric

CRUNCHY NUT TOPPING

3 tablespoons extra-virgin olive oil

½ cup shelled pumpkin seeds (pepitas)

½ cup shelled sunflower seeds

2 tablespoons sesame seeds

Kosher salt and freshly ground black pepper to taste

Honey Harissa (page 37 or store-bought), for serving

Serves
4 to 6

Active Time:
30 minutes

Total Time:
50 minutes

Make the soup: Heat the oil in a large (at least 4-quart) saucepan over medium heat. Add the onions and garlic and cook, stirring, until golden and slightly softened, 8 to 9 minutes. Add the orange vegetables and cook, stirring, until they begin to soften, 5 minutes. Add the coconut milk, 1¾ cups (one filled empty can's worth) water, honey, salt, and turmeric; bring to a boil, reduce the heat, and simmer until the vegetables are tender, 25 to 30 minutes. Cool slightly, transfer to a blender (or use an immersion blender or food processor), and puree until smooth, 30 seconds.

Make the topping: Heat the oil in a medium skillet over medium heat. Add the pumpkin seeds, sunflower seeds, and sesame seeds and cook, stirring, until they begin to turn golden and a few crackle or pop, 3 to 4 minutes. Drain on paper towels and season with salt and pepper.

Divide the soup among bowls, swirl each bowl with harissa, and garnish with the seeds. Extra topping will keep in an airtight container for up to 2 weeks.

Overnight Chicken Soup
(with a Yemenite Option)

This is the way my late mom, Steffi, used to cook her chicken soup: overnight for at least 12 hours, sometimes longer, until the soup turned golden, rich, and gorgeous. The chicken, wrapped in cheesecloth, gives everything it has to the soup. It defies logic, but the meat, and even the whole vegetables that simmer alongside it, emerge in shockingly good shape. Since we kept the Sabbath and had a low flame on our stove for warming food, the idea of going to sleep with a soup simmering away gives me great comfort; if it doesn't inspire the same feelings in you (no judgment), start the soup early in the morning, turn it off before you go to bed, then let it cool overnight on the stovetop before refrigerating. Since Yemenite hawaiij improves everything, I give you the option to add some in the last few hours of cooking; it will lend the most wondrous mildly spicy flavor and sunshiny hue to your broth.

1 whole 3- to 4½-pound chicken*

6 medium carrots, trimmed and peeled

3 large celery stalks, halved lengthwise

2 medium onions, peeled but left whole

1 medium parsnip, trimmed and peeled

1 medium turnip, trimmed and peeled

3 garlic cloves

1 whole bunch fresh dill, tied into a bundle with kitchen twine

1 tablespoon kosher salt

2 tablespoons hawaiij (page 27) (optional)

One 1-inch piece peeled ginger root (optional)

Lachuch (page 74), for serving

Serves 10 to 12

Active Time: 10 minutes

Total Time: About 13 hours

In a very large (at least 8-quart) stockpot*, arrange a large, overhanging double layer of cheesecloth. Place the chicken in the center of the cheesecloth and tie the cheesecloth into a knot so the chicken is totally enclosed. Add the carrots, celery, onion, parsnip, turnip, and garlic, cover with 3 inches of cold water, bring to a vigorous boil over high heat, and boil, skimming and discarding any scum, 15 to 20 minutes. Reduce the heat to a simmer, add the dill, and cook, checking every so often that the soup is moving with very small bubbles—almost like a tide washing in—but not boiling. After about 2 hours, add the salt. It should taste delicious and salty, like soup should taste. Cover with a tight-fitting lid and cook for a total of 12 hours, either a whole waking day or overnight. Occasionally, skim off the fat from the top (it's easy to do when the flame is so low; the fat pools on the top). Put that fat and broth with it in a bowl in the fridge; when it hardens, tip the bowl back into the soup; the broth slips out from underneath the disc of fat, which I use as schmaltz (chicken fat) in recipes like Medjool Date Gondi (page 167). If you're going Yemenite, add the hawaiij and ginger 2 hours before you're done cooking the soup. When ready to serve, remove and discard the dill. Remove the chicken to a bowl, cut the cheesecloth open to help it cool, then tip any broth back into the soup. Strip off and discard the skin and cheesecloth. Take all the meat off the bones. Discard the bones. Portion the meat out into bowls with the broth and vegetables (leave them whole, or cut them into large pieces if you like). Season with more salt if needed. Serve with lachuch.

*If you don't have an 8-quart pot, use a 6-quart pot. Start with a 3-pound chicken and use 2 carrots, 1 celery stalk, and 1 medium onion.

Chickpea and Spinach Harira

This Moroccan soup typically contains several cuts of meat but works equally well—and requires less time to prepare—in my vegetarian version, which becomes a main course with some crusty bread. Instead of the traditional method of thickening with flour, I use pastina, tiny pasta whose starch releases into the soup. I love tons of lemon here, but feel free to use less acid if you like.

⅔ cup dried chickpeas,* or one 15-ounce can chickpeas, drained and rinsed

¼ cup extra-virgin olive oil

1 large onion, diced

2 medium carrots, diced

3 garlic cloves, finely minced

1 tablespoon finely minced fresh ginger

1½ teaspoons ground turmeric

1½ teaspoons ground cumin

1 teaspoon ground cinnamon

1 teaspoon Honey Harissa (page 37 or store-bought), plus more for serving

2 tablespoons tomato paste

7 cups vegetable broth

6 medium tomatoes, chopped, or two 14½-ounce cans diced tomatoes in juice

½ cup dried red lentils, picked over

2 tablespoons kosher salt, plus more to taste

1 teaspoon freshly ground black pepper, plus more to taste

¼ teaspoon smoked paprika

⅓ cup pastina (tiny pasta), orzo, or broken vermicelli

6 cups baby spinach leaves

¼ cup freshly squeezed lemon juice

½ cup chopped fresh cilantro or parsley

⚬⚬⚬⚬⚬⚬⚬⚬⚬⚬

Serves 8

Active Time:
30 minutes

Total Time:
1 hour
50 minutes
(if using
soaked
chickpeas)

⚬⚬⚬⚬⚬⚬⚬⚬⚬⚬

In a large bowl, cover the chickpeas with at least 4 inches of water, cover the bowl, and soak for 10 to 12 hours at room temperature or for 24 hours in the refrigerator. Drain and rinse the chickpeas.

In a large (at least 5-quart) heavy pot, heat the olive oil over medium-high heat. Add the onions and carrots and cook, stirring occasionally, until the vegetables are tender and the onions are lightly golden, 9 to 10 minutes. Add the garlic, ginger, turmeric, cumin, cinnamon, and harissa and cook, stirring, until the spices are fragrant, 2 to 3 minutes. Add the tomato paste and cook, stirring, 2 more minutes. Add the broth, tomatoes, chickpeas, lentils, salt, pepper, and paprika; bring the liquid to a boil over medium-high heat, reduce the heat to low, and simmer, stirring once in a while, until the soup thickens as the lentils and chickpeas release their starch, 1 to 1½ hours. During the last 30 minutes of cooking, add the pastina to the soup, return to a boil, reduce the heat to low, and continue simmering, then add the spinach in handfuls until it wilts; 5 minutes before serving, add the lemon juice. Right before serving, stir in the cilantro and season with salt and pepper to taste.

*To quick-soak chickpeas, cover them with 3 inches cold water and bring the water to a boil over medium-high heat. Boil for 5 minutes, remove from the heat, and let the chickpeas sit in their hot water for 1 hour. Drain and proceed!

SALADS

- Arugula Salad with Dates, Feta, and Pistachios
- Cabbage, Apple, and Pomegranate Slaw with Cumin Dressing
- Sabich Fattoush Salad with Tahini-Amba Dressing
- Persimmon, Goat Cheese, and Pecan Salad with Very Lemony Dressing
- Rough-Chopped Salad with Yogurt and Dukkah
- Halloumi and Butternut Squash Salad with Crispy Chickpeas
- Toasted Challah Caprese Salad with Za'atar Vinaigrette

Arugula Salad with Dates, Feta, and Pistachios

Medjool dates can be sweet for straight snacking, but mixing them into a salad where they can fuse with creamy, sharp feta and bitter arugula balances their flavor without sacrificing any of their benefits. When cooked at a high temperature, the dates remain chewy and caramel-like, but their edges char into crispy bits you'll have to fight over with anyone nearby. For this salad, dinosaur kale or watercress would be great stand-ins for the arugula, and if you don't have any pistachios on hand, you can top with the Crunchy Nut Topping from my Orange Soup (page 170).

DRESSING

(Makes ⅔ cup)

4 tablespoons extra-virgin olive oil

2 tablespoons Pomegranate Molasses (page 48 or store-bought)

1 tablespoon silan (date syrup)

1 tablespoon Dijon mustard

1 tablespoon finely minced shallots

⅛ teaspoon kosher sea salt

⅛ teaspoon freshly ground black pepper

SALAD

8 cups (4 ounces) baby arugula leaves

1 cup (4 ounces) creamy, crumbled feta cheese

4 large or 6 medium Medjool dates, pitted and halved if small, quartered if jumbo

⅓ cup chopped toasted pistachios

○○○○○○○○○○

Serves 6

Active Time:
15 minutes

Total Time:
15 minutes

○○○○○○○○○○

Make the dressing: In a jar with a tight-fitting lid, combine the olive oil, pomegranate molasses, silan, mustard, shallots, salt, and pepper and shake until creamy.

Make the salad: Preheat the broiler. Arrange the arugula on a serving platter. Using your hands, separate the cheese into bite-sized chunks and scatter it over the arugula. Arrange the dates on a small foil-lined baking sheet and broil until slightly caramelized with charred edges, 2 to 3 minutes. Scatter the dates over the salad and top with the pistachios. Drizzle with some of the dressing.

Cabbage, Apple, and Pomegranate Slaw with Cumin Dressing

The joy of a tricked-out falafel stand is the unlimited supply of goodies you can stuff into your pita. It used to be you'd stand in front of the *miznon* (bar) and use tongs to refill your pita as many times as humanly possible. These days, in a development I've got mixed feelings about, more and more places give you tiny plastic receptacles to fill and take back to your table. This recipe is a fresher, more colorful version of the wilted cabbage salad you'll find on every self-serve falafel or shawarma bar. Tart apples and pomegranate seeds, loads of fresh herbs, two kinds of crunchy cabbage, and pumpkin seeds come together in a cumin-laced dressing that evokes the flavor profile of falafel itself. Stuff it into the sandwich of your choice, or use it as a more conventional side salad with meat or fish.

1 medium apple, cored and thinly sliced

⅓ cup apple cider vinegar

4 cups shredded green cabbage

4 cups shredded red cabbage

1 small red onion, thinly sliced

1 large carrot, shredded

2 scallions (green and white parts), very thinly sliced

2 medium radishes, very thinly sliced

½ cup extra-virgin olive oil

2 tablespoons whole-grain Dijon mustard

1½ tablespoons honey

1½ teaspoons ground cumin

1 teaspoon kosher salt

¼ teaspoon freshly ground black pepper

½ cup pomegranate seeds

¼ cup chopped fresh cilantro

¼ cup chopped fresh mint

½ cup lightly toasted shelled pumpkin seeds (pepitas)

Serves 8 to 10

Active Time:
10 minutes

Total Time:
30 minutes

In a large salad bowl, toss the apples with 1 teaspoon of the vinegar, then add the green and red cabbage, onion, carrot, and scallions and toss. In a jar with a tight-fitting lid, combine the olive oil, remaining vinegar, honey, mustard, cumin, salt, and pepper and shake until creamy. Pour the dressing over the salad, toss to coat, and let the slaw sit for at least 15 minutes (30 minutes will really mellow the acidity of the vinegar), then toss again with the pomegranate seeds, cilantro, mint, and pumpkin seeds before serving.

Sabich Fattoush Salad with Tahini-Amba Dressing

Along with shawarma and falafel, sabich completes the trinity of pita-bound street foods Israelis can't live without. In its traditional sandwich form, crispy fried eggplant, hard-boiled eggs, tomatoes, and often boiled potatoes are layered with hummus and dressed with amba into a handheld meal that's a riot of texture and flavor. Here's that beloved sabich, but laid out on a self-serve, family-style platter, with chickpeas replacing the hummus and spicy toasted pita triangles helping form a sort of free-form fattoush salad.

CHICKPEAS

⅔ cup dried chickpeas

1 teaspoon baking soda

1 teaspoon kosher salt

PITA CHIPS

¼ cup extra-virgin olive oil

1 teaspoon ground cumin

1 teaspoon sumac

½ teaspoon kosher salt

½ teaspoon paprika

Pinch of cayenne pepper

4 pitas, each split into two rounds

EGGPLANT

Vegetable oil

1 medium eggplant (1 pound), cut into ½-inch-thick rounds

Kosher salt and freshly ground black pepper to taste

EGGS AND POTATOES

4 smallish red potatoes

4 large eggs

TAHINI-AMBA DRESSING

(Makes ¾ cup)

½ cup pure tahini paste

¼ cup freshly squeezed lemon juice

¼ cup extra-virgin olive oil

2 tablespoons 40-Minute Amba (page 36 or store-bought)

¼ teaspoon kosher salt

Generous pinch of cayenne pepper

SALAD ASSEMBLY

2 cups chopped romaine lettuce

4 small ripe tomatoes, cut into wedges

1 cup fresh parsley leaves

Serves 4 to 6

Active Time:
30 minutes

Total Time:
45 minutes (not including chickpea soaking time)

Prepare the chickpeas: In a large bowl, cover the chickpeas with at least 4 inches of water, cover the bowl, and soak for 10 to 12 hours at room temperature or for 24 hours in the refrigerator. Drain and rinse the chickpeas.

Place the chickpeas in a medium saucepan and cover them with 2 inches of water, add the baking soda, and bring to a boil over medium-high heat. Reduce the heat and simmer, skimming off any scum, adding the salt after the first 15 minutes, until the chickpeas are tender-firm and salad-ready, 45 to 60 minutes. Drain the chickpeas and cover them.

Make the pita chips: Preheat the oven to 350°F.

In a small bowl, whisk together the olive oil, cumin, sumac, salt, paprika, and cayenne. Brush one side of each pita with the oil mixture, and cut through the stack four times to

RECIPE CONTINUES

yield 8 equal triangles per round, for a total of 32 triangles. Divide among 2 large rimmed baking sheets and bake until golden, switching the baking sheets midway through baking, 12 to 13 minutes total.

Fry the eggplant: In a high-sided skillet, heat ½ inch oil over medium-high heat. Season the eggplant generously on both sides with salt and pepper and fry until golden, 3 minutes per side. Drain on paper towels.

Cook the eggs and potatoes: In a medium pot, cover the potatoes with heavily salted cold water, bring to a boil, reduce the heat to a high simmer, and cook the potatoes until easily pierced with a fork but not mushy, 17 to 18 minutes. Using a slotted spoon, remove the potatoes to a plate; don't drain the water from the pot. When the potatoes are cool enough to handle, cut them into chunks. Set up an ice-water bath for the eggs. Gently lower the eggs into the boiling water that had been used for the potatoes and cook until the yolks are just cooked, 8 minutes. Remove the eggs with a slotted spoon, gently crack the shells to create little hairline cracks, and lower them into the ice water until cool, 5 minutes. Peel the eggs under cold running water and quarter them.

Make the dressing: In a jar with a tight-fitting lid, shake the tahini, lemon juice, ¼ cup water, olive oil, amba, salt, and cayenne until creamy.

Assemble the salad: On a serving platter, arrange the romaine, eggplant, tomatoes, eggs, pita chips, chickpeas, and parsley leaves and drizzle with the dressing.

Israeli Salad

Israeli salad is little more than the best vegetables you've got, chopped up, and seasoned to taste with lemon juice, olive oil, salt, and pepper. The only two nonnegotiable ingredients are firm, crunchy cucumbers and juicy, ripe tomatoes. Though small is often a way to show you've made some effort, cut them into the size you like—there is no wrong answer here!— and add radishes, red onions, carrots, kohlrabi . . . whatever you desire, really, as long as it's really fresh. Crunch is essential, and a bit of chopped fresh parsley is always a nice addition. Drizzling with Basic Tahini Sauce (page 120), loosened with a bit of extra water or lemon juice to get the pourable texture you want, completes this most simple, and most Israeli, of salads. If you're lucky, you'll find a pool of flavorful juices in the bottom of your bowl. At his restaurant in Philadelphia, my friend Michael Solomonov makes an Israeli Salad martini inspired by this heady brew, but I just tip the dregs straight into my mouth from the bowl, a chilled chaser that's as satisfying as the salad itself.

Persimmon, Goat Cheese, and Pecan Salad with Very Lemony Dressing

When the shuk is overflowing with persimmons, I'm helpless to resist them. Their complex flavor, sort of like a slice of spiced fruitcake picked off a tree, seduces me every time. If I see the tapered, longer Hachiya variety, I wait for them to get good and ripe, cut off the top, and scoop out the fruit with a spoon like pudding (or use them in my Triple Ginger Persimmon Loaf, page 326). If they're the firm, round Fuyu variety, I eat them like apples, or use them in salads, because I've never met a piece of lettuce that can't make friends with some delicious fruit. The key is to make sure your salad dressing is sufficiently sweet *and* acidic. This lemony one, mixed with a combination of silan, honey, and lemon juice, fits the bill. If you can't find persimmons, a firm, ripe peach or a tart apple work very well here.

DRESSING
(Makes ⅔ cup)
½ cup extra-virgin olive oil
¼ cup freshly squeezed lemon juice
1½ tablespoons Dijon mustard
1½ teaspoons silan (date syrup)
1½ teaspoons honey
¼ teaspoon kosher salt
¼ teaspoon freshly ground black pepper

SALAD
1 large head butter lettuce, torn into bite-sized pieces
1 large, firm persimmon, thinly sliced, or 1 firm peach or crisp apple, such as Honeycrisp or Pink Lady
½ small red onion, thinly sliced

½ cup toasted pecans (chopped if you want, or whole if that's the way you like them)*
4 ounces soft goat cheese, torn into chunks

○○○○○○○○○○○
Serves 4

Prep Time:
10 minutes

Total Time:
20 minutes
(including cooling time for the pecans)
○○○○○○○○○○○

Make the dressing: In a jar with a tight-fitting lid, shake the olive oil, lemon juice, mustard, silan, honey, salt, and pepper until unified and creamy.

Assemble the salad: Arrange the lettuce, persimmon slices, onion slices, pecans, and goat cheese on a platter. Shake the dressing again for a second or two and drizzle some of the dressing over the salad.

*To toast the pecans, preheat the oven to 350°F. Arrange the pecans on a small rimmed baking sheet and bake until slightly fragrant, 6 to 7 minutes. Remove from the oven and cool completely.

Rough-Chopped Salad with Yogurt and Dukkah

I like to keep the vegetables in this salad big, all the better for tasting the difference in textures and taste among carrots, radishes, cucumbers, tomatoes, kohlrabi, and whatever else I have available or decide to throw in that day. Next to it I put a bowl of Egyptian-inspired dukkah, my favorite all-purpose topping. Toasted hazelnuts and whole spices, sesame seeds, a hint of sugar, and a generous lashing of salt are all ground up into a Middle Eastern umami mix. Make a double batch, because it's killer sprinkled on popcorn, fish, or swirled into a bowl of olive oil as a dip for bread.

Dukkah (page 25)

Tomatoes

Kohlrabi

Cucumbers

Carrots

Radishes

Scallion greens

Yogurt

Extra-virgin olive oil

Freshly squeezed lemon juice

Kosher salt and freshly ground black pepper to taste

Serving size varies

Active Time: 20 minutes (if you've already made the dukkah)

Total Time: 20 minutes

Make sure you have the dukkah prepared before you begin making this recipe. Coarsely chop the vegetables to your desired size. Spread some yogurt on a plate or in a bowl, put the vegetables on top, drizzle with olive oil and lemon juice, season with salt and pepper, and top with as much dukkah as you like (which I predict will be a lot).

Kohlrabi

Though the name might sound like it has origins in the Middle East, it's actually German, and the word actually means "turnip cabbage," which should give you a heads-up on what to expect taste-wise. Widely available in Israel, kohlrabi is still relatively new to Western palates. Delicious raw, in soups, or roasted, its earthy, sweet flavor stays true in any preparation. When preparing kohlrabi, peel off a little more of the skin than you think you need to; it's got a fibrous layer that's virtually invisible but can be tough even when cooked.

Halloumi and Butternut Squash Salad with Crispy Chickpeas

Halloumi cheese is extremely popular in Israel, where it's grilled, pan-fried, or deep-fried and used to top salads for an unbeatable hot-cold combination. A sort of mozzarella on steroids, its firm, rubbery texture prevents the cheese from melting upon contact with high heat, allowing it to develop a charred, crispy exterior that can be sliced and eaten with a knife and fork. Though I usually see it paired with tomato-and-cucumber salads, I marry it here with roasted squash and crunchy, oven-baked chickpeas that are a great snack all on their own.

SALAD

1½ cups drained and rinsed canned or cooked chickpeas (see method, page 168)

2 tablespoons extra-virgin olive oil

1½ teaspoons kosher salt

1 teaspoon ground cumin

1 teaspoon ground sumac

¾ teaspoon freshly ground black pepper

½ teaspoon cayenne pepper

1 pound butternut squash, peeled, seeded, and cut into ½-inch-thick pieces

One 8-ounce package of halloumi cheese, sliced into ½-inch-thick pieces and patted dry

1 medium head romaine lettuce, torn into bite-sized pieces

Chopped scallion greens, for garnish

DRESSING (Makes ¾ cup)

4 tablespoons extra-virgin olive oil

2 tablespoons Pomegranate Molasses (page 48 or store-bought)

1 tablespoon red wine vinegar

1 tablespoon water

1 tablespoon silan (date syrup)

1 tablespoon Dijon mustard

1 tablespoon finely minced shallot

⅛ teaspoon kosher salt

⅛ teaspoon freshly ground black pepper

Serves 4

Active Time:
25 minutes

Total Time:
45 minutes

Prepare the salad: Preheat the oven to 425°F.

Dry the chickpeas between two clean kitchen towels (or paper towels) set on a large rimmed baking sheet; the more you dry them, the crispier they will be. In a medium bowl, toss the chickpeas in 1 tablespoon of the olive oil, 1 teaspoon of the salt, the cumin, sumac, ½ teaspoon of the pepper, and the cayenne. Spread evenly on the baking sheet.

In a medium bowl, whisk the remaining 1 tablespoon of the olive oil with the remaining ½ teaspoon salt and ¼ teaspoon pepper. Add the squash, toss until evenly coated, and spread on a second large rimmed baking sheet. Roast, switching the sheets halfway through, until the chickpeas are crispy and the squash is soft, 25 minutes total.

Make the dressing: While the chickpeas are roasting, combine all the ingredients in a jar with a tight-fitting lid and shake until creamy. The dressing will keep refrigerated in an airtight container for up to 1 week.

Sear the halloumi and assemble the salad: Over medium-high heat, sear the halloumi until browned, 2 minutes per side. Layer the lettuce, squash, scallion greens, and halloumi on a platter. Drizzle with the dressing, and scatter with the chickpeas. Serve immediately.

Toasted Challah Caprese Salad with Za'atar Vinaigrette

I sometimes let my challah go stale just so I can make my all-time favorite croutons. I tear them straight from whatever's left in the loaf and use them to top this summery, super-simple salad that gets a great hit of salt from cured Moroccan black olives and creamy contrast from fresh mozzarella. If you like a crunchier crouton, add the toasted challah at the end just before the dressing. But there's much joy to be had from letting the challah spend time absorbing the salad's summery flavor.

CROUTONS

3 cups torn challah, brioche, or other light, eggy bread of your choice

2 tablespoons extra-virgin olive oil

½ teaspoon kosher salt, plus more for seasoning

⅛ teaspoon freshly ground black pepper

DRESSING

⅓ cup extra-virgin olive oil

⅓ cup freshly squeezed lemon juice

1 tablespoon Za'atar Spice Blend (page 28 or store-bought)

½ teaspoon kosher salt

¼ teaspoon freshly ground black pepper

SALAD

4 medium ripe Roma or vine tomatoes, cut into chunks

8 medium Persian cucumbers, halved lengthwise and cut into chunks

One 6-ounce ball fresh mozzarella, torn into pieces

12 pitted oil-cured Moroccan olives, halved if desired

½ cup lightly packed basil leaves

○○○○○○○○○○

Serves 6

Active Time:
15 minutes

Total Time:
30 minutes

○○○○○○○○○○

Make the croutons: Preheat the oven to 350°F.

Place the challah on a large baking sheet, drizzle with the olive oil, season lightly with salt and pepper, and bake until golden and crisp, 12 to 13 minutes. Remove from the oven to cool on the baking sheet.

Make the dressing: In a jar with a tight-fitting lid, shake the olive oil with the lemon juice, za'atar, salt, and pepper until emulsified.

Make the salad: On a platter, arrange the tomatoes, cucumbers, mozzarella, olives, and basil. Pour most of the dressing on top, toss the salad, season with salt and pepper to taste, then scatter the challah on top and drizzle with the rest of the dressing.

PASTA AND GRAINS

Cinnamony Smoky Eggplant P'titim

Word to the wise: If you're in Israel shopping for pantry staples, don't ask for "Israeli couscous"; shopkeepers will look at you quizzically and give you regular semolina couscous. To Israelis, these are p'titim, and p'titim only. An after-school snack for generations of Israeli kids the way a box of mac 'n' cheese is for Americans, these tiny orbs of pasta were invented as a substitute for rice during Israel's so-called austerity period in the 1950s, when food was scarce and creativity was key. Israel's first prime minister, David Ben-Gurion, came up with the idea, so older Israelis know the product as "Ben-Gurion's Rice." Quick-cooking and absorbent, it soaks up any sauce you throw its way. No one's going to mistake this dish for rice, but p'titim deserve a place of their own in every kitchen. If you can't find them in a shop, Italian fregola works well, too.

1½ cups uncooked p'titim (Israeli couscous)

⅓ cup extra-virgin olive oil

½ small Italian eggplant, cubed (2 cups)

1 medium onion, chopped

1¼ teaspoons kosher salt

¼ teaspoon freshly ground black pepper

2 garlic cloves, finely chopped

1 tablespoon tomato paste

1 teaspoon ground cinnamon

½ teaspoon ground cumin

¼ teaspoon cayenne pepper

1 medium tomato, diced, or 1 cup canned diced tomatoes in juice

¼ teaspoon smoked paprika

¼ cup fresh parsley, chopped

○○○○○○○○○○

**Serves
4 to 6**

Active Time:
30 minutes

Total Time:
45 minutes

○○○○○○○○○○

In a dry skillet, toast the p'titim over medium heat, stirring frequently, until lightly golden and fragrant, 3 minutes. Transfer the p'titim to a plate. Add the olive oil to the skillet and raise the heat to medium-high. Add the eggplant, onions, ½ teaspoon of the salt, and the black pepper and cook, stirring often, until the onions are golden and softened and the eggplant has shrunk and is browned, 9 to 10 minutes. Add the garlic and cook 1 more minute. Add the tomato paste, cinnamon, cumin, cayenne, and another ½ teaspoon salt and cook, stirring, for 1 minute. Add the tomatoes and 1½ cups water to the pan, then stir in the p'titim, cover with a tight-fitting lid, reduce the heat to medium-low, and cook until the p'titim have absorbed all the liquid, 8 to 9 minutes. Remove from the heat and let rest for 2 minutes. Open the lid, stir in the paprika, the remaining ¼ teaspoon salt, and the parsley and serve immediately.

Lentils with Crispy Leeks and Fennel

I realized it was Mother's Day right before arriving at Zarafat Abu Dala's home in Yarka, a Druze village in the Lower Galilee (150,000 of the world's one million Druze, who are Arab but not Muslim, live in Israel, mostly in the Galilee). After handing over a bouquet of flowers I'd procured minutes before, I was rewarded with a plate of moist carrot cake, fresh mint tea, and a chat with Zarafat's daughter, Malak, who was our translator. Though Zarafat's husband, a television broadcaster, died four years ago, as Druze believe his soul inhabited a living person's body somewhere in the world. After he died, Zarafat began hosting meals at her house. We headed to the outdoor kitchen, stocked with homemade pickles olives and grape leaves stuffed into plastic jars and Coke bottles. We cooked a lot that day, but her fragrant lentils, loaded with soft onions, Baharat (page 24), and loads of fennel fronds, was my favorite. Since those fronds rarely make it to the market in Israel—much less in the United States—I swapped in a head of fennel to evoke that flavor. The crispy leek topping steers this dish in the direction of Lebanese mujadara.

1 cup green lentils, picked over

3 medium-large or 6 small leeks (1½ pounds), tender green and white parts only, thinly sliced into rounds

1 large head of fennel, with as many fronds attached as possible

6 tablespoons extra-virgin olive oil

1 teaspoon kosher salt, plus more for seasoning

1 teaspoon Baharat (page 24)

½ teaspoon ground cumin

2 cups low-sodium chicken broth

½ teaspoon freshly ground black pepper

Serves 4 to 6

Active Time: 25 minutes

Total Time: 60 minutes

Place the lentils in a medium bowl, cover with cold water, soak for 15 minutes, and drain.

Place the leeks in a large bowl, cover with cold water, and soak for 15 minutes to release any sand. Lift the leeks out into a strainer, drain well, and pat dry.

Trim and discard the stalks from the fennel, but remove and reserve the fronds. Halve the fennel through its core, then use the tip of the knife to cut out and discard the white inner core; thinly slice the fennel.

Heat 3 tablespoons of the olive oil in a large skillet over medium-high heat. Add half the leeks and cook, stirring, until deep brown and crisped, 10 to 11 minutes. Drain on a paper towel–lined plate; season with salt to taste.

In the same skillet, heat the remaining 3 tablespoons olive oil over medium heat. Add the other half of the leeks and cook, stirring, until tender, 4 minutes. Add the fennel, baharat, and cumin, and cook until the fennel starts to soften, 5 minutes. Add the drained lentils, broth, salt, and pepper to the skillet. Bring to a boil, reduce the heat to low, cover with a tight-fitting lid, and simmer until the lentils are tender and have absorbed the liquid, 20 to 25 minutes. Chop the fennel fronds, add most of them to the leeks, and transfer to a serving bowl. Top with the crispy leeks and a few fennel fronds.

Jeweled Rice

Because of its sweet, savory, and herby elements, this rice seems to go with everything. Basmati and jasmine rice both work well here, and though the barberries have a nice tartness, you can swap in whatever dried fruit you have around (same goes for the pistachios; use any nut you like).

6 tablespoons extra-virgin olive oil

1 jumbo onion, thinly sliced

1 teaspoon kosher salt

1½ cups basmati or jasmine rice

½ cup finely chopped dill, plus more for garnish

⅓ cup barberries or chopped dried cranberries

⅓ cup toasted pistachios, coarsely chopped

¼ cup toasted sliced almonds

Zest of 1 lemon

¼ teaspoon freshly ground black pepper

**Serves
4 to 6**

Active Time:
30 minutes

Total Time:
1 hour
10 minutes

In a large skillet, heat 3 tablespoons of the olive oil over medium-high heat. Add the onions and cook, stirring frequently at first to prevent the onions from burning, until the onions begin to soften, 5 minutes. Reduce the heat to medium and cook, stirring often, until the onions begin to turn light golden, another 20 minutes. Reduce the heat to medium-low, add ¼ teaspoon of the salt to the onions and cook, stirring, until the onions are caramelized and deep golden, another 15 to 20 minutes.

In a colander, rinse the rice until the water runs clear. In a large saucepan, bring the rice and 2¼ cups water to a boil, reduce the heat to low, cover, and simmer until the rice has absorbed all the water and is fluffy, 16 to 17 minutes. Uncover the rice and stir in the caramelized onions, dill, barberries, pistachios, almonds, and lemon zest with the remaining 3 tablespoons olive oil, ¾ teaspoon salt, and the pepper.

Freekeh and Roasted Grape Salad

Freekeh comes cracked or whole, which impacts its cooking time, but either way, it's chewy and mild, but not overwhelmingly smoky. It has a natural stickiness, and releases a gray film when cooked, but don't worry; you can skim it off after cooking. Though it's great warm, I love freekeh cold as the base for a salad with roasted vegetables or, better yet, fruit, which plays nicely in the flavor sandbox. Enter grapes, which I know you may be tempted to roast only after they began to wilt in the fridge. But I discovered that when starting with plump, fresh grapes—just the kind you'd want to eat out of hand—they shrivel slightly but maintain a concentrated burst of grapey flavor that's spot-on when combined with the crunch of toasted walnuts.

1½ cups freekeh, preferably whole (cracked is also fine!)

2½ cups (1 pound) seedless red grapes*

½ cup extra-virgin olive oil

1½ teaspoons kosher salt, plus more to taste

½ teaspoon freshly ground black pepper, plus more to taste

⅓ cup plus 2 tablespoons freshly squeezed lemon juice, plus more for seasoning

¼ teaspoon dried hot pepper flakes, such as Aleppo

Finely grated zest of 1 lemon

½ cup finely minced fresh chives or chopped parsley

½ cup chopped toasted walnuts

Serves 4 to 6

Active Time: 15 minutes

Total Time: 1 hour 15 minutes (including soaking time)

Preheat the oven to 400°F. Place the freekeh in a medium bowl, cover with water, and soak, 15 minutes for cracked and 30 minutes for whole. Drain and rinse the freekeh. Place the grapes on a large rimmed baking sheet, drizzle with 2 tablespoons olive oil, season with ½ teaspoon of the salt and ¼ teaspoon of the black pepper, and roast in the oven, shaking every 5 minutes or so, until the grapes shrivel and some are very caramelized and even a little burned on the edges, 20 to 25 minutes.

Place the drained freekeh in a medium saucepan with 2½ cups water and ½ teaspoon of the salt, bring it to a boil over medium-high heat, reduce the heat to medium-low and simmer, skimming off any scum and stirring occasionally once the water is partially absorbed, until the freekeh is cooked, 15 minutes for cracked and 25 to 30 minutes for whole (if water is absorbed but whole freekeh is not fully cooked through after 20 minutes, add ¼ to ⅓ cup water). Transfer to a large rimmed baking sheet and spread out to cool.

In a medium bowl, whisk ⅓ cup lemon juice with the remaining ⅓ cup olive oil, ½ teaspoon salt, ¼ teaspoon pepper, and the dried pepper flakes. Add the cooled freekeh and grapes along with the lemon zest and chives; gently toss and let sit for 5 minutes. Toss in the remaining 2 tablespoons lemon juice with walnuts. Season with salt, pepper, and lemon juice to taste.

*As seen on the cover, you can swap in ½ cup fresh pomegranate seeds for the grapes, or 2 tablespoons red onion for the chives, or ¼ cup toasted pine nuts for the walnuts.

Tahdig
(Crispy-Bottomed Persian Rice)

I love a recipe whose main ingredient is suspense. Tahdig, the iconic Persian rice dish, is named for the crispy layer at the bottom of the pot. Inverting the pot to reveal the tahdig never gets old! The secret is yogurt; I learned it from my Persian-Israeli friend Rottem Lieberson, who suspects that the extra fat and protein in the yogurt help stabilize the rice, brown it evenly, and prevent it from burning. Though there are many versions of tahdig with fruits, nuts, and potatoes, I find the additions increase your chances for failure. And since I'm all about crispy-rice victory, I offer the plain version here. Make sure not to skip the step of catching extra steam with a kitchen towel during cooking, which helps make the rice dreamily fluffy.

1½ cups good-quality jasmine or basmati rice

2 tablespoons kosher salt

¼ teaspoon ground turmeric

10 saffron strands (optional)

¼ cup Eight-Hour Labaneh (page 44 or store-bought), or Greek yogurt

¼ cup vegetable oil

Serves 6

Active Time:
25 minutes

Total Time:
1 hour

Place the rice in a medium bowl, cover with very cold water (warm water softens the rice too quickly), and soak for 20 to 25 minutes, swishing occasionally. Strain and rinse until the water runs clear (you'll be good after 1 minute).

During the last 15 minutes of rice soaking, fill a 6-quart pot halfway with water and bring it to a boil. Add the rice, salt, turmeric, and saffron, if using, return the water to a boil. Boil until the rice is a lovely golden color and is soft on the outside but still has a bit of a bite, exactly 4 minutes. Drain the rice well, then scoop 2 cups of the rice into a bowl and mix in the labaneh until well incorporated.

Arrange a large, clean kitchen towel on the counter. Place the lid of a 10-inch skillet in the center of the towel, bring the ends of the towel to meet on top of the lid, and tie them so the lid is wrapped in the towel. Heat the oil in the skillet over medium-high heat until a grain of cooked rice sizzles upon contact. Add the labaneh-rice mixture to the skillet; spread it out evenly, pressing down slightly. Add the rest of the rice, but don't press it down (you want this rice to steam and release some of its moisture). Cook until you see some browned bits around the edges of the rice, 9 to 10 minutes. Cover the rice with the cloth-wrapped lid, reduce the heat to very low, and cook until the edges have taken on a deep golden color, 35 minutes.

Remove the skillet from the stove and use a knife to loosen the sides. Fit a round serving platter slightly larger than the skillet's diameter over the rice. Using two oven mitt-lined hands, flip the rice; there should be a layer of fluffy rice underneath and a single layer of golden, burnished crispy tahdig on top. If not, simply do what millions have done before you and use a dull knife or offset spatula to gently dislodge the tahdig from the skillet. YUM!

Yerushalmi Kugel

During the year I spent between high school and college at a religious-studies program in Jerusalem, my dormitory was at the edge of Ge'ula, an ultra-Orthodox neighborhood where men shielded their eyes to avoid visual contact with women. We'd venture out late Thursday nights—knees, elbows, and any other potentially offensive parts covered—to watch as the city prepared for the Sabbath that would begin the next night. Thousands of people milled around running errands, buying holy books, and shopping for food from counters that sold delicious Ashkenazi takeout: roast chicken and oily paprika-dusted potatoes, endless varieties of yeast-risen cakes, and my favorite, Yerushalmi (Jerusalem) kugel. Towering and majestic, the peppery, golden noodle pudding was sweet-and-spicy comfort food, a side dish that ate like dessert. Our purchases almost never made it back to our dormitory unopened; on the way, we'd tear off the kugel piece by piece, the tender noodles surrounded by a chewy-crunchy crust where the *lukshion* (Yiddish for "noodles") had made contact with the pot. I've made Yerushalmi kugel many times, but one challenge has always been the oil-based caramel at its base (butter can't be eaten with meat dishes at a kosher Shabbat table), which tends to clump upon contact with the noodles. I solved the problem by loosening the caramel with just enough water so that it coated the still-warm noodles. In Jerusalem, the kugel is baked in giant, family-sized vessels, sometimes overnight. I bake my kugel for only 2 hours, but it still yields a delicious crusty layer, which hardens as it cools. You can go up in pot size; just remember—the larger your pot, the less dramatic height your final kugel will have.

3 cups sugar

Two 12-ounce packages of thin egg noodles

⅔ cup plus 1 tablespoon vegetable oil

1¾ tablespoons freshly ground black pepper, plus more if desired

1½ tablespoons kosher salt

6 large eggs, at room temperature, beaten

Serves 12

Active Time:
35 minutes

Total Time:
2 hours
55 minutes

Preheat the oven to 350°F.

Bring a large pot of salted water to a boil over medium-high heat, reduce to medium-low, cover, and keep at a simmer while you make the caramel.

Add the sugar to a 4-quart oven-safe saucepan (make sure there's a good amount of headroom on top of the sugar, like 5 or 6 inches, since there will be some sputtering later). Sprinkle ⅔ cup cold water evenly over the sugar so it's completely saturated and the consistency of wet sand, gently tilting the pan (but not stirring) to saturate any dry spots. Melt the sugar and water over medium heat until it reaches a uniform simmer, about 6 minutes, then raise the heat to medium-high and boil the liquid, not touching the caramel or swirling the pan, until it's a beautiful deep, dark maple color, 8 to 9 minutes. (At this point the difference between minutes is important, so don't move away from the pot. It can make the difference between a sweet kugel and a burnt, smoky one; the darker the caramel, the darker the kugel.) Turn off the heat and remove the caramel from the flame.

RECIPE CONTINUES

Using a ⅓ cup measure, lift out ⅓ cup hot water from the simmering pot and immediately add it to the caramel; the mixture will sputter and bubble wildly for a minute, then calm down and become a thick, dark golden liquid; swirl a couple of times, cover the caramel, and set it aside. While the caramel is cooling, return the pot of salted water to a boil over high heat and cook the noodles until al dente (no need to wait for the water to return to a boil), about 3 minutes.

Drain the noodles, rinse well in warm water, and return the noodles to the pot you cooked them in. Using a silicone spatula, scrape as much of the warm caramel as you can into the warm noodles and stir to combine; it's okay if there's a little sticky caramel left in the pot. Stir in the vegetable oil, followed by the pepper, and salt. Cool the noodle mixture until lukewarm, 10 to 15 minutes, then stir in the eggs to combine (if you do this too soon you might cook the eggs). Pour the mixture back into the pot you used to make the caramel (any hardened caramel will dissolve during baking).

Transfer to the oven and bake until the color deepens and the top develops a crust, 1 hour and 45 minutes to 2 hours. Cool for 30 minutes, loosen the edges of the kugel with a knife, and invert it onto a serving platter. Serve immediately, sliced into wedges, or allow to cool completely. If you wait, the outer shell of the kugel will be chewier.

Jerusalem (Kugel) of Gold

According to chef and food researcher Shmil Holland, kugel—a term that today is a catch-all for all sorts of baked, starchy casseroles—got its start in Alsace, France, where kugels were made of bread and apples bound with fat (as eloquently described in Joan Nathan's lovely cookbook *Quiches, Kugels, and Couscous: My Search for Jewish Cooking in France*). Eventually the tradition spread to Eastern Europe, where kugels were made with apples, berries, and nuts. When the first Hasidic Jews settled in Jerusalem in the 1800s, a lack of familiar ingredients led them to make a simpler, but no less delicious, kugel with little more than oil, sugar, noodles, and any eggs they had. The addition of pepper and the sour pickle with which Yerushalmi kugel is traditionally served (I skip the pickle) are nods to the local Israeli and Arabic traditions.

Potato Vareniki with Brown Butter and Drunken Salmon Roe

"Think of these as the Russian wontons," Sabina Valdman told me as we rolled out the dough for the vareniki she ate as a child in Riga, Latvia. Flour and water enriched with an egg yolk and a knob of butter created a pliant pasta that rolled like a dream, ready to be filled with a peppery mixture of potatoes and onions. Once Valdman's family moved to Israel in 1988—three years before communism fell and nearly a million former Soviets began their exodus to Israel—dishes like these kept them connected to their own life as they forged a new one that included being open about being Jewish for the first time in their lives. "We never talked about it in Russia," said Valdman, a well-known chef and TV cooking-competition veteran who did everything she could to lose her Russian accent and immerse herself in Israeli culture upon arrival. "That included the food." But over the past few years, perhaps because she got married and is now the mother of a newborn baby, she has found herself returning to her childhood for inspiration. That includes vareniki, which means "things cooked in boiling water" in Russian. After we filled, crimped, and cooked the dumplings, we riffed on the more traditional serving style—straight out of the water with a dollop of butter, and dill—by toasting them in browned butter and bedazzling them with salmon eggs we soaked in vodka. "What can I say?" said Valdman. "There's no escaping home."

DOUGH

1½ cups all-purpose flour, plus more for kneading

½ teaspoon kosher salt

½ cup boiling water

1 stick (½ cup) unsalted butter, at room temperature

1 large egg yolk

FILLING

2 medium Russet potatoes (1 pound), scrubbed

7 tablespoons unsalted butter, at room temperature

1 large onion, thinly sliced

¾ teaspoon kosher salt, plus more to taste

½ teaspoon freshly ground black pepper

ASSEMBLY

3 tablespoons salmon roe (optional)

2 tablespoons vodka (optional)

White vinegar, sour cream, and fresh dill, for serving

Makes
25 dumplings

Active Time:
1 hour
10 minutes

Total Time:
2 hours
15 minutes

Make the dough: In a medium bowl, combine 1 cup of the flour and the salt with the water and the butter and stir until combined. Stir in the remaining ½ cup flour, form a well in the center, add the yolk to the well, and use your hands to knead the egg into the dough. Transfer the dough to a lightly floured surface and knead the dough until smooth, 1 minute. Place the dough in a floured bowl, cover it with plastic wrap or a clean kitchen towel, and let it rest for 45 minutes and up to 1 hour.

While the dough is resting, make the filling: Add the potatoes to a medium saucepan and cover with cold water. Bring to a boil over medium-high heat, reduce the heat to medium (the water should still be bubbling and rolling but doesn't need to be raging), and boil until the potatoes can easily be pierced with a fork, 25 to 30 minutes. Drain the potatoes and cool.

RECIPE CONTINUES

While the potatoes are cooking, in a large skillet sauté 3 tablespoons of the butter with the onions over low heat, stirring occasionally, until the onions are translucent, 20 minutes. Raise the heat slightly and continue to cook, stirring occasionally, until the onions are deep golden but not burnt, another 20 to 25 minutes. Transfer the onions to a bowl (save the skillet with any onion bits for later). Peel the cooled potatoes, add them to the bowl with the onions, add the salt and pepper, and mash until smooth.

Gently stir the salmon roe and vodka together in a small bowl and refrigerate, if using.

Bring a large pot of generously salted water to a boil over medium-high heat. Flour a large work surface, uncover the dough, and roll it out into a large, thin circle about 20 inches in diameter; the dough should be pliable and easy to roll. Use a round 3-inch cookie cutter to cut out about 25 circles from the dough.* Place 1 tablespoon of the filling in the center of each round, then pull up the sides of the circle, stretching the dough to enclose the filling and creating a half-moon shape. Pinch with your fingers and crimp to seal.** Drop the vareniki into the water and cook them until they float and the water returns to a boil, 3 to 4 minutes. Drain the vareniki in a colander, removing as much liquid as possible.

Finish the vareniki and assemble: Add 2 tablespoons of the remaining butter to the skillet you used to cook the onions. Brown the butter over medium-low heat until small flecks appear, 3 to 4 minutes. Add half the vareniki and cook until they are slightly crisped and golden, 2 to 3 minutes per side. Using an offset spatula, transfer the vareniki to a platter and repeat with the remaining vareniki and butter. Drizzle with a tiny amount of white vinegar, and top with sour cream, vodka-soaked salmon roe (if using), and dill.

*Instead of rerolling the dough into more vareniki, gather up the scraps and throw the freeform noodles straight into the hot water, cook them for 1 to 2 minutes, drain them, and toss them with butter, cinnamon, and sugar. Dessert is served.

**At this point you can freeze the uncooked vareniki on a lightly buttered sheet pan in a single layer, then pop them into a resealable plastic bag. To cook them, drop them directly from the bag into boiling water and cook according to the instructions above.

Roasted Tomato and Labaneh Pappardelle

When labaneh is combined with roasted tomatoes, a new staple pasta sauce is born. The sweet and the tart mix together to cloak every bite of al dente pappardelle, which I chose specifically because its wide, flat surface is a great vehicle for the sauce. Fresh za'atar, if you can get it, really makes a difference; oregano, marjoram, or a sprinkle of dried za'atar spice blend would do great work here, too. Since labaneh can separate on its own, I add just enough cream to stabilize the sauce.

¾ pound dried pappardelle pasta

3 tablespoons extra-virgin olive oil, plus more for tossing the pasta

3 large garlic cloves, minced

1 teaspoon ground cumin

½ teaspoon dried red pepper flakes

1 recipe Roasted Sheet Pan Cherry Tomatoes (2½ cups roasted tomatoes, page 42)

3 tablespoons heavy cream or half-and-half

½ teaspoon kosher salt, plus more to taste

¼ teaspoon freshly ground black pepper, plus more to taste

½ cup 4-Hour Labaneh (page 44 or store-bought) or Greek yogurt

Chopped fresh or dried za'atar, chopped fresh or dried oregano or marjoram, or Za'atar Spice Blend (page 28), for serving

Serves 4

Active Time:
10 minutes

Total Time:
45 minutes (including Roasted Sheet Pan Cherry Tomatoes recipe)

Bring a large pot of generously salted water to a boil over medium-high heat and cook the pasta until al dente, about 3 minutes. Drain the pasta, reserving ¼ cup of the pasta water, and toss the pasta in a little bit of olive oil right in the colander to keep it from sticking. Add the 3 tablespoons of the olive oil to the empty pasta pot, reduce the heat to medium-low, then add the garlic, cumin, and red pepper flakes. Cook over medium heat, stirring, until the cumin is fragrant and the garlic is light golden, 2 minutes. Add the tomatoes, cream, salt, and black pepper, reduce the heat to medium-low, and warm through, 2 minutes. Add the labaneh, warm through for another minute, then add the pasta and toss it in the sauce, adding a little bit of the pasta water if needed to loosen the sauce. Season with salt and pepper, divide among 4 bowls, and garnish with za'atar.

Lemony Chili and Tuna Pasta

The seamy underside of being a recipe developer is that while there may often be lots of stuff in the fridge, sometimes there's just nothing for dinner. So one night I took the jar of "good" tuna from my cupboard (look for ones packed in olive oil in glass jars), grabbed a container of olives from the fridge, squired a bundle of bucatini from the cupboard, scraped the dregs of some 24-Hour Salted Lemon Spread (page 34) out of its little jar, and was well on my way to what has become one of our favorite dinners. Cooking the lemon condiment in olive oil for a bit before adding everything else caramelizes it slightly, rounding out some of its edges without losing the lemony sharpness you want here.

¾ pound bucatini or spaghetti

1 cup fresh shelled peas or frozen, thawed peas

¼ cup extra-virgin olive oil, plus more for tossing the pasta

6 garlic cloves, thinly sliced

⅓ to ½ cup 24-Hour Salted Lemon Spread (page 34)*

1 small hot red chili pepper, sliced into thin rounds

Two 6.7-ounce jars or three 5-ounce cans good-quality tuna in olive oil, drained

½ cup (¾ ounce) finely grated Parmigiano-Reggiano cheese, plus more for garnishing

¼ cup pitted cured Moroccan black olives, halved

1 cup finely minced fresh parsley

Freshly ground black pepper to taste

Serves 4

Active Time:
15 minutes

Total Time:
20 minutes

Bring a large pot of generously salted water to a boil over medium-high heat. Add the pasta and cook according to package directions until al dente, adding the peas during the last 30 seconds of cooking. Scoop out ¾ cup of the pasta water and reserve, then drain the pasta and peas. Toss them with a drop of olive oil right in the colander (the oil will keep the pasta from sticking). Return the pot to the stove, then add the ¼ cup olive oil, and heat over medium-low heat for 1 minute. Add the garlic and cook, stirring until fragrant and lightly golden, 2 minutes. Raise the heat to medium, add ⅓ cup of the lemon condiment and chilies and cook, stirring, until the mixture darkens slightly, 4 to 5 minutes. Add the reserved pasta water, stirring until everything is incorporated, then return the pasta and peas to the pot along with the tuna, cheese, and olives. Gently toss, taste, then toss with the remaining lemon condiment if you feel like it needs more punch. Toss with the parsley, season with black pepper, and garnish with more cheese.

*If you don't have any of the lemon condiment, you can sub in ¼ cup Preserved Lemon Paste (page 40), or more to taste, or the finely grated zest and juice of 1 large lemon.

Ricotta Dumplings with Pistachio-Cilantro Pesto

One spicy, pistachio-studded bite here tells you that you're in different pesto territory now. I've always struggled with pesto's richness. Adding spicy schug and a healthy amount of cilantro in the pesto brightens it up in surprising ways. OK, now the dumplings, which look like matzo balls but *so* aren't: I'd always wanted to try chef April Bloomfield's famous ricotta dumplings, but I was intimidated by a process that included rolling in semolina, and chilling overnight. Great news: Just mixing ricotta, flour, and egg yolks creates giant ricotta pillows in minutes. Just pull off pieces of dough, drop them in boiling water, and 3 minutes later—plus the time it takes to make the pesto—dinner is yours.

PISTACHIO-CILANTRO PESTO

1½ cups packed fresh basil leaves

½ cup packed fresh cilantro leaves

1½ cups (2¼ ounces) finely grated Parmigiano-Reggiano cheese

1 tablespoon Schug (page 35 or store-bought), or 1½ teaspoons chopped jalapeño

½ cup shelled pistachios, plus more, chopped, for garnish

½ teaspoon kosher salt

¼ teaspoon freshly ground black pepper

½ cup extra-virgin olive oil

DUMPLINGS

1 pound whole-milk ricotta cheese

1 cup (1½ ounces) finely grated Parmigiano-Reggiano cheese

1 large egg yolk

1 teaspoon kosher salt, plus more to taste

½ teaspoon freshly ground black pepper, plus more to taste

½ cup all-purpose flour

Serves
3 or 4

Active Time:
20 minutes

Total Time:
40 minutes

Make the pesto: In the bowl of a food processor, process the basil, cilantro, Parmigiano-Reggiano, schug, pistachios, salt, and pepper. With the motor running, drizzle in the olive oil in a thin stream until a smooth pesto forms, about 20 seconds. Measure out ½ cup and store the rest in an airtight container in the refrigerator for up to 1 week.

Make the dumplings: Bring a medium pot of generously salted water to a boil over medium-high heat. Stack three heavy-duty paper towels on a plate. Dollop the ricotta on top of the towels, spread it out, stack three more paper towels on top, and press down for 5 minutes to absorb the liquid. Peel away and discard the towels. Transfer the ricotta to a bowl and stir in the Parmigiano-Reggiano, egg yolk, salt, and pepper. Gently sift in the flour and stir just until a loose dough is formed. Form the dough into 10 golf ball–sized rounds. (Don't handle or pack the dough too much. The balls don't need to be perfectly round, either.) Drop the dough into the water, return to a boil, and cook until the dumplings float to the top and are cooked through, 4 to 5 minutes. Use a slotted spoon to transfer the dumplings to a paper towel–lined plate. Reserve ¼ cup pasta cooking water.

Finish the dish: In a large skillet, cook the reserved ½ cup pesto and ¼ cup pasta cooking water over medium heat until simmering, 2 to 3 minutes. Move the drained dumplings to the skillet, toss to coat with the pesto, and warm through for 2 minutes. Season with salt and pepper and garnish with pistachios.

POULTRY AND MEAT MAINS

- Crispy Sesame Schnitzel
- Harissa-Honey Pargiyot (Boneless Chicken Thighs)
- Sumac Grilled Chicken, Citrus, and Avocado Salad
- Shawarma Pargiyot
- Za'atar Roasted Chicken over Sumac Potatoes
- Sour Lime and Pomegranate Chicken Wings
- Grilled Chicken and Corn Salad with Avocado-Za'atar Green Goddess Dressing
- Root Vegetable and Medjool Date Stew
- Turkish Coffee–Rubbed Rib Eyes with Seared Broccoli
- Hawaiij-Braised Short Ribs with Roasted Kohlrabi Mash
- Mafroum (Stuffed Eggplant in Tomato Sauce)
- Schug-Marinated Baby Lamb Chops
- Mini Herb and Garlic Kebaburgers
- Rice and Beef–Stuffed Tomatoes

Crispy Sesame Schnitzel

Israeli schnitzel used to be pounded from inexpensive turkey cutlets, breaded and fried to approximate Austrian wiener schnitzel made with veal. Today, nearly all of it is made with chicken breasts you can buy, thinly sliced and stacked between pieces of cellophane, at butchers and supermarkets. Frozen, breaded schnitzel is a classic staple, too, but it's so much better to make your own. So many creative varieties abound, but to me the classic version is still the best. Letting the breaded schnitzel rest for even half an hour ensures that the breading adheres to the chicken like a glove, meaning minimal runaway crumbs during the frying process.

1 cup dried breadcrumbs

½ cup panko breadcrumbs

¼ cup sesame seeds

1 teaspoon fine sea salt, plus more for seasoning

½ teaspoon garlic powder

½ teaspoon paprika

½ teaspoon freshly ground black pepper, plus more for seasoning

¼ teaspoon cayenne pepper, or more if you like it hot

2 large eggs, beaten

½ cup all-purpose flour

Four 6-ounce boneless, skinless chicken breast halves

½ cup vegetable oil, for frying, plus more as needed

Serves 4

Active Time:
10 minutes

Total Time:
30 minutes

In a shallow dish, combine the dried breadcrumbs, panko, sesame seeds, ½ teaspoon of the salt, garlic powder, paprika, ¼ teaspoon of the black pepper, and the cayenne. Place the beaten eggs in another shallow dish.

In a third shallow dish, combine the flour with the remaining ½ teaspoon salt and ¼ teaspoon black pepper.

Season the chicken generously with salt and black pepper. Place each piece between 2 pieces of plastic wrap and pound lightly with a mallet to achieve a thickness anywhere between ⅛ and ¼ inch. If you prefer your schnitzels to be smaller, this is the time to halve them.

Line a sheet tray with parchment. Dredge the cutlets in the flour, then the egg, then the breadcrumb mixture, shaking off the excess after each step and pressing the crumbs in firmly on both sides. Arrange them on the sheet tray as you finish the breading process. If desired, wait 30 minutes before frying (this helps the crumbs adhere better).

In a heavy skillet, heat the vegetable oil over medium heat for 2 to 3 minutes; the oil should be hot but not smoking. Working in batches, lay 2 cutlets in the pan and fry until the underside is golden brown and crisp, 2 to 3 minutes. Flip and fry for 2 to 3 more minutes. Drain on paper towels, season with salt and pepper to taste, and serve hot.

Note

To add extra seasoning to your schnitzel, add ¼ cup dukkah (page 25) to the breadcrumb mixture.

Harissa-Honey Pargiyot
(Boneless Chicken Thighs)

Though the actual definition of *pargit* is "baby chicken" or "Cornish hen," what we're actually talking about here are dark-meat boneless chicken thighs. Juicy, marinade-friendly, and pleasingly rich, they're as popular here as skinless, boneless chicken breasts are in the United States. For this recipe, I ask the butcher to leave the skin on. The harissa-honey glaze helps burnish and crisp the skin, and does its part in creating a pan sauce. To take advantage of the loquat's very short season, I threw some of those in the pan, but apricots, peaches—even tomato wedges—work beautifully here.

1¼ cups low-sodium chicken broth

3 tablespoons Honey Harissa (page 37) or 2 tablespoons store-bought, plus more for brushing chicken

2 tablespoons honey, plus more for drizzling

1 tablespoon sherry vinegar

1½ teaspoons kosher salt, plus more for seasoning

1½ teaspoons cornstarch

5 to 6 skin-on, boneless chicken thighs (about 1¾ pounds), patted dry

Freshly ground black pepper to taste

2 tablespoons extra-virgin olive oil

3 small onions (red or white), each cut into 4 wedges through the root*

3 medium loquats or apricots, halved

Thinly sliced scallions (green parts only) or chopped chives, for garnish

Rice, for serving

○○○○○○○○○○
Serves 4

Active Time:
15 minutes

Total Time:
45 minutes
○○○○○○○○○○

Arrange a rack in the upper third of the oven and preheat the broiler.

In a medium bowl, whisk together the broth, harissa, honey, vinegar, salt, and cornstarch. Season the chicken thighs generously with salt and pepper.

Heat the olive oil in a large (at least 10-inch) oven-safe skillet over medium-high heat. Add the chicken to the skillet, skin-side down, and cook without moving until the skin is browned and crisp, 4 to 5 minutes. Flip the chicken and cook until the underside is browned, 4 more minutes. Remove to a plate and drain and discard all but 2 tablespoons of the fat from the skillet. Reduce the heat to medium and arrange the onions in the skillet with one of the flat sides touching the surface of the skillet. Cook until the onions are golden on the underside, 2 to 3 minutes. Flip the onions and brown the underside an additional 2 to 3 minutes. Add the harissa-honey liquid to the skillet, raise the heat to medium-high, and cook until the mixture thickens, 3 to 4 minutes. Nestle the chicken skin-side up in the pan. Add the fruit and cook the chicken, spooning some of the sauce over the skin, until the fruit begins to soften slightly, 2 to 3 minutes. Transfer the skillet to the oven and broil until the skin crisps, the liquid thickens further, and the chicken is cooked through, 3 to 4 minutes for smaller thighs, 6 to 7 minutes for larger ones. Remove the chicken from the oven and garnish with scallions. Divide among plates and spoon the sauce over the top. Serve with rice.

*Leaving the root end of an onion intact ensures that when you cut the onion into wedges, they have a better chance of holding their shape.

Sumac Grilled Chicken, Citrus, and Avocado Salad

This may be the perfect sunny winter salad: juicy citrus, creamy avocados, crunchy lettuce, and a tangy sumac marinade and dressing. Since the chicken is also great served cold, you can basically make all the elements in advance and assemble it when you're ready to eat.

CHICKEN

½ cup extra-virgin olive oil

½ cup fresh clementine or orange juice (from 2 clementines), plus 3-inch-thick strips of clementine zest

1 tablespoon sumac

1 teaspoon kosher salt, plus more for seasoning

½ teaspoon freshly ground black pepper, plus more for seasoning

4 scallions (white and green parts), cut into 2-inch lengths and bruised lightly

5 sprigs thyme

1½ pounds thin-cut chicken cutlets (about 8 pieces)

Canola oil, for greasing the pan or grates

DRESSING
(Makes ⅔ cup)

⅓ cup extra-virgin olive oil

¼ cup freshly squeezed lemon juice

2 tablespoons freshly squeezed clementine or orange juice

½ teaspoon kosher salt

¼ teaspoon freshly ground black pepper

¼ teaspoon sumac, plus more for sprinkling

SALAD

2 medium heads romaine, leaves washed and torn

1 large ripe avocado, sliced

1 medium orange, rind removed, cut into ¼-inch rounds

1 clementine, rind removed, cut into ¼-inch rounds

1 medium grapefruit, rind removed, cut into ¼-inch rounds

¼ cup pomegranate seeds

2 tablespoons chopped toasted pistachios

1 tablespoon chopped fresh mint, or tiny mint leaves

ooooooooooo

Serves 4

Active Time:
30 minutes

Total Time:
1 hour
30 minutes
(including
minimum
marinating
time)

ooooooooooo

Marinate the chicken: Combine the olive oil, clementine juice and zest, sumac, salt, pepper, scallions, and thyme in a gallon-sized resealable plastic bag. Using your hands, move the ingredients around to incorporate them. Add the chicken to the bag, move it around to coat it, seal the bag, and chill to marinate for at least 1 hour and up to 8 hours. Ten to 15 minutes before cooking, remove the chicken from the refrigerator to come to room temperature.

Make the dressing: In a jar with a tight-fitting lid, combine the olive oil, lemon juice, clementine juice, salt, pepper, and sumac and shake until creamy.

Preheat a grill pan over medium-high heat. Remove the chicken from the marinade, shake off excess liquid, and season with salt and pepper. Brush the pan or grates with canola oil, then grill the chicken until caramelized and grill marks form, 2 to 3 minutes per side. Transfer to a plate and cool slightly.

Assemble the salad: Arrange the romaine, avocado, and citrus on a platter. Arrange the chicken on the salad, shake the remaining dressing again, and drizzle the dressing on top. Garnish with pomegranate seeds, pistachios, and mint.

I Love Ettingers

With their jade-green interiors and shiny, bright-green skin so thin it can often be peeled, Ettinger avocados—first planted here in 1947 and picked in the fall and early winter—have a fresh, less oily, but still rich flavor I've grown to love. Though I don't want to pit one avocado against another, locally grown Pinkertons—which taste like a cross between Ettinger and Haas-style avocados—run a close second.

Shawarma Pargiyot

When the hunger for shawarma overtakes me, I won't be deterred until I bite into a pita stuffed full of sizzling, highly seasoned meat with all the trimmings. By using the flavor profile of my hawaiij spice blend as inspiration for the seasoning, a whole world of near-instant gratification dinners presented themselves to me. Shawarma-stand shawarma is usually made out of lamb or turkey crowned with lamb fat, which drips down onto the meat as it rotates on a spit, but I always have pargiyot (skinless, boneless chicken thighs) in the house, so they're the natural choice for me. They stay juicy and take on marinade quickly, whether you have only half an hour or can wait longer for the flavors to permeate. After you cook the pargiyot, chop then stuff the meat into warm pita. A slick of amba mayo, a quick-pickled onion, a simple green slaw, and you've got a great version of the going-out shawarma experience at home. If you're planning ahead, the cabbage salad and onions can certainly be made the day before.

PARGIYOT

3 tablespoons extra-virgin olive oil or canola oil

1½ teaspoons ground cumin

1 teaspoon freshly ground black pepper

1 teaspoon ground turmeric

1 teaspoon kosher salt

¾ teaspoon ground coriander

½ teaspoon ground cardamom

½ teaspoon sweet paprika

½ teaspoon garlic powder

¼ teaspoon dried oregano

⅛ teaspoon ground cinnamon

Pinch of ground cloves

Pinch of ground ginger

Five 4-ounce skinless, boneless chicken thighs (pargiyot)

PICKLED RED ONIONS (Makes 2 cups)

1½ cups apple cider vinegar

2 tablespoons sugar

5 whole black peppercorns

1 bay leaf

½ teaspoon kosher salt

1 medium red onion, sliced into thin rings

CABBAGE SALAD (Makes 4 cups)

⅓ cup vegetable oil

¼ cup white vinegar

1 teaspoon kosher salt, plus more to taste

1 teaspoon sugar

¼ teaspoon freshly ground black pepper, plus more to taste

½ medium green cabbage, thinly sliced

FOR ASSEMBLY

4 pitas (page 92 or store-bought)

Cilantro sprigs

Honey Harissa (page 37) or your favorite hot sauce

Amba Mayo (page 36)

○○○○○○○○○○

Serves 4

Active Time:
30 minutes

Total Time:
1 hour
30 minutes
(including
minimum
marinating
time)

○○○○○○○○○○

Marinate the pargiyot: In a medium bowl, whisk together the olive oil, cumin, pepper, turmeric, salt, coriander, cardamom, paprika, garlic powder, oregano, cinnamon, cloves, and ginger. Add the chicken thighs and toss to coat, unfurling any folded-over chicken so the spices coat it all over. Cover and refrigerate for 30 minutes and up to 12 hours.

Make the pickled onions: In a small saucepan over medium-high heat, bring the vinegar, sugar, peppercorns, bay leaf, and salt to a boil. Add the onions and cook for 1 more minute. Remove from the heat and let the onions rest in the liquid for 10 minutes. Drain the liquid from the onions and reserve the liquid. Let the onions and liquid cool to

RECIPE CONTINUES

room temperature. Place the onions in a small jar, cover with the liquid, seal the jar, and refrigerate until chilled.

Make the cabbage salad: In a large bowl, whisk together the vegetable oil, vinegar, salt, sugar, and pepper. Add the cabbage, toss to coat, cover, and let sit for at least 30 minutes and up to 24 hours. Season with additional salt and pepper to taste.

Grill the pargiyot: Heat a large, heavy skillet or grill pan over medium-high heat. Cook the chicken until it is golden with crispy edges, 5 to 6 minutes per side. Transfer to a cutting board, rest for a minute, and chop into pieces.

Assemble the sandwiches: Toast the pitas lightly and stuff them with the cabbage salad, chicken, cilantro sprigs, and pickled onions. Serve with harissa and amba mayo.

Za'atar Roasted Chicken over Sumac Potatoes

On countless visits here before I made Israel my home, I'd buy giant bags of za'atar from the shuk; that way, after I left and no matter where I was, if I was pining for the sun and spice of this magical place, I could sprinkle it back into my life, if even just for the duration of a meal. For something that takes 10 minutes to throw together, the roasted chicken is a masterpiece. I rest the bird right on top of the potatoes, so the za'atar-scented drippings coat the tangy, sumac-coated potatoes while they cook in unison. If you're having a crowd, throw this in the oven during cocktail hour, then pull it out for oohs and aahs. If you're feeding a smaller group, be happy, because this chicken, pulled off the bone and tossed into a salad, makes a killer next-day lunch.

4 to 5 medium red potatoes (1½ pounds), scrubbed

4 medium shallots, quartered

4 tablespoons extra-virgin olive oil

2 tablespoons sumac

Kosher salt and freshly ground black pepper to taste

1 small roasting chicken (about 3½ to 4 pounds), patted dry

1 small lemon

5 tablespoons Za'atar Spice Blend (page 28 or store-bought)

¼ teaspoon dried red pepper flakes

2 garlic cloves

6 thyme sprigs

Serves 4

Active Time:
20 minutes

Total Time:
2 hours
5 minutes
(including
resting time)

Preheat the oven to 425°F.

Cut each potato into 6 wedges. In a 9 x 13-inch metal or glass baking dish, toss the potatoes and shallots with 1 tablespoon of the olive oil and the sumac, salt, and black pepper.

Season the cavity and exterior of the chicken well with salt and pepper. Zest the lemon into a small bowl, halve the lemon and set aside. Add the remaining 3 tablespoons olive oil to the bowl along with 4 tablespoons of the za'atar and the red pepper flakes and gently stir. Stuff the lemon halves, garlic, and thyme sprigs inside the chicken, then rub the chicken all over with the za'atar mixture. (If you want to, you can tie the legs of the chicken together; it's easier than doing a full chicken trussing, which is impressive but not necessary for a dish like this.) Sprinkle with the remaining tablespoon of za'atar. Place the chicken, breast-side up, on top of the potatoes. Roast the chicken for 15 minutes, then reduce the heat to 350°F and continue to roast the chicken until a chicken leg jiggles when pulled, the juices run clear, and the potatoes underneath the chicken are soft and the ones on the edges are crisp and golden, about another hour and 20 minutes (the rule is 23 to 25 minutes per pound of chicken, but the high roasting temperature at the beginning of the recipe shaves off a little time). Remove the chicken from the oven and let rest for 10 minutes. Remove the lemon, garlic, and thyme springs from the cavity, discarding the garlic and thyme. Carve the chicken right on top of the potatoes, letting the juice coat the potatoes, then squeeze one or both halves of the reserved lemon on the chicken and potatoes.

Sour Lime and Pomegranate Chicken Wings

Dried Persian limes (see page 30) come in two shades—black and a sort of walnut-y tan—and are traditionally dropped whole into Persian stews and soups to add a hint of citrus and the singular funk that only fermentation can. I wanted to spread the love to other preparations, so I crushed the limes into a powder to form the base for a dry rub that perfectly counterbalances the fattiness of chicken wings (you can also find dried lime powder on Amazon and Kalustyans.com). Sprinkling the rub on the wings, then letting it sink in, sends that distinctive pucker all the way down to the bone. I arrange the wings on a rack set over a baking dish and roast them until almost done, then brush them with pomegranate molasses for both high gloss and an extra layer of sour power.

1 teaspoon vegetable oil

2 pounds chicken wings (10 to 12 wings)

Juice and zest of 1 lime

4 small dried Persian limes,* or 2 tablespoons Persian lime powder (known as Lemon Omani powder)

1 tablespoon ground turmeric

2 teaspoons garlic powder

2 teaspoons sweet paprika

2 teaspoons kosher salt, plus more for seasoning

2 teaspoons sugar

1 teaspoon onion powder

1 teaspoon freshly ground black pepper, plus more for seasoning

1 teaspoon ground cumin

⅓ cup Pomegranate Molasses (page 48 or store-bought)

Chopped scallion greens, for serving

Pomegranate seeds, for serving

Serves 6 to 8, as an appetizer

Active Time: 15 minutes

Total Time: 3 hours (including minimum marinating time)

Line a large rimmed baking sheet with foil, set a rack on top of the sheet, and grease the rack lightly with vegetable oil. In a large bowl, toss the wings with the lime juice and zest, then arrange them on the sheet, fleshy-side down, leaving space between each wing. Using the heel of a large chef's knife, smash the Persian limes into a couple of pieces to break them up. In a spice grinder, pulverize them into a fine powder, 30 seconds. Add the turmeric, garlic powder, paprika, salt, sugar, onion powder, pepper, and cumin and pulse the grinder a few more times to create a unified mixture. Sprinkle half the mixture evenly over the wings, pressing it in gently with your hands. Flip the wings then sprinkle and press in the other half of the mixture. If you have time, place the wings in the refrigerator for at least 2 hours and up to 24 hours (if you have room, leave them uncovered; this helps dry out the skin and crisp it up).

Preheat the oven to 400°F.

RECIPE CONTINUES

Leaving the wings on the rack over the baking sheet, bake them until they're sizzling and the meat is cooked, 40 to 45 minutes. Remove the wings from the oven, brush both sides with the pomegranate molasses, arrange the wings fleshy-side up on the rack, and return to the oven until the wings caramelize slightly, 5 to 6 minutes. Remove from the oven and season generously with salt and pepper.

To serve, transfer to a plate and sprinkle with the scallions and pomegranate seeds.

*If you can't find dried Persian limes, using only fresh lime juice and zest works great, too. Simply toss the wings in the juice and zest of 2 limes as your first step, then combine all the other spices and proceed with the recipe.

Grilled Chicken and Corn Salad with Avocado-Za'atar Green Goddess Dressing

Not a dressing Israelis are familiar with, Green Goddess is a great foil for a basket's worth of herbs and avocado, which I use in place of buttermilk to keep it dairy-free. I throw in a little za'atar for intrigue before hitting "blend," and behold—a tangy dressing even the most skeptical Israelis have been unable to resist. I serve pieces of bread, rubbed generously with garlic and oil and grilled, to dip into an extra bowl of the creamy, thick dressing.

DRESSING
(Makes about 2 cups)

⅓ cup mayonnaise

1 large ripe avocado, peeled and pitted

½ cup freshly squeezed lemon juice

¼ cup lightly packed parsley leaves

½ cup lightly packed fresh basil leaves

¼ cup minced chives

1 tablespoon fresh tarragon leaves, or 1 teaspoon dried

1 tablespoon Za'atar Spice Blend (page 28 or store-bought) or 1 teaspoon fresh za'atar or oregano leaves

1 large garlic clove, minced

½ teaspoon kosher salt

¼ teaspoon freshly ground black pepper

CHICKEN, CORN SALAD, AND BREAD

2 baby chickens or 1 regular whole chicken (about 3 pounds total)

½ cup extra-virgin olive oil

Peeled strips of zest and juice of 1 lemon

4 cloves fresh garlic, smashed, plus 1 clove, halved

4 thyme sprigs

Kosher salt and freshly ground black pepper to taste

Six 1-inch-thick slices country bread or French bread

2 ears corn, shucked

1 small bunch kale, spines removed and thinly sliced

1 head romaine lettuce hearts, thinly sliced

1 cup cherry tomatoes, halved

½ small red onion, thinly sliced

Serves 6

Active Time:
30 minutes

Total Time:
1 hour 30 minutes (including minimum marinating time)

Make the dressing: Combine all the dressing ingredients in a blender or the bowl of a food processor and blend until smooth, thick, but still just barely pourable, 15 to 20 seconds, stopping and scraping down the sides of the blender and adding water by the tablespoonful to achieve your desired consistency.

Make the chicken, corn salad, and bread: To flatten the chickens, use kitchen shears to cut out the backs of the chickens, then turn the chickens over so the breasts are facing up. Use your hand to press down in the center of the chickens until they collapse slightly. Combine ¼ cup olive oil, lemon zest and juice, 4 cloves smashed garlic, thyme, salt, and pepper in a glass dish or large resealable plastic bag, then add the chicken and move it around to coat in the marinade. Seal the bag. Refrigerate for at least 1 hour and up to 4 hours. Preheat a grill over medium-high heat. Grill the chickens until an instant-read

RECIPE CONTINUES

thermometer reads 165°F or a leg comes loose easily when pulled, 7 to 8 minutes per side if using baby chickens, and 12 to 13 minutes per side if using a regular chicken.

Rub both sides of the bread with the halved clove of garlic, brush the bread with the remaining ¼ cup olive oil, and season generously with salt and pepper. During the last 6 minutes of grilling the chicken, place the corn and bread on the grill. Grill, turning occasionally and flipping the bread once, until the corn is slightly charred, and the bread is toasty and has developed grill marks, 5 to 6 minutes total for the corn, and 2 to 3 minutes per side for the bread. Transfer the chicken, corn, and bread to a tray. Stand the corn on one end and use a sharp knife to cut the kernels from the cobs; discard the cobs. Combine the kale, romaine, corn, tomatoes, and onions in a salad bowl. Cut the chicken into pieces, drizzle the salad with the dressing, and serve with the chicken. Serve the grilled bread alongside with extra dressing.

Root Vegetable and Medjool Date Stew

The Medjool dates in this wintery stew soak up the sauce but still hold their shape during cooking. I use white wine instead of red. It helps prevent the lighter-colored root vegetables from getting too dark (though if you use beets, you'll have a pinkish—but no less delicious—stew), and I love the way its flavor melds with the chopped preserved lemon I stir in toward the end.

2½ pounds beef stew meat, cut into 2-inch chunks

2 teaspoons kosher salt, plus more for seasoning

Freshly ground black pepper

2 tablespoons all-purpose flour

2 tablespoons olive oil

1 large onion, cut into chunks

5 whole garlic cloves

3 tablespoons tomato paste

1 teaspoon paprika

1 cup dry white wine

3½ cups beef or chicken broth

2 thyme sprigs

½ teaspoon dried red pepper flakes

2 pounds root vegetables (celery root, carrots, parsnips, potatoes, Jerusalem artichokes, beets), peeled and cut into 2-inch chunks

8 small or 6 medium Medjool dates, pitted but left whole

1 tablespoon chopped Preserved Lemon (page 38 or store-bought) or finely chopped fresh lemon

Serves 6 to 8

Active Time: 30 minutes

Total Time: 3 hours

Season the meat generously with salt and pepper. Place the flour in a resealable plastic bag, add the meat, and shake to coat. Heat the oil in a large pot over medium-high heat. Working in batches, brown the meat until seared on all sides, 8 minutes total. Remove the meat to a plate. Add the onions and garlic to the pot and cook, stirring, until slightly softened, 6 to 7 minutes. Add the tomato paste and paprika and cook, stirring, until slightly caramelized, 2 minutes. Add the wine and 2 teaspoons salt, bring to a boil, reduce the heat to medium, and cook until the wine is mostly evaporated, 2 to 3 minutes. Return the meat to the pot along with 2½ cups of the broth, the thyme, and red pepper flakes. Bring to a boil, reduce the heat, and cook until the meat begins to become tender, 1 hour. Add the root vegetables and dates with the remaining broth, return to a boil, reduce the heat to medium-low, and cook, stirring occasionally, until the vegetables are tender, 1 hour more. Stir in the preserved lemon 5 minutes before serving.

Turkish Coffee–Rubbed Rib Eyes with Seared Broccoli

Get thee a good steak, rub it in coffee and spices, and you've got yourself a killer dinner. A Turkish coffee–inspired rub (Turkish coffee often has cardamom in it—I add cardamom and cayenne) does magical things when applied to meat and grilled, quickly transmitting a jolt of flavor while helping the steak develop an irresistible crust. And the broccoli, which picks up just enough smoke to be interesting, stands up to the meat bite for bite.

One 1-inch-thick rib-eye steak (about 1½ pounds)

1 small head broccoli, with a nice stem attached

2 tablespoons extra-virgin olive oil

1 tablespoon kosher salt, plus more for seasoning

1 tablespoon coarsely ground fresh black pepper, plus more for seasoning

¼ cup coarsely ground coffee beans (such as for French press coffee)

1 tablespoon ground cardamom

½ teaspoon cayenne pepper

Dukkah (page 25), for serving (optional)

Serves 2

Active Time:
10 minutes

Total Time:
35 minutes

Let the steak come to room temperature while you prepare the broccoli and spice rub. Using a peeler, peel the tough outer layer from the broccoli stem. Trim off the end of the stem, then cut through the broccoli to create steaks about ¼ inch thick. Brush the broccoli steaks with the olive oil, season with salt and pepper, and set aside. In a small bowl, combine the coffee, 1 tablespoon salt, 1 tablespoon pepper, the cardamom, and the cayenne. Pour the coffee mixture onto a large dinner plate or small rimmed baking sheet and shake gently to distribute all over the plate. Press the steak into the spices, applying pressure so it sticks to the steak. Lift the steak up and shake the plate to redistribute the coffee mixture evenly. Flip the steak and press the other side into the spices.

Preheat a grill, grill pan, or cast-iron skillet over medium-high heat. For a medium-rare result, grill the steak, making sure not to move it around, until the underside has developed a crust and is deeply browned and the fat is sizzling, 5 to 6 minutes per side (grill an extra minute or two for medium). Remove the steak, tent it lightly with foil, and let it rest for 5 minutes before slicing. While the steak is resting, place the broccoli on the grill and cook it until charred, 2 to 3 minutes per side. Uncover the steak, slice it against the grain, and serve with the broccoli. Serve the dukkah on the side if desired.

Hawaiij-Braised Short Ribs with Roasted Kohlrabi Mash

The centerpiece of a Yemenite Shabbat meal is often soup laced with Hawaiij (page 27), a yellow, peppery spice mix similar to Indian curry that Yemenites brought with them when they immigrated, first in smaller numbers at the end of the 1800s and then in waves when they were airlifted to a new Israel soon after the founding of the modern state. I love the spice in its traditional application, but why stop there? When rubbed into rich cuts of meat before a long, slow braise in a heavy pot, the turmeric, pepper, and cumin permeate the meat and infuse it with deep flavor. Ask your butcher to cut the short ribs English-style, then again across the bone into large hunks—larger than you might think you need. Long cooking shrinks the meat down, and you want to be left with substantial pieces of meat to swirl around in the rich sauce. The kohlrabi slow cooks at the same time as the ribs; it's a worthy, earthy, mildly sweet substitute for starchier options (use turnips if you can't find kohlrabi). Mash them by hand, or whir in the bowl of a food processor for extra smooth results. And here's a bonus recipe idea: Don't mash the kohlrabi. Simply let it cool to room temperature and slice it thick. You may never eat potatoes again.

SHORT RIBS

4 pounds English-style bone-in short ribs, cut across the bone into 3-inch pieces (ask your butcher to do this)

2 teaspoons kosher salt, plus more for seasoning

1 teaspoon freshly ground black pepper, plus more for seasoning

2 tablespoons vegetable oil, plus more as needed

6 tablespoons Hawaiij (page 27)

2 jumbo onions, cut into thick slices

5 garlic cloves, peeled

6 medium carrots, halved lengthwise

2 tablespoons tomato paste

2 tablespoons all-purpose or gluten-free flour of your choice

2 cups dry red wine

10 sprigs thyme

¼ small bunch parsley

¼ small bunch cilantro

1 bay leaf

4 cups low-sodium beef or chicken broth, plus a little more if needed

KOHLRABI MASH
(Makes 3 cups)

8 large (4½ to 5 pounds) whole kohlrabi or turnips

6 tablespoons extra-virgin olive oil

2 teaspoons kosher salt, plus more to taste

¼ teaspoon freshly ground black pepper to taste

½ cup low-sodium chicken or vegetable broth

Schug (page 35), for serving (optional)

○○○○○○○○○○○

**Serves
4 to 6**

Active Time:
1 hour

Total Time:
4 hours

○○○○○○○○○○○

Preheat the oven to 325°F.

Prepare the short ribs: Fit one rack in the oven to accommodate the pot you're cooking the ribs in, and the other to fit the baking dish for the kohlrabi (they will cook at the same time). Arrange the short ribs on a rimmed baking sheet, pat dry with paper towels, and season generously with salt and pepper. Heat the vegetable oil in a large, heavy-bottomed Dutch oven over medium-high heat. Working in 2 batches, brown the ribs until very deeply caramelized, 3 to 4 minutes per flat surface or about 12 minutes total per batch. Move the

RECIPE CONTINUES

ribs to a plate and, while still warm, sprinkle both sides with ¼ cup of the hawaiij. Drain and discard all but 2 tablespoons of the fat from the Dutch oven (if the oil seems burned, drain it all and use 2 tablespoons of fresh oil), reduce the heat to medium, add the onions and garlic and cook, stirring, until the onions are translucent, 7 to 8 minutes. Add the carrots and cook, stirring, 3 to 4 more minutes. Add the tomato paste and flour and cook, stirring, until absorbed into the vegetables, 2 to 3 minutes. Add the wine, raise the heat to medium-high, bring to a boil, and cook until only about ½ cup of wine remains, 12 to 13 minutes. Tie the thyme, parsley, cilantro, and bay leaf together with kitchen twine and add to the pot along with the broth, the remaining 2 tablespoons hawaiij, the 2 teaspoons salt, and the 1 teaspoon pepper. Nestle the short ribs in the pot among the vegetables; the liquid should come about two-thirds of the way up the sides of the meat. Bring to a boil, cover with a tight-fitting lid, and immediately transfer to the oven. Cook until the meat is fork-tender and the sauce is reduced and thickened, 2½ to 3 hours.

While the meat is cooking, get the kohlrabi started: Use a sharp knife to cut the rind and fibrous white outer membrane away from the kohlrabi to expose snowy whitish jade-green flesh. Poke a few holes in each kohlrabi with a fork and place them in a large glass or metal baking dish. Drizzle the kohlrabi with 4 tablespoons of the olive oil, sprinkle with ½ teaspoon salt and pepper, and shake the pan to coat. Add the broth, cover tightly with aluminum foil, and bake along with the short ribs until the kohlrabi are tender and golden in spots, 2½ hours. To test for doneness, pierce a kohlrabi with a fork or toothpick; if it yields easily it's ready; if not, cover it back up and return it to the oven for another 20 minutes. Transfer the kohlrabi and any juices collected in the pan to a large bowl. Add the remaining 2 tablespoons olive oil and 1½ teaspoons salt and mash the kohlrabi with a potato masher (or process to your desired texture in a food processor, 20 to 30 seconds).

Spread the kohlrabi mash on a serving platter. Remove the ribs from the oven, discard the herb bundle, and arrange the meat (on the bones or off, up to you), onions, and carrot halves on top of the kohlrabi. Use a spoon to skim any fat you can off the sauce and drizzle the sauce over the platter. Serve with schug, if desired.

Mafroum
(Stuffed Eggplant in Tomato Sauce)

I've loved mafroum ever since I first had it at Guetta, a Libyan joint at the edge of Jaffa not far from where we live. Libyan-inspired food, nicknamed *Tripolitani* cuisine after the country's capital, feels a little less spicy than some other North African cuisines, with thicker tomato sauces—perhaps because Libya was once an Italian colony. Mafroum is sometimes made with potatoes, or even cauliflower, but there's no beating the way the eggplant, slit open to create receptacles for the highly seasoned filling, absorbs the delicious tomato-based sauce. Many recipes call for just cinnamon in the meat, but I like the way baharat, with its notes of allspice, warms up the filling.

EGGPLANT FILLING

1 medium onion, grated

1 small sweet potato (6 ounces), peeled and grated

1 slice white bread, torn and sprinkled with 1 tablespoon water

1 pound 80/20 ground beef

½ cup chopped fresh parsley

¼ cup chopped fresh chives

1 teaspoon Baharat (page 24 or store-bought)

3 large eggs, beaten

2 garlic cloves, minced

1 teaspoon kosher salt

¼ teaspoon freshly ground black pepper

EGGPLANT

2 medium globe eggplants (8 to 10 ounces each)

Vegetable oil, for frying the eggplant

¾ cup all-purpose flour

3 large eggs

½ teaspoon fine sea salt

½ teaspoon paprika

SAUCE

1 large onion, finely minced

3 large garlic cloves, minced

¼ cup tomato paste

2 teaspoons sweet paprika

½ teaspoon Baharat (page 24)

1 teaspoon kosher salt

¼ teaspoon cayenne pepper

2 cups chicken broth or water

1 medium tomato (6 ounces), diced, or 1 cup canned, diced tomatoes in juice

Couscous (see base recipe for Vegetable Stew with Easy Homemade Couscous, page 286, or store-bought), for serving

○○○○○○○○○○

Serves 6

Active Time:
1 hour

Total Time:
1 hour
30 minutes

○○○○○○○○○○

Make the filling: Arrange a clean kitchen towel on a work surface and pile the onion, sweet potato, and soaked bread in the middle of it. Close up the towel and, working over the sink, twist the towel from the sides until you have squeezed out as much liquid as you can from the contents. Open the towel, dump the contents into a large bowl, use your fingers to break up any large bits of bread, and add the beef, parsley, chives, baharat, beaten eggs, garlic, salt, and pepper and mix gently with your hands until everything is incorporated.

Prepare the eggplant: Whisk the eggs and salt in a small bowl. Combine the flour and paprika in a second bowl. Place each eggplant on a cutting board, trim off and discard the ends, and cut twelve ¾-inch rounds from the 2 eggplants, trying to make all the rounds as

RECIPE CONTINUES

equal in diameter as possible. Reserve the leftover eggplant for the Sabich Fattoush Salad (page 182) or P'titm (page 196). To make the mafroum pockets, lay each eggplant round flat on the cutting board and slice through the middle, moving the knife through the center slice but stopping short of cutting through it by about ½ inch so the ends on one side are still attached (it should look like an almost split pita). Stuff each sliced eggplant with meat filling; using between ¼ and ⅓ cup filling per eggplant silce, depending on the diameter of the eggplant. Press the top to "seal" it all together—you'll have filling that is exposed, but don't worry—it won't fall out.

Fry the eggplant: Heat ½ inch vegetable oil in a 12-inch skillet over medium-high heat. While the oil is heating, coat each filled eggplant pocket completely in the flour and then the egg, shaking off the excess between dips. Working in 2 batches, fry the eggplant until each side is golden, 2 to 3 minutes per side. Transfer the eggplant to a tray and drain and discard all but 3 tablespoons of the oil in the pan (or replace with new oil if yours seems burned).

Make the sauce: Add the onions to the pan and cook over medium heat, stirring, until softened and golden, 8 to 9 minutes. Add the garlic and cook 1 more minute. Add the tomato paste, paprika, baharat, salt, and cayenne and cook, stirring, until fragrant and the tomato paste is slightly caramelized, 2 minutes. Add the broth and tomatoes and bring to a boil, then gently nestle the fried stuffed eggplants in the sauce. Reduce the heat to a simmer, cover with a tight-fitting lid, and cook until the eggplant is tender and has absorbed some of the sauce, 40 minutes. Uncover and cook for 5 more minutes. Serve with couscous.

Schug-Marinated Baby Lamb Chops

Lamb chops may seem fancy, but nothing could be easier to make at home. In recent years, Israel has begun to raise a small amount of good-quality, hormone-free, pasture-raised lamb, and it's delicious, capped with luscious fat and meat that melts in your mouth. When I can get them, I make this simple dish. The minty schug marinade tenderizes the lamb and makes it extra juicy and flavorful. In addition to being gorgeous, grilled lemons and red onions add sharpness and zest.

¼ cup extra-virgin olive oil

¼ cup coarsely chopped fresh mint

3 tablespoons Schug (page 35), plus more for serving

Kosher salt and freshly ground black pepper to taste

8 to 10 baby lamb chops (about 2 pounds)

1 lemon, thinly sliced

2 small red onions, each cut through the root into 6 wedges

Serves 4

Active Time:
20 minutes

Total Time:
1 hour
20 minutes
(including
minimum
marinating)

Combine the olive oil, mint, schug, salt, and pepper in a large resealable bag and smush the mixture around until combined. Add the lamb chops and move them around in the bag until they are coated in the marinade. Marinate for at least 1 hour and up to 8 (you can marinate on the counter if it's only an hour; refrigerate if it's longer than that).

Preheat a grill or grill pan over medium-high heat. Remove the chops from the marinade and remove as much of the mint and most of the schug from the chops as you can. Working in batches if using a grill pan and all at once if grilling, grill the chops, lemons, and onions until the chops are medium-rare, the onions are charred, and the lemons are slightly caramelized, 3 to 4 minutes per side (the lemons may be done earlier; if so, remove them from the grill). Serve the chops with the onions and lemons, with additional schug on the side.

Mini Herb and Garlic Kebaburgers

The traditional way to make kebab is to wrap the ground meat around long, flat metal skewers known as *shipudim*, but I find this method challenging. The meat needs to be really finely chopped, and sometimes it has a hard time adhering to the skewers. Making patties and cooking them straight on the grill—like little burgers but so much better—makes this an easy every-night thing instead of a production.

BURGERS

1 small red onion, roughly chopped

½ small red bell pepper, seeded

3 large garlic cloves

1 cup lightly packed parsley leaves

1 cup lightly packed cilantro leaves

½ cup lightly packed mint leaves

2 tablespoons fresh za'atar or oregano, or 2 teaspoons dried

¾ pound ground lamb (at least 20–25% fat)

¾ pound ground beef (at least 20–25% fat)

2 teaspoons kosher salt

1½ teaspoons ground cumin

½ teaspoon ground coriander

½ teaspoon freshly ground black pepper

2 teaspoons Honey Harissa (page 37 or store-bought), or ½ teaspoon cayenne pepper

¼ teaspoon baking soda

FRIES

2 large Russet potatoes (about 1½ pounds), scrubbed

3 tablespoons vegetable oil

¾ teaspoon kosher salt, plus more for seasoning

¼ teaspoon freshly ground black pepper, plus more for seasoning

Spicy Lemony Carrot Salad (page 137), Basic Tahini Sauce (page 120), and green salad, for serving

BURGERS

Makes
12 mini burgers

Active Time:
15 minutes

Total Time:
1 hour

FRIES

Active Time:
10 minutes

Total Time:
40 minutes

Prep the burgers: Preheat the oven to 400°F. In the bowl of a food processor, pulse the onion, bell pepper, and garlic until finely chopped, 20 pulses. Add the parsley, cilantro, mint, and za'atar and pulse until the herbs are finely chopped, 15 pulses. Transfer the mixture to a large bowl. Add the lamb, beef, salt, cumin, coriander, black pepper, harissa, and baking soda and gently mix with your hands to incorporate. Form the mixture into 12 equal-sized round patties about 1 inch thick, arrange on a plate, cover, and refrigerate for 30 minutes.

Make the fries: Preheat the oven to 425°F. Cut the potatoes into ½-inch batons, then pat them dry with paper towels. In a large bowl toss the potatoes with the oil, salt, and pepper. Arrange in a single layer on a large rimmed baking sheet and bake until crisp and golden, flipping the fries once after 20 minutes only if they seem like they're burning, 30 to 35 minutes.

Grill the burgers: Preheat a grill, grill pan, or cast-iron skillet over medium-high heat. Cook the patties, trying not to move them, until a slight crust forms and the meat is cooked to medium, 3 to 4 minutes per side.

Serve the kebabs with the spicy lemony carrot salad, fries, tahini sauce, and green salad.

Rice and Beef–Stuffed Tomatoes

"Stuffed tomatikas are really personal to me," Roy Yerushalmi told me, using his nickname for tomatoes as we hit the shuk to pick up the raw ingredients for his beloved Turkish great-grandmother Fortuneé's filled vegetables. "Istanbulites didn't use a lot of rice," he told me, sipping the pre-measured cognac that was supposed to go into the recipe. "It was considered déclassé." When I left a tiny scrap of meat in the bowl, he gasped. "Part of my family lived through the siege of Jerusalem," he told me. "Letting the meat run down the drain? NEVER!" Into the skillet went lemon juice, a splash of that cognac (or what was left of it), and the stuffed tomatoes, which came out homey but rich. The fat from the meat and olive oil carrying the subtle flavor of the cognac, they were as good at room temperature as they were hot.

10 to 11 large firm, ripe tomatoes, depending on the size of your pot (about 4 pounds)

¾ pound ground beef (at least 20% fat)

⅔ cup uncooked round rice, such as carnaroli

¼ cup chopped parsley, plus more for garnish

¼ cup chopped dill, plus more for garnish

¼ cup extra-virgin olive oil

1 large egg

1¼ teaspoons kosher salt, plus more for seasoning

½ teaspoon freshly ground black pepper, plus more for seasoning

¼ cup sugar

⅓ cup freshly squeezed lemon juice

Generous splash of cognac or chicken broth, plus 1 to 2 cups additional broth, as needed

Serves 6 to 8

Active Time: 35 minutes

Total Time: 1 hour 45 minutes

Choose the oven-safe pot you're going to use; a 6-quart stockpot should work well. Fit the whole tomatoes into the pot to gauge how many tomatoes you'll need; they can be tight-fitting. Remove the tomatoes from the pot. Using your hands, gently combine the beef, rice, parsley, dill, olive oil, egg, salt, and pepper in a large bowl and chill until ready to use.

Preheat the oven to 400°F. Cut off the top ½ inch of the tomatoes; reserve the tops. Using a small teaspoon, hollow out the centers of the tomatoes, leaving as much flesh intact as possible on the inner walls; reserve the tomato liquid and seeds. Season the insides of the tomatoes lightly with the salt. Remove the filling from the fridge and fill the tomatoes about three-quarters of the way up, leaving room for the rice to expand when cooked. Put the sugar and lemon juice in the bottom of the pot and cook, stirring, until the mixture caramelizes slightly, 2 to 3 minutes. Add the cognac and swirl around to deglaze for 1 to 2 minutes. Remove the pot from the heat, fit the tomatoes inside, then gently pour the tomato liquid and enough broth into the pot so it comes about halfway up the tomatoes, opening the tomatoes and splashing a bit of the broth on top of the filling.

Preheat the oven to 350°F. Place the tops on the tomatoes, place the pot over medium heat, and bring to a boil. Reduce the heat to low, cover with a tight-fitting lid, and cook until the tomatoes soften, the rice looks swollen, and the broth has reduced by about one-third, 20 to 25 minutes. Uncover, transfer the pot to the oven, and continue to cook until the tops are a little browned, 20 to 25 minutes. Serve immediately, or at room temperature.

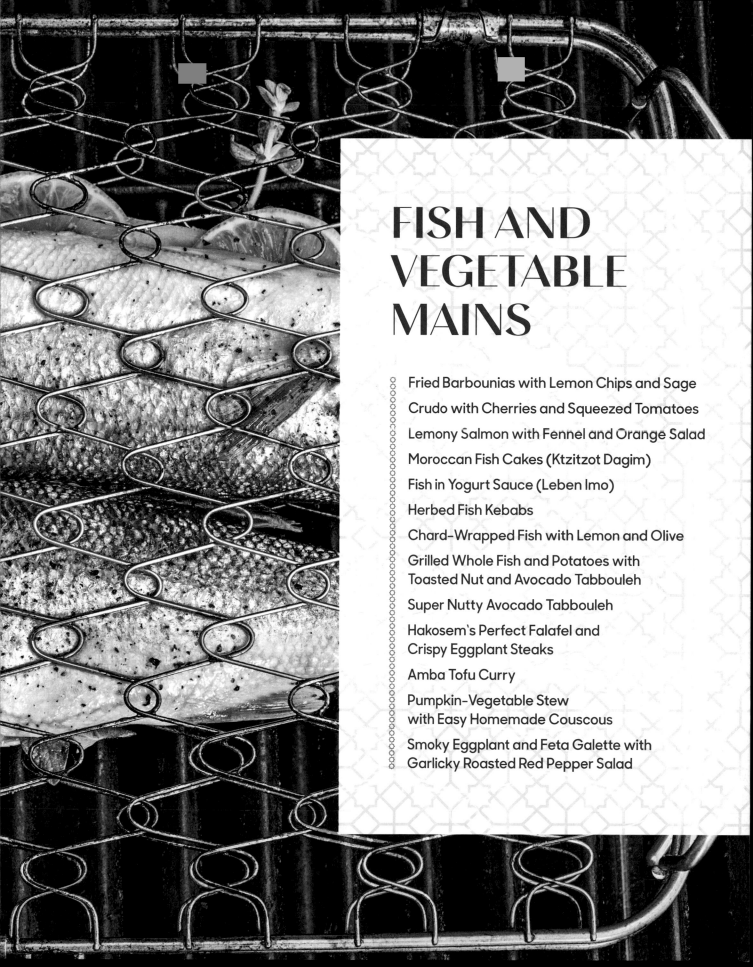

FISH AND VEGETABLE MAINS

- Fried Barbounias with Lemon Chips and Sage
- Crudo with Cherries and Squeezed Tomatoes
- Lemony Salmon with Fennel and Orange Salad
- Moroccan Fish Cakes (Ktzitzot Dagim)
- Fish in Yogurt Sauce (Leben Imo)
- Herbed Fish Kebabs
- Chard-Wrapped Fish with Lemon and Olive
- Grilled Whole Fish and Potatoes with Toasted Nut and Avocado Tabbouleh
- Super Nutty Avocado Tabbouleh
- Hakosem's Perfect Falafel and Crispy Eggplant Steaks
- Amba Tofu Curry
- Pumpkin-Vegetable Stew with Easy Homemade Couscous
- Smoky Eggplant and Feta Galette with Garlicky Roasted Red Pepper Salad

Fried Barbounias with Lemon Chips and Sage

It's a banner day when you can find barbounias (tiny red mullets), identified by their yellow neon stripes, in the market. There's little to do but dredge them in flour (add a little cornmeal if you like) and fry them until you've got little crispy morsels you must, MUST eat right away—preferably by hand. Half the fun is cleaning them to the bone, leaving their tiny skeletons behind in a pile. The wheels of fried lemon and shards of sage are like chips; I like to take a bite of rich fish, then clean my palate with a crispy lemon and an earthy bite of sage. It's not always easy to find these babies in Israel, much less stateside, so feel free to use chunks of meaty whitefish instead.

Vegetable oil, for frying

1 cup flour

2 tablespoons cornmeal (optional)

Kosher salt and freshly ground black pepper

1½ pounds whole baby red mullet fish*

1 thin-skinned lemon, sliced into very thin rounds, seeds removed, plus lemon wedges for serving

12 sage leaves

Serves 4 to 6

Active Time: 30 minutes

Total Time: 30 minutes

Fill a large pot halfway with vegetable oil and heat to 350°F (use a deep-fry thermometer to gauge the oil temperature, or drop a piece of bread in the oil; if it begins to brown and sizzle, the oil is ready). Arrange a rack over a paper towel–lined plate or sheet pan. In a large bowl, season the flour (and cornmeal, if using) generously with salt and pepper, then dredge the fish, a few at a time, shaking off the excess flour. Working in batches so as not to lower the temperature of the oil too much, drop the fish into the oil and fry until crisp and cooked through, 3 to 4 minutes. Drain on the rack. Dredge the lemon slices in the flour, shake them off, drop them into the oil, and fry until the edges are caramelized and the lemons crisp up, 1 minute per side; remove with a spider to the paper towels to drain. Gently lower the sage leaves into the oil and fry until crisp, 10 seconds. Remove with a spider to the paper towels to drain. Pile the fish, lemon chips, and sage onto a platter, season with salt and pepper, and serve with lemon wedges.

*If you can't find baby mullets, use 1½ pounds skinless, thick whitefish fillets, such as haddock, cod, or halibut, cut into 1½-inch chunks.

Crudo with Cherries and Squeezed Tomatoes

This preparation really shines in the summer but can work all year. All you need is a really good piece of sushi-grade fish; keep it in the coldest part of the fridge—ideally use it on the same day. Since most of the flavor from a perfect cherry tomato comes from its seeds and jelly-like insides, that's what I use here to help dress the fish. Toss in the most beautiful produce you can find, and make sure to lavish it with lemon and olive oil at the end.

½ pound sushi-grade fish
(such as tuna, yellowtail, or salmon),
thinly sliced

8 fresh cherries, pitted and halved*

1 small Persian cucumber, peeled
into thick ribbons

1 hot red or green chili pepper,
seeded and thinly sliced

8 cherry tomatoes

3 tablespoons extra-virgin olive oil

Lemon or lime wedges

Kosher salt

Serves 4

Active Time:
5 minutes

Total Time:
10 minutes

Arrange the fish, cherries, cucumber, and chili pepper slices on a plate. Halve the tomatoes, then squeeze them directly onto the plate (eat the squeezed tomatoes). Drizzle the plate with olive oil, then squeeze lemon juice to taste on the fish and season with salt to taste.

*If you can't find cherries, swap in ¼ cup diced ripe mangos, peaches, plums—even avocados.

Shishi in the Shuk

Shishi, or Friday, in the shuk is by turns magical and maddening, as seemingly half of the country converges to join in the frenzy of a nation preparing for relaxation come sunset, when Shabbat (the Sabbath) begins. This is technically the beginning of the weekend, but since most businesses are closed on Saturdays, Friday becomes a time for combining errands with a little bit of fun. Whether you're religious or not, Shabbat is a time of repose, with families gathering for at least a Friday-night meal, and possibly several more the next day, so a bit of a siege mentality prevails, with shoppers laying in provisions for one day without a lot of food available for purchase (oh, the horror).

By ten o'clock the shuk is full of people ready to engage in commerce as a contact sport. "Haideh!" ("Let's go!"), the vendors chant in a sort of call-and-repeat, ratcheting up their salesmanship to 10-plus levels. Challah, the traditional bread for a Shabbat meal, is bought by the hundreds.

Music streams, the scents of falafel and stone fruit, briny olives and suntan lotion mingle and change meter by meter. On side streets, cafés, restaurants, and bars set up extra tables and chairs as Tel Avivans come to drink beer, arak, and seemingly anything else they can get their hands on.

Over at Musi Dagim, Musl Fenster, whose father established one of Tel Aviv's top fishmongers in 1948, pours shots as the day comes to a close. Over at Shabtai, a fishmonger on the edge of the Yemenite Quarter, Hilla Mayer Batish, the daughter-in-law of the owners, sets up a tiny stand where she makes beautiful plates of crudo and ceviche to order using Shabtai's fish tossed with seasonal fruits and vegetables from the market. The freshest fruit and vegetables, seaweed strands, and chunks of fish are mixed with citrus and handed out in takeout bowls. People stand around a small table, taking bites with plastic forks, washing it all down with cold beer or glasses of Champagne.

At produce stalls, prices fall in fifteen-minute increments, with vendors eager to rid themselves of produce in anticipation of a new week just around the corner. By late afternoon, as the sun weakens, the crowds thin, and people head home or to the beach nearby to watch the sunset, the shuk prepares for its own, well-deserved, day of rest.

Left: Top right: Hilla Mayer Batish. Bottom right: Musi Fenster and his son, Nimrod.

Lemony Salmon with Fennel and Orange Salad

This is winter dinner, Tel Aviv–style. During the rainy season in January and February, I like to create meals that bring sunshine into the kitchen. I basically created Preserved Lemon Paste (page 40) for this purpose: to cover a whole side of creamy salmon with something that could stand up to its richness. While the salmon cooks, make the fennel salad, filled with juicy citrus. By the time the salad's done, the salmon will be about ready to take out of the oven.

SALMON

One 2-pound salmon fillet, skin on

⅔ cup Preserved Lemon Paste (page 40)

Paprika and thin preserved lemon slices (page 38), for garnish

FENNEL SALAD

1 medium orange

1 medium blood orange

3 tablespoons freshly squeezed lemon juice

2 tablespoons extra-virgin olive oil

1 large head fennel

Kosher salt and freshly ground black pepper to taste

Serves 4

Active Time:
10 minutes

Total Time:
30 minutes

Bake the salmon: Arrange a rack 4 to 6 inches from the broiler and preheat the oven to 300°F.

Arrange the salmon in a baking dish, spread with preserved lemon paste, scatter with paprika and lemon slices, and bake until the salmon is just cooked through, 20 minutes. Turn on the broiler and broil until the lemon paste is slightly golden, 2 to 3 minutes.

Make the salad: While the salmon is baking, make the salad. Using a sharp knife, cut the top and bottom of the oranges off, stand the oranges on a cutting board, and cut the peel and rind from the oranges, following the shape of the fruit and trying to cut off as little of the flesh as possible. Squeeze any small amounts of juice from the rind pieces into a bowl and discard the rind. Hold an orange in your hand over the bowl. Using a sharp paring knife, cut between the white membranes that divide the flesh of the orange wedges. Release the orange flesh into the bowl, discarding as many pits as you can. Squeeze any extra juice out of the remaining web of orange membranes and discard. Repeat with the second orange. Whisk in the lemon juice and olive oil. Trim and discard the stalks from the fennel, but remove and reserve the fennel fronds. Halve the fennel through its core, then use the tip of the knife to cut out and discard the white inner core; thinly slice the fennel. Add the fennel to the bowl, and gently toss to coat with the dressing. Season with salt and pepper and garnish with fennel fronds.

Serve the salmon with the salad.

Moroccan Fish Cakes
(Ktzitzot Dagim)

As one of Tel Aviv's most creative and talented pastry chefs, Rinat Tzadok works with her professional and life partner, Uri Scheft of Lehamim and Breads bakeries (see page 95), on everything from product development to food styling. What many don't know about Rinat is that her savory cooking is her secret weapon; everything she touches is simultaneously light and indulgent. Rinat, who has a side business of her own creating showstopping private dinners and small events for private clients, is the kind of cook who says she's throwing together a simple dinner, which to her means three kinds of crudo, four salads, a few vegetable dishes, and two main-course *sirim* (pots) bubbling away on the stove. One of my favorites is her Moroccan fish patties, which I was lucky to taste at a Shabbat dinner one Friday night with her, Uri, and their four-year-old daughter, Hallel. First, she makes a sauce with long, dried shoshka peppers, a variety not readily available in the United States; I sub in sweet paprika. I always thought the sauce had a lot of tomatoes, so I was surprised to see she added only a few thin slices along with bell peppers that get silky right in the pan. Keep the temperature relatively low throughout cooking; this prevents the patties from breaking apart and allows the sauce to come together without too much darkening or burning. Make sure to have challah on hand for dipping!

½ cup extra-virgin olive oil

1 small (4 ounce) red onion, finely diced

1 pound skinless, boneless whitefish fillets, such as cod or snapper, cut into large chunks

4 cups packed cilantro leaves and tender stems, chopped (1 cup)

1 large egg yolk

2½ teaspoons kosher salt

¼ teaspoon crushed whole coriander seeds

2 medium (¾ pound) red bell peppers, seeded and thinly sliced

5 whole garlic cloves and 5 sliced garlic cloves

1 small tomato, cored and sliced into very thin rounds

2 medium jalapeños, slit down the center but kept in one piece

5 lemon segments (from ½ small lemon)*

2 teaspoons sweet paprika

○○○○○○○○○○○
Serves 6 as an appetizer and 4 as a main course

Active Time:
1 hour
30 minutes

Total Time:
1 hour
30 minutes
○○○○○○○○○○○

To make the fish cakes: Heat 2 tablespoons of the olive oil in a 10- or 12-inch skillet over medium heat. Add the onions and cook, stirring, until softened but not browned, 6 to 7 minutes. Transfer to a large mixing bowl. Pulse the fish in the bowl of a food processor until very small, distinct pieces remain but the fish isn't totally ground, 15 pulses. Gently fold the chopped fish into the cooled onions and add ¼ cup chopped cilantro with 2 tablespoons of the olive oil, the egg yolk, 1¼ teaspoons of salt, and the coriander seeds. Gently form the mixture into 12 equal patties (about 3 tablespoons per patty), place them on a plate in a single layer, cover with plastic wrap, and chill while you make the sauce.

To make the sauce: While the fish cakes chill, in the same skillet you used to sauté the onions, heat an additional 2 tablespoons of the olive oil over medium-low heat, add the bell peppers with the whole and sliced garlic cloves and cook, stirring, until very soft, 10 minutes. Add the tomato slices, jalapeños, ¼ cup chopped cilantro, lemon segments,

RECIPE CONTINUES

paprika, the remaining 1¼ teaspoons salt, and the remaining 2 tablespoons of olive oil and cook, stirring, until the tomatoes begin to soften, 3 to 4 minutes. Add 1 cup water, bring to a boil over medium-high heat, reduce the heat to medium-low, and simmer until the mixture thickens, 9 to 10 minutes. Gently arrange the fish cakes in the skillet and cook, spooning the sauce over the cakes, until the underside is just cooked, 4 minutes. Gently flip the fish cakes, add ¼ cup cilantro, and cook until the patties are just cooked through, spooning more sauce on top as you cook, another 4 minutes. Garnish with the remaining ¼ cup cilantro before serving.

*To make lemon segments, slice the top and bottom off of the long ends of a lemon so it can sit flat on the counter. Using a sharp knife and starting from the top, cut away the zest and white pith beneath, leaving the lemon flesh exposed, until you have a lemon-shaped orb of pure lemon. Hold the lemon in your hand over a bowl. Release the segments by cutting the flesh away from the white membrane surrounding the segments.

Fish in Yogurt Sauce
(Leben Imo)

"Back when I was a kid my grandmother had dishes like this waiting for me when I came home from school," said Osama Dalal of his leben imo ("mother's yogurt"), a dish of tender braised spinach topped with white fish fillets cooked in coriander-scented yogurt sauce. "But it was made with meat, and was really labor intensive. You had to stand over the yogurt for hours, cooking it over a super-low temperature so it wouldn't break," he told me. He solved that problem by creating a sort of béchamel that you can make in advance and hold until you're ready to cook the fish and spinach, making this great dinner-party food. It's a bit richer than you might expect, but that much more delicious, too. Serve with Jeweled Rice (page 200) or even Tahdig (page 206), either of which would be a great landing spot for the creamy sauce. The accompanying salad is generously dressed with the one-two punch of Pomegranate Molasses (page 48) and lemon as well as a hint of spice.

FISH

6 tablespoons (¾ stick) unsalted butter

5 tablespoons minced garlic

2½ tablespoons ground coriander

⅓ cup all-purpose flour

¾ cup half-and-half or whole milk

2½ cups full-fat yogurt, preferably made from goat's milk or sheep's milk

1 tablespoon kosher salt, plus more for seasoning

Eight 4-ounce skinless center-cut whitefish fillets (2 pounds), such as halibut

Freshly ground black pepper to taste

3 tablespoons extra-virgin olive oil

One 1-pound bunch spinach, stems removed and discarded, or 10 ounces prewashed baby spinach

2 teaspoons freshly squeezed lemon juice

1 teaspoon ground sumac

3 tablespoons toasted pine nuts

Chopped fresh mint, for garnish

OSAMA'S SALAD

8 cups (8 ounces) assorted fresh greens and tender herbs (arugula, mustard greens, mint, dill), coarsely chopped

5 scallions (white and green parts), thinly sliced

2 medium blood oranges (or regular oranges), segmented, juice reserved*

2 medium radishes, thinly sliced

¼ cup pine nuts, lightly toasted

1 hot chili pepper, seeded and sliced

¼ cup extra-virgin olive oil

3 tablespoons freshly squeezed lemon juice

1 tablespoon Pomegranate Molasses (page 48)

Generous seasoning of kosher salt and freshly ground black pepper to taste

---

○○○○○○○○○○
Serves 6

Active Time:
45 minutes

Total Time:
1 hour
15 minutes
○○○○○○○○○○

Make the fish: In a 9- or 10-inch skillet, heat the butter over medium-low heat. Add 2 tablespoons of the minced garlic and the coriander and cook, stirring, until the garlic is slightly softened but not browned and the coriander is fragrant, 2 to 3 minutes. Add the flour all at once and cook, whisking, until the flour absorbs the butter and turns a light golden color, 2 minutes. Add the half-and-half and cook, stirring, until a thick paste forms, 2 to 3 minutes. Add the yogurt and salt and cook, whisking often, until thickened, silky, and pourable, 9 to 10 minutes. Remove from the heat and press foil on the surface of the sauce so that it doesn't form a skin.

RECIPE CONTINUES

Preheat the oven to 350°F.

Pat the fish dry and season it generously on both sides with salt and pepper. In a large (at least 10-inch), oven-safe high-sided skillet (nonstick or coated cast-iron if you have it), heat 2 tablespoons of the olive oil over medium heat and brown the fish lightly, 2 to 3 minutes per side (the fish won't be fully cooked through; this will happen in the oven). Transfer the fish to a plate, using a spatula to gently dislodge the fish if it's slightly stuck to the skillet (don't wash the skillet; you'll be using it again).

With the heat still at medium, add the remaining 1 tablespoon olive oil to any juices and oil in the skillet you used to cook the fish, then add the remaining 3 tablespoons of garlic and cook, stirring, for 1 minute. Add the spinach in batches and cook while stirring until wilted, 2 to 3 minutes. Stir in the lemon juice, then set the fish on top of the spinach. Pour the reserved yogurt sauce over the fish, shaking the skillet gently so the sauce settles well into the greens and between the pieces of fish. Transfer to the oven and bake, uncovered, until the top is very lightly golden and the edges are bubbly, 16 to 17 minutes. Use a paring knife to cut one piece of the fish to make sure it's just opaque and cooked through; if not, return to the oven for 2 to 3 more minutes. Remove from the oven and sprinkle with the sumac, pine nuts, and mint.

Make the salad: In a large salad bowl, combine the greens, scallions, orange segments, radishes, pine nuts, and chili pepper. Add the olive oil, lemon juice, any reserved blood orange juice, pomegranate molasses, and salt and pepper and to taste and toss to coat.

*To make orange segments, slice the top and bottom off of an orange so it can sit flat on the counter. Using a sharp knife and starting from the top, cut away the zest and white pith beneath, leaving the orange flesh exposed. Hold the orange in your hand over a bowl. Release the segments by cutting the flesh away from the white membrane surrounding the segments. Squeeze the juice from the web of membranes into a small bowl.

Herbed Fish Kebabs

OK, let's clear up some semantic confusion, because a kebab is not always just a kebab. Shish kebab usually refers to marinated chunks of meat, skewered and grilled, while kebab is basically a burger by another name: ground meat, seasoned, sometimes skewered, sometimes not, then grilled. These are basically shish kebabs, but with fish, coated in a chimichurri-esque mixture. Use the thickest, firmest fish you can find, and do your best to thread everything on the skewers in a way that makes them sit evenly on the grill—this helps develop a nice char on the fish and vegetables.

1 cup packed parsley leaves and tender stems

1 cup packed cilantro leaves and tender stems

½ cup packed tender mint leaves

1 tablespoon fresh za'atar or oregano leaves

2 scallions (white and green parts), coarsely chopped

3 garlic cloves, smashed

1 small shallot, quartered

1 small jalapeño, seeded and finely chopped

½ cup extra-virgin olive oil

2 tablespoons freshly squeezed lemon juice

1 teaspoon finely grated lemon zest

½ teaspoon kosher salt

3 medium tomatoes, each cut into 8 wedges

1 jumbo or 2 medium red onions, cut into 1-inch chunks

1½ pounds thick, firm, center-cut skinless white fish fillets, such as halibut or mahimahi, cut into 1-inch chunks

Serves 4

Active Time:
20 minutes

Total Time:
40 minutes

In the bowl of a food processor, pulse the parsley, cilantro, mint, za'atar, scallions, garlic, and shallot until finely minced but not pasty and liquidy, 20 to 25 pulses. Add the jalapeño, olive oil, lemon juice, lemon zest, and salt and pulse 5 more times. Divide the mixture in half. Create 8 to 10 skewers by threading the tomatoes, onions, and fish on the skewers in any order you like. Arrange the skewers on a rimmed baking sheet and brush them with half the herb mixture. Clean, lightly grease, and preheat a grill (or a flat griddle or grill pan, to allow the skewers to lie flat) over medium-high heat. Working in batches if using a grill pan but all at once if on a grill, grill the skewers, turning once, until the fish is cooked through, 3 to 4 minutes per side. Serve the kebabs with the remaining green sauce.

Chard-Wrapped Fish with Lemon and Olive

I grew up before the advent of self-serve olive bars. To this California kid, olives were spongy, black (possibly dyed), and used primarily to fit over tiny fingertips for dinnertime entertainment. I didn't develop a taste for them until I moved here and started shopping at the original olive bars, the *bastot* (stalls) selling a dozen varieties out of bins: wrinkly, oil-cured Moroccans; purple-blushed kalamatas (imported from Greece); the cracked, flat-green local *suri* variety. Now it's hard to imagine a meal *without* a little bowl of olives for snacking. I like to chop up whatever I have around, spread it on fish, and wrap it in chard before simmering it in a lemony, cilantro-y sauce.

2 lemons

⅓ cup pitted mixed olives, plus 12 whole pitted olives

4 tablespoons extra-virgin olive oil

3 cups cilantro leaves, finely chopped (about ¾ cup)

4 garlic cloves, finely minced (4 teaspoons)

1 teaspoon dried red pepper flakes

5 very large Swiss chard leaves (or more as needed), tough ends trimmed

1½ pounds skinless, center-cut white fish fillets, such as halibut or cod

1 teaspoon kosher salt, plus more for seasoning

¼ teaspoon freshly ground black pepper, plus more for seasoning

1 small onion, diced

1½ tablespoons all-purpose flour

1½ cups chicken stock

½ cup yellow cherry tomatoes, halved

Rice, couscous, or other cooked grain

Serves 4

Active Time:
20 minutes

Total Time:
45 minutes

Finely zest and juice both lemons. Reserve the juice and half the zest. In a small bowl, combine the remaining zest with the olives, 1 tablespoon of the olive oil, 2 tablespoons of the chopped cilantro leaves, 1 teaspoon garlic, and the red pepper flakes until incorporated.

Bring a small pot of water to a boil over medium-high heat. Use a knife to separate the leaves from the chard stems so you have 2 leaves from each stem. Thinly slice the stems crosswise. Dip the chard leaves in the boiling water for 10 seconds to soften; drain, cool slightly, and pat dry. Cut the fish into 8 equal-sized pieces, season with salt and pepper, and spread 2 teaspoons of the olive mixture on each piece of fish.

Place 1 piece of fish on a piece of chard and roll it up; use the extra 2 leaves to patch any parts that need extra wrapping. Heat the remaining 3 tablespoons olive oil in a large skillet over medium heat. Add the onion and cook, stirring, until tender and lightly golden, 8 to 9 minutes. Add the chard stems with the remaining 3 teaspoons garlic and cook, stirring, until softened, 3 to 4 minutes. Add the flour and cook, stirring, until absorbed, 1 minute. Add the reserved lemon zest and juice with the stock, salt, and pepper and cook, stirring, until the liquid thickens and bubbles, 2 to 3 minutes. Stir in most of the remaining cilantro. Nestle the fish in the skillet, scatter the tomatoes and whole olives over the fish, reduce the heat to medium-low, cover, and cook until the fish is opaque and the chard can be cut easily, 10 minutes. Serve over the grain of your choice with sauce spooned over the top; garnish with cilantro.

Grilled Whole Fish and Potatoes with Toasted Nut and Avocado Tabbouleh

Come summer, we love to head up north and have fresh grilled fish in and around Tiberias, a city on the shores of the Kinneret lake, also known as the Sea of Galilee. The best restaurants do very little to it except dress it with a drop of salt and lemon. Now that we have a grill, we do the same thing at home, using smaller whole fish like *denis* or *levrak* (sea bream and sea bass, respectively). We ask the fishmonger to clean the fish but leave the heads and tails on; it really keeps it moist, and after you make it once, you'll be converted to whole-fish cooking. I'm partial to serving the fish with tabbouleh. A raft of chopped herbs is tossed with more lemon juice and less bulgur than you'd expect (you can use any other grains you have, too, or even very finely chopped cauliflower). In addition to toasted nuts I fold in a firm, finely diced ripe avocado. It almost disappears visually into the salad but adds a creamy-crunchy textural element that makes it irresistible. Make sure your herbs are well washed. (You might not notice how sandy parsley can be when you're just using a tablespoon or two, but when it's the star ingredient, it needs to be pristine.) Dry the herbs very well before using; any moisture that remains can cause them to clump and blacken.

5 tablespoons extra-virgin olive oil, plus more for greasing and drizzling

4 small Russet potatoes, scrubbed

4 whole fish (about 1 pound each), such as sea bass or sea bream

Kosher salt and freshly ground black pepper to taste

1 lemon, half very thinly sliced, the other half cut into wedges

Thyme, rosemary, and oregano sprigs

1 teaspoon sweet paprika

Serves 4

Active Time:
10 minutes

Total Time:
30 minutes

If you're using a grilling cage, grease it lightly with oil, then preheat the grill over medium-high heat. If you're using the oven, lightly grease a rack and set it over a large rimmed baking sheet and preheat the oven to 500°F.

Use a fork to poke deep holes in the potatoes. Wrap them in a clean kitchen towel, making sure they're covered on all sides. Microwave until almost cooked but still a bit firm, 8 to 9 minutes. Remove from the microwave and let cool. Season the cavities of the fish generously with salt and pepper, then layer a few lemon slices inside each one along with a few herb sprigs. Rub the outsides of the fish generously with 2 tablespoons of olive oil, then season with salt and pepper. Halve the potatoes and toss them in a medium bowl with the remaining 3 tablespoons olive oil and the paprika; season generously with salt and pepper.

If grilling, place the fish in the grilling cage and then onto the grill (or directly onto very well-greased grill grates), along with the potatoes, and grill, flipping midway through, until the skin of the fish is crispy and the flesh is opaque, and the potatoes are tender and crispy, 5 to 6 minutes per side. If using the oven, preheat it to 500°F. Roast the fish and potatoes until the skin starts to blister, the lemons brown at the edges, and the potatoes are tender and crispy, 11 to 12 minutes total. Brush the potatoes with any remaining paprika oil and serve with the fish. Serve with lemon wedges.

RECIPE CONTINUES

Super Nutty Avocado Tabbouleh

½ cup bulgur, preferably fine*

½ cup extra-virgin olive oil

⅓ cup freshly squeezed lemon juice, plus more to taste

1 teaspoon ground cumin

1 teaspoon kosher salt, plus more to taste

3 large bunches fresh parsley (about ½ pound)

½ large bunch fresh mint (about 1 ounce)

8 scallions, trimmed and thinly sliced (1 cup)

4 medium, firm ripe red tomatoes, cored, seeded, and diced

½ cup toasted pine nuts

½ cup sliced or chopped toasted almonds

1 large, firm, ripe avocado, finely diced

Serves 4 to 6

Active Time: 20 minutes

Total Time: 1 hour

Place the bulgur in a medium bowl, cover with 1 cup hot water, cover tightly with plastic wrap, and let sit for 20 minutes if using fine bulgur or about 55 minutes if using coarse, until all the water has been absorbed; uncover the bulgur and fluff it with a fork. In a small bowl, whisk together the olive oil, lemon juice, cumin, and salt. Pick the leaves and tender stems from the parsley and mint, place them in a large bowl, cover them with very cold water, and swish them around for a few seconds. Using your hands, pull the herbs out of the water, transfer them to a salad spinner, and dry them very well; if they're still damp after spinning, lay them out on a large, clean kitchen towel and gently roll up the towel to absorb any excess liquid. Working with a few handfuls of herbs at a time, chop the parsley and mint, making sure to move the herbs around while chopping them; if you go over the herbs too many times in the same spot, they'll blacken. Add the herbs to a large bowl with the bulgur, scallions, tomatoes, pine nuts, almonds, and avocado. Toss with the lemon–olive oil mixture, season with more lemon and salt to taste, let sit for 5 minutes, and serve right away; tabbouleh isn't one of those foods that improves as it sits around!

*Bulgur typically comes in fine and coarse varieties; if you use fine bulgur, chances are it will absorb more water than coarse. So if you end up using coarse bulgur, make sure to drain all the excess liquid before proceeding.

Hakosem's Perfect Falafel and Crispy Eggplant Steaks

Falafel

Fast, filling, and cheap, a street-stand falafel is the meal I crave more than any other. The times I've made breakfast, lunch, or dinner out of a mana (portion) of falafel are too numerous to count, and here are some of the reasons: the crunch of the falafel against the smushy pita, the hot and crispy falafel flirting with the cool salad, all unified under a blanket of tahini. The good news is that with a few dried chickpeas and a little patience, you can pull it off at home with relative ease. There are many opinions about what makes a falafel perfect; the seasonings, condiments, and ways to stuff a pita vary. Hakosem makes one of the most consistently crispy, greaseless, and delicious falafel balls in town thanks to a handful of fresh herbs and the surprise of sesame and nigella seeds in the mix. Unlike other proprietors, who try to keep the mixture on the less-wet side, Ariel Rosenthal from Hakosem believes oil and water *do* mix. "It needs to have moisture to be juicy after fried," Ariel told me. He doesn't add extra flour or breadcrumbs to his falafel mix. Instead he takes extra care with his frying oil, and you should, too. Try to keep your oil clean, fresh, and consistently heated. Though many people will tell you that you can, don't reuse old oil for this purpose. Use a candy or deep-fry thermometer if you have one. The results a fluffy, crunchy, juicy falafel—are well worth the effort.

Makes 24 falafel balls
Active Time: 45 minutes
Total Time: 25 hours (including soaking time)

⅔ cup dried chickpeas

1 cup coarsely chopped parsley leaves and tender stems

1 cup coarsely chopped cilantro leaves and tender stems

½ medium onion, coarsely chopped

2 garlic cloves

½ small jalapeño, seeded and coarsely chopped

1 teaspoon kosher salt, plus more for seasoning

½ teaspoon ground cumin

½ teaspoon ground coriander

1 teaspoon sesame seeds

½ teaspoon nigella seeds

¼ teaspoon baking soda

Grapeseed, canola, or another neutral-flavored vegetable oil, for frying

Cauliflower and Turnip Pickles (page 282), and Salt-Brined Dill Pickles (page 32), for serving

Prepare the chickpeas: Place the chickpeas in a bowl, cover with 4 inches of water, and soak in the refrigerator for 24 hours.

Drain and rinse the chickpeas, place them in the bowl of a food processor, and process until they're pulverized into large crumb-like pieces, stopping to scrape down the sides of the bowl if necessary, 30 to 45 seconds. Add the parsley and cilantro to the processor with the onion, garlic, jalapeño, and 2 tablespoons of water and pulse until a unified and bright

RECIPE CONTINUES

green mixture is formed, stopping to scrape down the sides of the bowl if necessary, 20 to 30 seconds (add an extra tablespoon of water if necessary).

In a small bowl, combine the salt, cumin, coriander, sesame seeds, nigella seeds, and baking soda. Just before frying the falafel, add the spices to the food processor and pulse until incorporated, 15 pulses.

Heat 2 inches of grapeseed oil in a high-sided skillet over medium-high heat until it reads 360°F on a candy thermometer, or a small piece of white bread begins to sizzle and brown immediately when dropped into the oil. Set a colander over a bowl or line a plate with paper towels. Using two spoons, your hands, or a small Pal Ed falafel mold (see photo and description, page 283), form the falafel into balls the size of small walnuts. Fry in batches, making sure not to overcrowd the skillet or let the oil temperature drop below about 340°F, until deep golden, 1 to 2 minutes but no more. Serve hot, seasoning with more salt if desired. The falafel mixture and spice mixture can be held separately for up to 24 hours, then combined at the last minute and fried fresh.

To build sandwiches, layer crispy eggplant or falafel in pitas with Israeli salad, hummus (page 116 or 118), amba (page 36), and schug (page 35).

Serve with Cauliflower and Turnip Pickles (page 282) or Salt-Brined Dill Pickles (page 32).

Crispy Eggplant Steaks

Ariel's crispy, juicy fried eggplant steaks (bottom of photo at right) have become famous in Tel Aviv and beyond, and I dare say they're as satisfying as a real steak. If you want to serve these together, prep the eggplant, then prep the falafel. Then you'll be ready to fry the eggplant followed by the falafel.

Makes 10 pieces
Active Time: 35 minutes
Total Time: 1 hour 15 minutes (including resting time)

1 medium eggplant (1 pound), preferably long and thin over fat and squat	Kosher salt	½ cup cornstarch
	Grapeseed, canola, or another neutral-flavored vegetable oil, for frying	½ cup all-purpose flour

Peel the eggplant, then halve it lengthwise so you have 2 pieces about 4 to 5 inches long. Using a sharp knife, slice the eggplant into ½-inch-thick steaks. Arrange them on a rack set over a rimmed baking sheet and season each side generously with salt. Let them sit for 45 minutes.

RECIPE CONTINUES

Heat 2 inches of grapeseed oil in a high-sided skillet over medium-high heat until it reads 360°F on a candy thermometer, or a small piece of white bread begins to sizzle and brown, but not burn, immediately when dropped into the oil. In a medium bowl, combine the cornstarch and flour. After the eggplant slices sit for 45 minutes, rinse them under cold running water, let the excess moisture drip off, then dredge the eggplant pieces in the cornstarch-flour mixture, shaking off any excess (don't worry if some parts are more coated than others; this makes for an incredibly craggy topography of fried goodness). Two or 3 pieces at a time, fry the eggplant, making sure not to overcrowd the pan or let the oil temperature drop below about 340°F, until the eggplant pieces are golden and crisp, 2 to 3 minutes per side. Drain on the salting rack, season with salt to taste, and serve hot.

Cauliflower and Turnip Pickles

Turmeric dyes the cauliflower a lovely shade of yellow, and a few beets transform turnips into perfectly pink batons. This isn't classic canning; these are fresh veggies meant to be eaten soon after making.

Makes 4 cups of each variety
Active Time: 30 minutes
Total Time: 1 day (including minimum pickling time)

2 medium turnips (1 pound), peeled and cut into ½-inch-thick batons

1 medium head cauliflower, stem removed, head cut into small and medium florets (about 4 cups)

2 cups white vinegar

4 tablespoons sugar

2½ tablespoons kosher salt

1½ teaspoons mustard seeds

1 teaspoon whole peppercorns

2 bay leaves

1 tablespoon ground turmeric (for the cauliflower pickles)

½ small beet, peeled and thinly sliced (for the turnip pickles)

Place the turnip batons in a medium bowl. Place the cauliflower florets in another medium bowl.

In a medium saucepan over medium heat, bring the vinegar, 2 cups of water, sugar, salt, mustard seeds, peppercorns, and bay leaves to a boil. Reduce the heat to low and simmer until the sugar and salt dissolve, 2 to 3 minutes. Pour half the mixture, including half the spices and a bay leaf, over the turnips. Add the turmeric to the remaining half, return it to the heat, and let simmer for 2 minutes. Pour the turmeric liquid plus the remaining spices and bay leaf over the cauliflower. Let both bowls sit for 20 minutes. Pack the turnips tightly into 1 quart-sized jar, wedge the beets into the jar, and carefully pour the turnip liquid into the jar all the way to the top. Pack the cauliflower into another quart-size jar and pour its liquid into the jar all the way to the top. Seal each jar and chill. The pickles will be ready to eat after 1 day but ideal after 3 days, and will last in the refrigerator for up to 1 month.

The Pal Ed Falafel Mold

If you've ever watched Israeli falafel vendors forming and shaping falafel batter into balls (well, more like little pucks), chances are they're using a Pal Ed falafel mold. This ingenious spring-loaded aluminum gadget perfectly portions the falafel batter every time, ensuring even frying and uniform shape and appearance. Invented by European immigrant Pesach Bash in the years following World War II, the device has become an icon of the Israeli kitchen, made in assorted sizes—even double molds for vendors in a real hurry—some even suitable for forming patties out of meat, fish, or vegetables. Though Pal Ed makes many other products, this is the one to get—or bring home from Israel as a gift for yourself or someone else.

Amba Tofu Curry

It seems like half of Israel travels to India and the rest of Asia after their mandatory army service ends, and they come craving the faraway flavors they learned to love overseas. My husband's son, Nadav, was my guinea pig for this curry, which is sort of an Indian-Asian hybrid that uses amba, the savory mango pickle with Jewish-Iraqi-Indian roots, instead of red or green curry paste or Indian curry spices, in a coconut-based sauce. It may sound like a bit of a stretch, but the sour, pungent notes in the viscous yellow amba are a great foil for the sweetness of coconut milk. I used the tiny baby eggplants I found in the market, which cook up fast and tender, but regular eggplant works great, too. I like to use baby okra here since their cooking time matches that of the eggplant; the smaller and younger, the less slimy.

One 13.5-ounce can coconut milk, preferably full-fat

⅓ cup 40-Minute Amba (page 36 or store-bought), or more to taste

3 tablespoons lightly packed light brown sugar

½ teaspoon kosher salt

One 14-ounce package firm or extra-firm tofu

3 tablespoons vegetable oil

10 baby eggplants, trimmed and halved, or 1 regular eggplant (1 pound), cut into 1-inch chunks

1 small onion, thinly sliced

2 large garlic cloves, minced

½ pound very small okra (the smaller the better) or frozen okra, defrosted, trimmed

½ cup cherry tomatoes, halved

1 teaspoon red or green jalapeño, seeded and chopped

Rice, for serving

Lime wedges, for serving

Handful of fresh Thai or regular basil, for garnish

Serves 4

Active Time:
45 minutes

Total Time:
45 minutes

In a medium bowl, whisk together the coconut milk, amba, brown sugar, and salt. Slice the tofu into 8 equal-sized rectangles, then pat each rectangle dry with paper towels. Heat a large, dry, nonstick skillet over medium-high heat (don't put any oil in the skillet). Working in batches if necessary, arrange the tofu in the skillet and cook, pressing down often with a metal spatula, until no more water seems to be releasing from the tofu and the underside is browned, 2 to 3 minutes (the tofu will make strange howling noises; this means it's doing what it's supposed to, which is drying out on the inside so it can soak up the sauce). Flip the tofu and cook, pressing, another 2 to 3 minutes. Transfer the tofu to a plate and slice each piece lengthwise into 3 equal-sized batons. Add 1½ tablespoons of the vegetable oil to the skillet, then add the eggplant, cut-side down, and cook until the underside is golden, 2 to 3 minutes. Flip and cook another 2 to 3 minutes. Transfer the eggplant to the plate with the tofu and add the remaining 1½ tablespoons of the vegetable oil to the skillet. Add the onions and cook until slightly softened, 5 minutes. Add the garlic and cook, stirring, 1 minute more. Return the tofu and eggplant to the skillet along with the okra, tomatoes, and jalapeño, then add the coconut mixture and bring to a boil. Reduce the heat to a simmer, coating the mixture in the sauce occasionally, until the liquid thickens, 6 to 7 minutes. Serve over rice with the lime wedges, and garnish with the basil.

Pumpkin-Vegetable Stew with Easy Homemade Couscous

◇◇◇◇◇◇◇◇◇◇

**Serves
8 to 10**

Active Time:
1 hour
30 minutes

Total Time:
14 hours
(including
chickpea
soaking
time)

◇◇◇◇◇◇◇◇◇◇

"You don't make couscous on a day of mourning," my friend chef Nofar Zohar told me as we prepped the ingredients for a rich vegetable stew that would be ladled atop homemade couscous. "This is a happy dish for a happy day." Since it is considered a good luck talisman for new homes, Nofar's mother prepares couscous for friends and neighbors as a housewarming gift. "You want to leave all the vegetables big," she told me as we carved hunks of cabbage and squash. "You want them to be sexy." Adding a touch of brown sugar and caramelizing the vegetables adds both sweetness and depth. The vegetables may be a bit softer than you're used to, but trust me—you'll love them. If you've ever made your own couscous, you know it's typically a multi-hour process of pinching, sieving, and steaming semolina. Nofar's method, learned from her mother, takes 30 minutes from start to finish and yields pretty darned good couscous: light, fluffy, and deliciously salty. In Israel it's easy to find coarse semolina, which yields a slightly sturdier couscous. Stateside, the standard semolina is a little finer; if you use fine couscous, the finished product will be a little less toothsome but no less delicious (you can also sub in store-bought couscous). To make it we used a kish kash, a traditional flat, high-sided wide-mesh sieve designed for the job. You can order one online or use a gardening soil sifter, which I found online (see Shopping Guide).

⅔ cup dried chickpeas, or one 15-ounce can chickpeas, drained and rinsed

7 cups low-sodium vegetable broth

⅓ cup grapeseed oil

3 medium carrots, peeled, trimmed, halved lengthwise then crosswise

2 medium onions, peeled, furry ends trimmed, quartered through the root

1 medium celery root, peeled and cut into 8 wedges

3 large celery stalks, outer layers peeled, cut into large chunks

2 tablespoons dark brown sugar

6 sprigs fresh dill

6 sprigs fresh parsley

6 sprigs fresh cilantro

3 tablespoons sweet paprika

4 teaspoons kosher salt, plus more to taste

1 tablespoon freshly ground black pepper

1¼ teaspoons ground cinnamon

1 teaspoon ground mace or ½ teaspoon ground nutmeg

¼ teaspoon ground turmeric

¼ cup tomato paste

1½ pounds seeded pumpkin or kabocha squash, rind on and cut into 4-inch chunks

3 small zucchini (or 2 medium), trimmed but left whole (halved if medium)

½ very small green cabbage, cut into 4 wedges

2 medium ripe tomatoes, cored and quartered

3 small potatoes, halved

COUSCOUS (Makes 8 cups)

½ cup canola oil

1 tablespoon kosher salt

2¾ cups (1 pound) semolina, preferably coarse

Soak the chickpeas: Place the chickpeas in a bowl, cover with 4 inches of water, cover, and soak on the counter for 10 to 12 hours or in the refrigerator for 24 hours. Drain and rinse the chickpeas.

Make the stew: In a medium saucepan, keep the broth at a simmer, covered, over very low heat until ready to use. In a large (6- or 8-quart), wide-bottomed soup pot with a tight-fitting lid, heat the grapeseed oil over medium heat. Add the carrots and onions and

RECIPE CONTINUES

cook, turning occasionally, until the outer parts of the carrots and the onions caramelize, 6 minutes total. Add the celery root and celery and cook until the vegetables soften, 5 minutes. Add the chickpeas, stir in the brown sugar, cover, and cook until the vegetables release liquid, 5 minutes. While the vegetables cook, tie the dill, parsley, and cilantro into a bundle with kitchen twine.

Stir in the paprika, salt, pepper, cinnamon, mace, and turmeric. Cook 1 minute. Add the tomato paste and cook, stirring, until absorbed, 2 minutes. Add the pumpkin, zucchini, and herb bundle. Add 3 cups of the simmering broth just to cover. Bring to a boil over medium-high heat, reduce the heat to a medium-low, cover, and simmer until the vegetables soften slightly, 15 minutes. Uncover, then add the rest of the broth to the pot. Nestle the cabbage, tomatoes, and potatoes into the pot; return to a vigorous boil; reduce the heat to a simmer again; cover; and cook until the potatoes are tender, 40 minutes.

While the soup is cooking, make the couscous: In a large pot over medium-high heat, bring 2¾ cups of water, the canola oil, and the salt to a boil. Add the semolina and cook, stirring, over high heat, until the semolina drinks up the water and pulls away from the sides of the pot, 1 minute. Reduce the heat to low and continue to cook until the semolina becomes more solid and harder to stir but is still lush and full of moisture, adding up to ¼ cup of water to help stir, 3 minutes. Turn off the heat, cover (this is critical! The semolina continues to steam and soften), then let the semolina sit, covered, for 15 minutes. Set a large-holed sieve over a large rimmed baking sheet and uncover the pot. Let it cool a bit, then, about 1 cup at a time, using a dish-gloved hand or silicone spatula, push and smear the semolina through the sieve; it will fall out the other side like little perfect fluffy snowflakes.

To serve, remove and discard the herb bundle, mound the couscous into bowls, and top with some of the vegetables and broth.

Couscous Condiments

The series of side dishes and condiments that Nofar taught me how to make turn her couscous meal into a party. Caraway-laced chirshi is actually a Libyan specialty, but her family adopted it as part of their couscous ritual. While most recipes call for boiling the pumpkin, mine uses roasted butternut squash, which deepens the flavor. The mildly spicy charred tomato salsa tastes better as it sits around. I am also obsessed with her free-form pickled vegetables; cured with nothing more than lemon juice, salt, and sugar, you can get them on the table in less than 45 minutes.

Charred Tomato Salsa
Makes 2½ cups

4 medium tomatoes
(1½ pounds)

1 jalapeño

⅓ cup extra-virgin olive oil

2 tablespoons chopped
Preserved Lemons
(page 38)

3 garlic cloves, thinly sliced

1 teaspoon kosher salt

½ teaspoon sugar

Char the tomatoes and jalapeño directly over a high flame until the tomato skin is slightly charred on all sides and the pepper is blistered, 5 minutes for the jalapeño and 10 minutes for the tomatoes. Transfer to a medium bowl and cool for 15 minutes. Core and peel the skins off the tomatoes and remove the stem from the jalapeño. Chop the tomatoes and jalapeños. Place them in the bowl and stir in the olive oil, preserved lemons, garlic, salt, and sugar. Let the flavors meld for 1 hour before serving.

Fresh Moroccan Pickles
Makes 4 cups

1 small fennel bulb

1 lemon, ends trimmed

1 small red bell pepper, seeded and sliced

2 tender celery stalks, cut into 3-inch lengths, plus tender leaves

2 small carrots, halved lengthwise and cut into thin sticks

2 small radishes, cut into ⅛-inch-thick slices

3 tablespoons freshly squeezed lemon juice

2 tablespoons kosher salt

1 tablespoon sugar

Halve the fennel through its core, then use the tip of the knife to cut out the white inner core; discard the core and cut the fennel into ⅛-inch-thick pieces. Slice the lemon lengthwise into quarters, remove as many seeds as you can, then cut each quarter into very thin slices. In a medium bowl, toss the sliced fennel and lemon with the bell pepper, celery, carrots, radishes, lemon juice, salt, and sugar. Let sit for 30 minutes, toss again, and chill until ready to use. Refrigerated pickles keep for 1 week.

Roasted Chirshi
Makes 2½ cups

6 tablespoons extra-virgin olive oil

2 tablespoons tomato paste

1 tablespoon plus ½ teaspoon paprika

2 teaspoons ground caraway

2 teaspoons kosher salt, plus more to taste

¼ teaspoon freshly ground black pepper, plus more to taste

¼ teaspoon plus generous pinch cayenne pepper

One 1½-pound peeled butternut squash, cut into 1½-inch cubes

2 medium carrots (8 ounces), cut into 1-inch pieces

5 garlic cloves

2 teaspoons freshly squeezed lemon juice

Preheat the oven to 400°F.

In a large bowl, whisk together 3 tablespoons of the olive oil with the tomato paste, 1 tablespoon of the paprika, the caraway, salt, pepper, and ¼ teaspoon of the cayenne. Add the butternut squash, carrots, and garlic. Toss to coat, transfer to a 9 x 13-inch glass baking dish, seal tightly with foil, and bake until the vegetables are tender, and slightly darkened around the edges, 40 to 45 minutes. Cool for 10 minutes. Transfer to a large bowl. Add the remaining 3 tablespoons olive oil with the lemon juice, the remaining ½ teaspoon of paprika, and a pinch of cayenne. Mash with a potato masher until almost smooth. Season with salt and pepper and serve warm or at room temperature.

Smoky Eggplant and Feta Galette with Garlicky Roasted Red Pepper Salad

Shaily Lipa spent many a Saturday morning at her *savta* (grandma) Levana's side, watching as she made the *borekitas* that were the centerpiece of the family's weekly Shabbat breakfast. Filled with smoky eggplant and feta, the flaky pockets epitomized the traditions so dear to Levana, while serving as a weekly reminder of the Greek coastal city of Thessaloniki, or Salonika, that was home to a vibrant Jewish community of fifty thousand before the Holocaust wiped it out. One sunny morning at her home outside of Tel Aviv, Shaily, who grew up to become a respected food editor, cookbook author, and television personality, showed me how to make the magical dough at the heart of those borekitas. The method, which involves dumping flour all at once into boiling liquid, calls to mind pâte à choux, the classic French dough used to make cream puffs and eclairs, albeit here in different proportions. The addition of humble white vinegar transformed the dough into a pliant, velvety ball with no stickiness whatsoever. Shaily and I followed Levana's recipe to a tee, filling, stamping, folding, crimping, and baking them to a golden glow. I loved the dough so much, I went home dreaming about how I could honor Levana's recipe while making it the starting point for a main course. I rolled the dough into one huge circle, filled it with that same mix of eggplant and feta, topped it with olives and tomatoes, and folded it over to make a rustic galette that emerged from the oven sturdy enough to cut, yet as deliciously flaky as I remembered (the eggplant filling can be made a day in advance). Served with a side of the silky roasted peppers, a wedge of this galette hits the spot.

FILLING

1 jumbo or 2 medium Italian eggplants (1½ pounds), charred (see method, page 133)

1 cup (4 ounces) crumbled feta cheese

3 tablespoons chopped fresh dill

2 tablespoons extra-virgin olive oil

1 small jalapeño, seeded and sliced into thin rings (1 tablespoon)

1 teaspoon kosher salt

¼ teaspoon freshly ground black pepper

DOUGH

3 cups all-purpose flour, plus more for flouring your hands

½ teaspoon baking powder

1 cup vegetable oil

1 teaspoon kosher salt

2 tablespoons white vinegar

TOPPING

1 large egg, whisked with ½ teaspoon water and a pinch of salt

½ cup (¾ ounce) finely grated kashkaval or Parmigiano-Reggiano cheese

1 small Roma tomato, sliced into thin rounds

6 pitted kalamata olives

---

ooooooooooo

Serves 6

Active Time:
40 minutes

Total Time:
2 hours

ooooooooooo

Make the filling: Chop the charred eggplant until chunky and transfer it to a large bowl. Gently fold in the feta, dill, olive oil, jalapeño, salt, and black pepper until incorporated.

Make the dough: In a medium bowl, whisk together the flour and baking powder. In a medium saucepan, bring the vegetable oil, ⅔ cup water, and salt to a boil over high heat (the water will form ½-inch bubbles that begin to pop through the oil; that's what boiling looks like here). Remove the saucepan from the heat, add the vinegar, then add the flour

RECIPE CONTINUES

mixture all at once and stir vigorously with a wooden spoon until the flour drinks up the liquid and a unified, velvety dough forms; let the dough cool for 10 minutes.

Preheat the oven to 400°F.

Set a large piece of parchment paper on the counter. Using lightly floured hands, form the dough into a ball. Place it in the center of the parchment paper and gently roll it into a 12-inch round about ¼ inch thick (the dough is soft, go easy on it). Transfer the dough-topped parchment paper to a baking sheet.

To assemble and bake: Dollop the filling into the center of the dough round and spread it out, leaving a 1-inch border around the edges. Fold the dough up and over the filling (if you've ever made a galette, it's the same idea—very rustic!) so that the dough forms a 1-inch frame around the filling. Brush the edges of the dough with the egg mixture, then sprinkle the edges with the cheese. Arrange the tomato slices and olives on top of the galette and bake until the tomatoes are wilted and the dough is golden and flaky, 35 to 40 minutes. Cut into wedges and serve warm or at room temperature. Serve with Garlicky Roasted Red Peppers (recipe follows).

Garlicky Roasted Red Peppers

Since I wanted these peppers to be a bit meatier and less smoky, they are roasted on a slightly lower temperature than my charred peppers (see method, page 133). But if you have some of those on hand, by all means feel free to swap them in.

Makes 3 cups
Active Time: 15 minutes
Total Time: 1 hour 15 minutes

6 large firm red bell peppers

¼ cup extra-virgin olive oil, or oil from Garlic Confit (recipe follows)

8 cloves Garlic Confit (recipe follows), or store-bought roasted garlic

2 tablespoons chopped fresh dill

1 teaspoon salt

¼ teaspoon freshly ground black pepper

Preheat the oven to 400°F.

Place the bell peppers (stems and all) on a large, foil-lined rimmed baking sheet and roast, turning occasionally without piercing them, until they appear puffed up with hot air and are slightly charred in spots (they don't need to be totally black), 30 to 35 minutes. Place in a large bowl, seal tightly with plastic wrap, and let cool completely. Uncover, slip the skins off the bell peppers with your hands (they should peel off easily), then discard the skins along with the stems and all the seeds so all you're left with is silky roasted pepper flesh. Rinse out and dry the bowl, slice the peppers into strips, and toss them in the bowl with the olive oil, garlic, dill, salt, and pepper.

Garlic Confit

You can use store-bought roasted garlic cloves, but if you have an hour you can make your own, which yields a bonus product: deliciously garlicky olive oil you can swap in virtually anywhere olive oil is called for.

Makes 1 cup each roasted garlic cloves and roasted garlic oil
Active time: 1 minute
Total time: 50 minutes

2 cups peeled garlic cloves   **1½ cups extra-virgin olive oil**

Place the garlic cloves in the smallest saucepan you have. Pour the olive oil over the garlic; it should just cover the cloves. Warm the garlic and oil over a very low flame until the cloves are light golden and totally soft, but not caramelized or dark brown, 45 to 50 minutes. You don't want the oil to boil and fry the garlic; you're going for a very low, slow process of turning the cloves golden. Refrigerated in an airtight container, confit and oil will keep for up to 2 weeks.

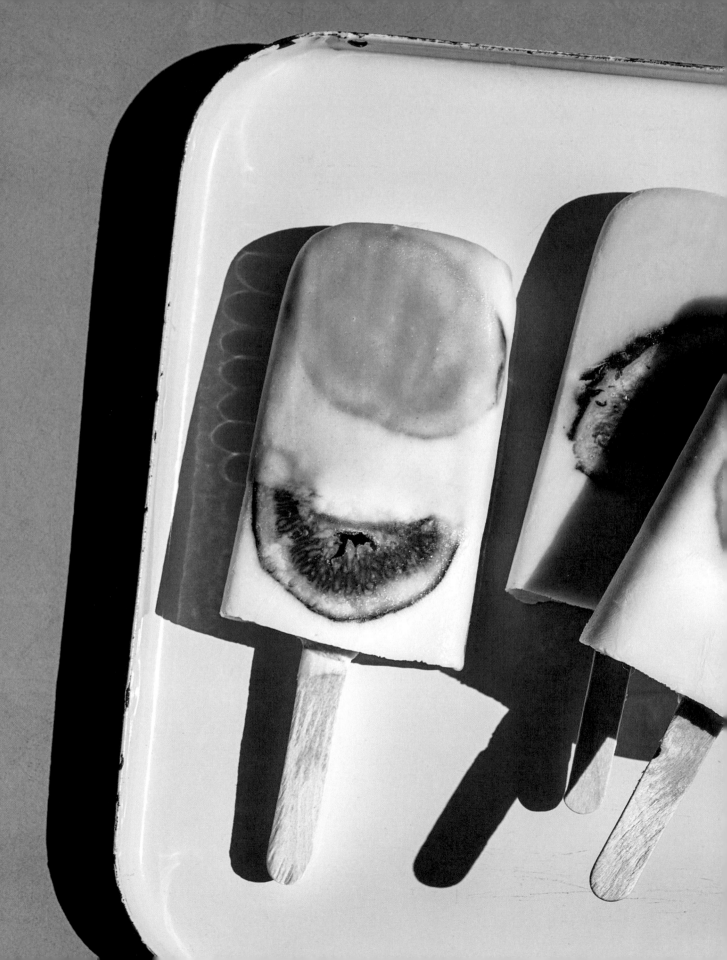

COCKTAILS, DRINKS, AND FROZEN TREATS

Fig and Yogurt Pops with Tahini Magic Shell

Popsicles (known here as *artikim*) are a national obsession, delivering a refreshing blast chill when the temperatures spike from hot to hades. From the cheap, delicious, artificially flavored ices you can buy along the beach to Mexican-style paletas, which come in a million gourmet flavors, it's easy to get a frozen/sweet fix on a stick. To show off the gorgeous fruit in season, I based these pops (see photo, pp. 294–295) around thick, juicy slices of figs. I slide them into popsicle molds, then tip a tart, honey-sweetened yogurt mixture around them before freezing. If you can, try to arrange your pops so the figs remain visible (see instructions in recipe), but no matter how you build them, they're delicious. The tahini magic shell really is two-ingredient heaven; dip once and you've got a semi-translucent sesame slick that hardens on contact with the pops; dip twice for a thicker layer. I make a generous amount of the magic shell because it makes dipping the pops easier; you can refrigerate any leftover shell, then gently rewarm it in the microwave. If you want to halve it, you'll just have to tip and swirl the pops around to coat them.

POPS
1 cup plain yogurt
¼ cup honey

Generous pinch of ground cardamom
Pinch of fine sea salt
2 or 3 large, plump fresh figs

TAHINI MAGIC SHELL
1 cup pure tahini paste
½ cup coconut oil, melted

ooooooooooo

Makes
4 pops

Active Time:
15 minutes

Total Time:
4 hours

ooooooooooo

Make and freeze the pops: In a medium bowl, whisk together the yogurt, honey, cardamom, and salt. Take a look at your popsicle molds and gauge how thick you need to slice your figs; you want to be able to slide the figs into the molds so they are fairly tightly wedged in place (this will mean you'll see fig after they're frozen). Slide 1 large or 2 smaller fig slices into the molds, then press a wooden popsicle stick through the figs down into the bottom of the molds. Pour the yogurt mixture around the figs, moving the figs slightly with your fingers and tapping the molds against the counter to allow the yogurt to fill any gaps and air pockets. Freeze until solid, 3 to 4 hours (or if you have an instant popsicle maker, by all means use that).

Make the magic shell and finish the pops: Once the pops are frozen, combine the tahini and coconut oil until smooth in a glass that can fit the popsicle without it touching its sides. Line a plate with wax paper and place it in the freezer. Loosen the pops by letting them sit out for 5 minutes, or run the outside of the molds carefully under warm water in 15-second increments until they release. Dip each pop in the tahini mixture, pull it out, and let the excess mixture drip off. If desired, dip again; the mixture should harden almost immediately. Place each pop on the wax paper–lined plate as they're done. Freeze for a few minutes before serving, or wrap each pop in wax paper, then in plastic wrap, and store in the freezer for up to 1 week.

Jewels for Sale

I noticed Edgar Asis's tiny fruit stand one morning as I made my rounds in the shuk. No more than three feet across, the table was lined with newspapers and covered in small containers of the most beautiful, unblemished figs I had ever seen. They were stacked in perfect pyramids and they were very expensive. "Every one of them will be perfect, down to the bottom layer," he promised me. I took them home; they were, indeed, flawless, and every day since that day I've been buying fruit from Edgar. Born in Halabi, Syria, in 1940, he came to Israel as a two-year-old with his family, and soon his father began selling vegetables from a cart. Though Edgar studied the diamond trade, life in the shuk eventually drew him back, and he worked with his father until his death in 1988. Rather than close up shop, Edgar chose to focus on selling one thing and selling it well. From September to January that means pomegranates, whose seeds he individually sorts into cups sold with jaunty spoons peeking out of the tops. From January through May it's strawberries, and the summer is for cherries, figs, and apricots—but only if he can find the best, and always, perhaps owing to his brief foray in the diamond trade, arranged like jewels.

Mixed Herbal Tea

Most mornings I brew a pot of tea like this, known in Hebrew as a *chalita*, or infusion. This has pretty much come to *mean* tea in Israel; every café has fresh mint, and often people just skip the tea and get the mint combined with whatever other herbs the kitchen has on hand. I start out drinking mine hot, then let it sit around, eventually pouring over ice as the day progresses. Other than rosemary, there's hardly an herb I haven't thrown in here, from sage and thyme to lemongrass, and my beloved louisa, or lemon verbena. Throw in fresh turmeric or ginger for a kick, or a drop of honey if you like it sweetened. Herbs here can be pretty sandy, so I make sure to wash them well by throwing them into a giant bowl of cold water, pulling the herbs out and leaving any grit behind. And don't fret: If you don't end up drinking it, just strain it into a pitcher, discard the wilted herbs, and chill.

½ bunch mint, rinsed

½ cup fresh or dried lemon verbena leaves (or more mint)

1 sage leaf (optional)

One 3-inch piece ginger, peeled and cut into matchsticks

One 2-inch piece fresh turmeric, peeled and cut into thin coins

1 strip fresh lemon or orange peel

Honey (optional)

Serves 6

Active Time:
10 minutes

Total Time:
15 minutes (including minimum infusion time)

Add the mint, verbena, sage (if using), ginger, and turmeric to a pot of boiling water or an infusing tea carafe filled with hot water. Let it infuse for as little as 5 minutes and up to 4 hours. Drink hot or chilled over ice; garnish with a lemon peel and sweeten with honey as desired.

Cardamom-Cinnamon Cold Brew

For me, drinking hot coffee ceases in June and only resumes in September, when the days start to shorten and the Tel Aviv temperatures return to near normal. Until then, I cold-brew endless pitchers of coffee with cinnamon sticks and cardamom. Cold-brewing results in coffee that is clearer, stronger, and less bitter all at the same time. I lighten it with homemade almond milk sweetened with dates or date syrup (page 302), both of which seem born for this job. The flavor of the coffee is evocative of classic hot Turkish coffee, but cooled down for the purposes of summer consumption.

1½ cups (5 ounces) coarsely ground coffee beans (French press grind) of your choice (I like dark roast)

1 cinnamon stick
10 cardamom pods, slightly crushed

Date-Sweetened Almond Milk (page 302), for serving

Makes
4 cups concentrate; serves 8

Active Time:
5 minutes

Total Time:
about 12 hours (including minimum steeping time)

Place the coffee, cinnamon stick, and cardamom pods in a large lidded jar (lined with a nut-milk bag, if you have one) or cold-brew pitcher and slowly add 5 cups cold water (filtered or bottled if you prefer). Cover and refrigerate for at least 12 hours and up to 24. If you made the coffee in a cold-brew pitcher, you're good to go; pour and enjoy. If you made it in a jar, remove and discard the cardamom pods and cinnamon sticks. Line a fine-mesh strainer with a double layer of cheesecloth and strain the coffee into a bowl, pressing down or forming a sack and squeezing as much liquid as possible into the bowl (or strain through the nut-milk bag, if using). Transfer to a bottle. To serve, dilute with up to an equal amount of water (but less if you're adding Date-Sweetened Almond Milk). Refrigerate and use for up to 1 week.

Date-Sweetened Almond Milk

2 cups (10 ounces) raw almonds

2 or 3 pitted Medjool dates, or
1 tablespoon silan (date syrup)

4 cups cold water

1 teaspoon pure vanilla extract

¼ teaspoon fine sea salt

○○○○○○○○○○

Makes
4 cups

Active Time:
20 minutes

Total Time:
about
8½ hours
(including
minimum
refrigeration
time)

○○○○○○○○○○

In a medium jar or container, cover the almonds with at least 3 inches of cold water and refrigerate for at least 8 hours and up to 24. Drain and rinse the almonds well. Place the almonds and dates in a blender with the 4 cups of cold water and blend until smooth, 1½ to 2 minutes (the more powerful your blender is, the less time this will take. Also, the more you blend, the hotter the mixture will get, which will make its fridge life a little shorter). If you have a nut-milk bag, strain the blended liquid and solids through the bag, squeezing out as much liquid as you can with clean hands. If you don't have a nut-milk bag, strain through a double layer of cheesecloth fitted into a fine-mesh strainer and do the solid-squeezing thing. Discard the almond meal, or use it (or freeze it in an airtight container for up to 3 months for later use) to make Almond-Coconut Basbusa Snack Cake (page 355). Stir in the vanilla and salt. Store in the coldest part of the refrigerator in a tightly sealed bottle or jar, for 2 to 3 days, shaking before serving.

Instant Entertaining

When I need to entertain but am short on time, out comes the *ja'aleh,* a perfect accompaniment to the cocktails and other drinks in this chapter. A Yemenite custom designed to give people the opportunity to make extra blessings over food on the Sabbath morning, ja'aleh has evolved into a feast any day of the week. The genius of ja'aleh is its instantaneous bounty: all you've got to do is some strategic shopping. I stock up on roasted and raw almonds; dried apricots, plums, and raisins from Uzbekistan; Turkish figs; Israeli dates; and *kabuki* (crispy-coated peanuts)—not to mention sunflower, pumpkin, even watermelon seeds salted and roasted in their shells. Some people make homemade cookies to accompany the spread, but my feeling is, if you're keeping it simple, keep it *really* simple.

Bloody Miriam

If you happened to be in Jerusalem in the winter between 1979 and 1980 and saw an eight-year-old girl walking around with orange palms . . . that was me. It was the year I discovered fresh carrot juice, and from my first glass of juice made right before my eyes from this country's candy-sweet carrots, I was hooked. My family cut me off when my tender young palms turned a spooky shade of light orange, a thankfully temporary condition known as carotenemia caused by beta-carotene overload. While I still indulge in carrot juice quite often—there are at least five juice bars within a five-minute walk of my house—as an adult I sometimes find it a tad sweet on its own. So one brunchy Friday morning at home, after picking up a juice I couldn't finish, I found myself mixing it up into what has become a house favorite: the Bloody Miriam (sorry, Mary). Fresh horseradish, a few mashed cherry tomatoes to thicken the base, preserved lemon, gin, and the kick of harissa have revealed a new way to love this drink.

2 teaspoons celery seeds

½ cup (4 ounces) carrot juice

5 or 6 yellow cherry tomatoes, finely chopped

1½ ounces (3 tablespoons) gin

1 ounce (2 tablespoons) Preserved Lemon liquid (page 38), or 3 tablespoons freshly squeezed lemon juice plus ¼ teaspoon salt

2 teaspoons freshly grated or prepared white bottled horseradish, drained

1 teaspoon Honey Harissa (page 37), or hot sauce of your choice

Pinch of celery salt

Pinch of fine sea salt

Pinch of freshly ground black pepper

Celery sticks and lemon or lime wheels, for garnish

Makes
1 drink

Active Time:
10 minutes

Total Time:
10 minutes

Place the celery seeds on a small, round plate. Moisten the rim of a rocks glass; invert and dip it in the celery seeds. In a shaker combine the carrot juice, tomatoes, gin, preserved lemon liquid, horseradish, harissa, celery salt, salt, black pepper, and 3 or 4 ice cubes. Shake vigorously, then carefully pour everything, including the ice, into the rimmed glass. Garnish with celery sticks and lemon or lime wheels.

Note

To make this a pitcher drink for a crowd, ditch the celery-seed rim, multiply everything else by 8, stir in a pitcher, chill, and add ice just before serving.

Spiced Silan Bourbon Cocktail

The caramelized, dark, and complex flavors of both bourbon and silan make them seem like long-lost friends reunited in a glass. By infusing the silan with the warmest of spices plus a bit of a kick courtesy of a dried hot chili, you've got a winning elixir on your hands. The longer you infuse the syrup, the deeper its flavors become. I like to serve this cocktail with my Seeded Za'atar Crackers (Za'atar Malatit, page 104) at cocktail hour; the sweet-edged drink and the super-savory, crunchy crackers are a killer combination.

SILAN SYRUP
(Makes ¾ cup)
1 cup silan (date syrup)
1 cinnamon stick
10 whole black peppercorns

10 whole cloves
4 cardamom pods
1 small dried hot chili pepper, such as chile de arbol

COCKTAIL
4 ounces (½ cup) bourbon
1½ ounces (3 tablespoons) silan (date syrup)
Orange twists

○○○○○○○○○○
Makes
2 cocktails

Active Time:
10 minutes

Total Time:
1 hour
10 minutes
(including
minimum
infusing
time)

○○○○○○○○○○

Make the syrup: In a small saucepan over medium heat, combine the silan, 2 tablespoons water, cinnamon stick, peppercorns, cloves, cardamom pods, and dried chili. Bring just to a boil over medium heat, then reduce the heat to low and simmer until the mixture thickens slightly, 5 minutes. Remove from the heat, cool for 10 minutes, transfer to a glass jar with a tight-fitting lid, cover, and let sit for at least 1 hour and up to 1 week in the fridge. If you like, remove and discard the cinnamon stick, peppercorns, cloves, and cardamom pod or just leave them in and they'll remain in the cocktail strainer when you make your drinks). Sealed in an airtight jar, the syrup lasts for up to 3 months in the refrigerator.

Make the cocktail: In an ice-filled cocktail shaker, vigorously shake the bourbon and silan. Strain into two ice-filled rocks glasses and garnish each glass with an orange twist. Serve with Seeded Za'atar Crackers (Za'atar Malatit, page 104), if desired.

Pomegroni

As I juiced my millionth pomegranate of the winter using the hand-cranked press that sits on our counter, it occurred to me: Who needs Campari when you've got fresh pomegranate juice? The fruit's tannic, sweet-bitter taste stands in perfectly for the classic Italian aperitif, especially with a shake or two of bitters to steer the drink firmly out of the sugary column. Of course, a blood orange slice makes positively everything look gorgeous and calls to mind yet another element of Campari, orange peels.

6 ounces (¾ cup) pomegranate juice

2 ounces (¼ cup) sweet white vermouth or Lillet

2ounces (¼ cup) dry gin

Generous splash Angostura bitters

Blood orange or other orange wheels

○○○○○○○○○○
Makes
2 cocktails

Active Time:
5 minutes

Total Time:
5 minutes

○○○○○○○○○○

In an ice-filled cocktail shaker, vigorously shake the pomegranate juice, vermouth, gin, and bitters. Pour into two ice-filled rocks glasses, add more bitters to taste, and garnish with orange wheels. The recipe can be multiplied (minus the ice) and stored in a pitcher for up to 1 week and can be freshened with more bitters as needed.

Almondy Vodka Limonana

It isn't summer in Israel if there isn't a huge frosty pitcher of minty *limonana* (lemonade) on the table. It helps that the words for lemon and mint, *limon*, and *nana* respectively, meld together effortlessly on the tongue—and in the glass—into a singular expression of the season. So popular is the combination that it comes in frozen and popsicle versions. I make mine with Roasted Almond Rosetta Syrup (page 356), or any good-quality orgeat (see Shopping Guide), which gives the drink a Sicilian twist. If you don't like the flavor of almonds, you can sweeten with honey, simple syrup, or even maple syrup.

4 ounces (½ cup) vodka

2½ ounces (5 tablespoons) Roasted Almond Rosetta Syrup (page 356) or store-bought orgeat (almond syrup; see Shopping Guide)

3 ounces (6 tablespoons) freshly squeezed lemon juice

4 mint sprigs, plus more for garnish

Thinly sliced lemons, for garnish

○○○○○○○○○○

Makes
2 cocktails

Active Time:
5 minutes

Total Time:
5 minutes
(if using premade or store-bought syrup)

○○○○○○○○○○

In an ice-filled cocktail shaker, vigorously shake the vodka, syrup, lemon juice, and mint sprigs. Strain into two ice-filled rocks glasses and garnish with lemon slices and more mint sprigs.

Watermelon Arak Granita

I like to think of this frosty dessert as the anise-averse drinker's gateway to arak, our version of ouzo, raki, Pernod, or Sambuca. A beloved spirit in this part of the world, it's traditionally made by distilling grapes, then infusing the resulting liqueur with anise. It's mixed with water, then poured over ice, and once it turns cloudy you know it's reached its ideal temperature for sipping. When watermelon is at its peak, I whip it up in the blender with arak and lime juice, place the mixture in the freezer, and scrape, scrape, scrape my way to the coolest dessert around.

4 cups (1¼ pounds) cubed, very ripe, very pink seedless watermelon

¼ cup freshly squeezed lime juice

1½ ounces (3 tablespoons) arak (Israeli anise liqueur), ouzo, or anisette

1 to 2 tablespoons sugar (optional)

Fresh mint, for garnish

○○○○○○○○○○

Serves 4

Active Time:
15 minutes

Total Time:
3 hours
45 minutes
(including
freezing
time)

○○○○○○○○○○

Clear space for a 9 x 13-inch glass or metal baking dish or a larger rimmed sheet pan in your freezer; the larger the surface area, the quicker the granita comes together. In a blender, combine the watermelon, lime juice, arak, and sugar, if using, and blend until smooth, 15 to 30 seconds. Pour the mixture into the baking dish and place it in the freezer. After 1 hour, open the freezer and run a fork through the mixture; at this point it will feel like wet slush, but it's important to get it moving before it freezes too solidly. Close the freezer and, every 30 minutes, open the freezer and scrape the granita with a fork; with every half hour, it will create more ice crystals and, after 2½ to 3 hours, will become granita. Serve immediately, or transfer to a large lidded container (you don't want to pack the granita down too much) and store in the freezer for up to 1 week.

DESSERTS

Pistachio-Crusted Lemon Bars

With a crumbly pistachio crust and a filling that includes olive and coconut oils, these bars are so rich and tart, you'll hardly notice they're dairy-free. Dried rose petals, which are edible, have a more subtle taste than rosewater, but a little bit goes a long way—so use in moderation.

PISTACHIO CRUST

6 tablespoons cold (solid) coconut oil, plus more for greasing the pan

½ cup shelled pistachios

½ cup all-purpose flour

½ cup confectioners' sugar

1 teaspoon freshly grated lemon zest

¼ teaspoon fine sea salt

LEMON CURD

3 large eggs

4 large egg yolks

¾ cup sugar

3 tablespoons cornstarch

¼ teaspoon fine sea salt

1 cup freshly squeezed lemon juice (from about 5 lemons)

4 tablespoons finely grated lemon zest

⅓ cup extra-virgin olive oil

2 tablespoons chopped toasted pistachios

1 teaspoon crushed rose petals, for garnish (optional)

Makes
16 bars

Active Time:
45 minutes

Total Time:
6 hours
(including minimum cooling time)

Make the pistachio crust: Grease an 8-inch square baking pan with coconut oil. Line the pan with 2 crisscrossing strips of parchment paper, greasing between each layer and leaving a 2-inch overhang on all sides. Grease the top and sides of the parchment-lined pan. Place the coconut oil in a small bowl in the refrigerator until it is solid, 30 minutes to 1 hour. In the bowl of a food processor, pulse the pistachios until almost fine, 30 seconds. Add the flour, confectioners' sugar, lemon zest, and salt and pulse until incorporated, 15 pulses. Using a spoon, addt the coconut oil in small chunks to the food processor, and pulse until the mixture looks like uniform large breadcrumbs, 15 to 20 pulses. Pour into the prepared pan, pressing down to form a crust but not overpacking; chill for 30 minutes.

Make the lemon curd: In a small saucepan, whisk together the eggs, egg yolks, sugar, cornstarch, and salt, then whisk in the lemon juice and zest until smooth. Set a fine-mesh strainer over a bowl. Place the saucepan over medium heat and cook, whisking constantly, until the mixture becomes thick and the whisk leaves an impression in the curd and coats the back of a spoon, 8 to 9 minutes. Patience! The thickening will happen quickly at the end.

Remove the saucepan from the heat and use a silicone spatula to push the curd through through the strainer into the bowl below; discard the solids. Whisk in the olive oil until smooth, cool slightly, then press plastic wrap onto its surface to keep it from forming a skin.

Bake the crust and curd: Preheat the oven to 325°F. Bake the chilled crust until it has puffed, then sunk, and is lightly golden, 20 to 22 minutes. Remove it from the oven and cool for 2 to 3 minutes. Raise the oven temperature to 350°F, then pour the filling over the crust, smoothing it evenly with a knife or offset spatula. Bake until the curd has firmed up but the center still moves a bit, 16 to 17 minutes. Remove from the oven, cool completely, seal with plastic wrap, and chill at least 4 hours. Cut into 16 equal pieces and garnish with crushed rose petals (if using) and chopped pistachios.

Sabras

Originally brought to the region by Arab traders who'd encountered them in Spain, sabras are considered Israel's national fruit, and natural representation of the Israeli personality: prickly on the outside, soft and sweet inside. Also known as prickly pears, sabras grow wild near beaches, in the desert, in people's gardens—and are picked for sale in markets and roadside stands where, if you're lucky, they've been denuded of their sharp thorns. Professional sabra cutters use chain-mail gloves to remove the spikes and peel them for consumption, but it can also be easily done at home. Simply (carefully) cut the top and bottom off of the fruit, then score the skin lengthwise down one side through the skin. Peel it back to reveal the moderately sweet flesh, whose taste falls somewhere between honeydew, guava, and cucumber. Slightly mealy and only moderately sweet, it's filled with black seeds you chew around and swallow along with the fruit itself. I serve the cut sabras on a bed of ice on a hot night, letting people pick them up and eat them whole.

Chewy Tahini Blondies

I've made these so many times, so you won't have to. On the surface this seems like a dead-simple recipe, but it took quite a bit of tinkering to nail. Tahini has a complex molecular structure made up of lots of tiny carbohydrate molecules that cling to liquid for dear life, seizing up the way chocolate does if you add liquid to it at the wrong time. But if you play your carbs right and add the tahini last, after all of the other ingredients, it stirs in smoothly and bakes up into these sexy little squares that get better as they sit around. To make these non-dairy, swap in a neutral-flavored olive oil or vegetable oil instead of the butter.

½ cup (1 stick) unsalted butter, melted and cooled, or ½ cup olive oil or vegetable oil, plus more for buttering the pan

1¼ cups all-purpose flour

¾ teaspoon baking powder

½ teaspoon ground cardamom (or more to taste if you really like this flavor)

½ teaspoon fine sea salt

¼ teaspoon freshly ground black pepper

2 tablespoons lightly toasted black sesame seeds

2 tablespoons lightly toasted white sesame seeds

1¼ cups lightly packed light brown sugar

2 large eggs

1 teaspoon pure vanilla extract

½ cup pure tahini paste

○○○○○○○○○○

Makes
16 squares

Active Time:
10 minutes

Total Time:
40 minutes

○○○○○○○○○○

Preheat the oven to 350°F. Butter an 8-inch square baking pan, then line the pan with 2 crisscrossing strips of parchment paper, buttering between each layer and leaving a 2-inch overhang on all sides. Butter the top and sides of the parchment.

In a medium bowl, whisk together the flour, baking powder, cardamom, salt, pepper, and the black and white sesame seeds. In another medium bowl, whisk together the brown sugar, ½ cup melted butter, eggs, and vanilla until smooth. Fold the dry ingredients into the wet ingredients until just incorporated, then fold in the tahini until smooth. Pour the batter into the prepared pan and bake until golden on the outside and the center doesn't jiggle but is still soft, 25 to 30 minutes. Remove from the oven, cool in the pan, and cut into 16 equal squares.

Tahini Caramel Tart
(aka the Gal Gadot of Tarts)

Gal Gadot, the Israeli star of the *Wonder Woman* movies, is a national hero here. When someone called this the "Gal Gadot of tarts," I gave myself a superhero high-five before cutting off another slice. Salty, sweet, rich, and savory, it's a showstopper that comes together with pantry staples. A butter-and-cream caramel is finished with tahini, which contributes to a gorgeously pourable texture. The press-in chocolate shortbread crust, studded with sesame seeds, is dense and flaky at the same time, a cookie with larger-format aspirations. A small slice, in tandem with a strong cup of coffee, is enough. Bonus: Kept warm, the filling works as a tahini caramel sauce begging for a bowl of vanilla ice cream.

CHOCOLATE SHORTBREAD CRUST

½ cup (1 stick) unsalted butter, slightly softened

½ cup confectioners' sugar

¾ cup all-purpose flour

⅓ cup unsweetened cocoa powder

¼ teaspoon fine sea salt

3 tablespoons sesame seeds

TAHINI CARAMEL

½ cup granulated sugar

¾ cup heavy cream

½ cup lightly packed light brown sugar

6 tablespoons (¾ stick) unsalted butter, cut into 6 pieces

3 tablespoons silan (date syrup)

½ teaspoon fine sea salt

⅓ cup pure tahini paste

LABANEH WHIPPED CREAM

⅔ cup heavy cream

½ cup 4-Hour Labaneh (page 44 or store-bought), or Greek yogurt

1 tablespoon confectioners' sugar

Serves 12 to 14

Active Time: 45 minutes

Total Time: 4 hours 45 minutes (including minimum cooling time)

Make the crust: Preheat the oven to 325°F.

In the bowl of a stand mixer fitted with the paddle attachment, beat the butter and confectioners' sugar at medium-high speed, scraping down the sides of the bowl if necessary, until light and fluffy, 2 to 3 minutes. Add the flour, cocoa powder, salt, and sesame seeds and beat until just incorporated, 15 to 20 seconds. Gather the dough, then press it into the bottom and up the sides of a 9-inch tart pan with a removable bottom. Freeze for 10 minutes, then bake until the crust is golden and flaky but still soft, 25 minutes. Cool completely.

While the tart is cooling, make the caramel: Place the granulated sugar in a medium saucepan (try to use one with a few inches' headroom) and sprinkle 3 tablespoons water on top of it. Turn the heat to medium, bring to a boil, then increase the heat to medium-high and boil until the sugar turns syrupy and the color of light caramel, 7 minutes (be careful here; it can burn, so take it off the heat a few seconds early if you're in doubt, and swirl gently if one area begins to darken more than others). Remove the syrup from the heat,

RECIPE CONTINUES

then immediately add the cream, brown sugar, butter, and silan and stir until the butter is melted; the mixture will sputter, then may harden in parts, but don't worry. Place the saucepan back on the stove. Bring the mixture to a low simmer over low heat and simmer until it's a deep mahogany color, 11 to 12 minutes. Remove from the heat, whisk in the salt and then the tahini until smooth, and pour into the baked tart crust. Cool slightly, then chill until the tart is set, at least 4 hours (but overnight is best).

Make the whipped cream: Just before serving, in a stand mixer fitted with the whisk attachment, whip the cream until soft peaks form, 2 minutes. Add the labaneh and confectioners' sugar and whip until soft peaks return, 1 minute. Remove the tart from the fridge, slice, and serve with the whipped cream.

Fluffy Israeli Cheesecake with Fresh Plum Compote

Every spring, Israelis raid the dairy case to prepare dishes both savory and sweet for Shavuot, a harvest festival that also commemorates the day the Jewish people were said to have received the Torah at Mount Sinai. According to legend, this is when they began observing dietary restrictions separating meat and milk. More than any Shavuot recipe, cheesecake defines the holiday. The classic Israeli version—which bears similarities to German Käsekuchen—virtually floats in comparison to its dense New York–style cousin. It starts with *g'vina levana* ("white cheese"), a uniquely Israeli spreadable cheese that's most similar to German quark (if quark is hard to find, Greek yogurt mixed with sour cream yields similar results). Separating the eggs and folding the fluffy whites back in before baking ensures a levity I've come to treasure. If you're a nocturnal baker, you're in luck. Leaving this cake in the oven overnight after baking allows the cake to relax into itself without collapsing too quickly, further developing its unique texture. You will open the oven in the morning to discover a deeply browned surface and, if you're lucky (yes, I said lucky), there may be a gorgeous crack somewhere on the top of the cake.

CRUST

One 8.8-ounce package of Biscoff (Lotus) cookies (32 cookies)

5 tablespoons unsalted butter, melted, plus more for buttering the pan

Generous pinch of fine sea salt

CHEESECAKE

5 large eggs, separated

1 cup sugar

1 medium lemon

2½ cups *g'vina levana* (Israeli white cheese; see Shopping Guide), quark, or 1¼ cups each full-fat Greek yogurt and sour cream

1 cup full-fat sour cream

¼ cup cornstarch

1 vanilla bean, scraped, or 1 teaspoon pure vanilla extract

PLUM COMPOTE
(Makes about 1¾ cups)

5 ripe (but not too soft) plums (1 pound), pitted and cut into 6 wedges each

⅓ cup sugar

2 teaspoons freshly squeezed lemon juice

Pinch of fine sea salt

Serves 10 to 12

Active Time: 45 minutes

Total Time: 6 hours 45 minutes (including minimum baking and cooling/ resting time)

Make the crust: Preheat the oven to 350°F.

In the bowl of a food processor, process the cookies until fine crumbs form, 15 seconds (you should have about 1½ cups crumbs). Add the butter and salt and pulse until the crumbs are moistened, 10 pulses. Lightly butter the bottom of a 10-inch springform pan, then press in the crust, using a flat-bottomed glass to pack in the crumbs. Bake until fragrant, deep golden, and crisp, 15 minutes. Remove from the oven, let cool completely, then butter the sides of the pan.

RECIPE CONTINUES

Make the cheesecake: Raise the oven temperature to 375°F. Position two racks in the oven, one as low as possible (this will be for the bain-marie, or steam bath, you will create for the cheesecake) and one centered in the oven.

In the bowl of a stand mixer fitted with the whisk attachment, beat the egg yolks and ¾ cup of the sugar on medium-high speed until fluffy and light, 2 minutes. Zest the lemon straight into the mixer bowl (reserve the zested lemon), then add the *g'vina levana*, the sour cream, cornstarch, and vanilla bean seeds and whip until fluffy, 1 more minute. Transfer the mixture to a large mixing bowl.

Wash and dry the stand mixer bowl and whisk, then halve the zested lemon. Squeeze 1 tablespoon lemon juice onto a paper towel and wipe the inside of the mixer bowl and the whisk with the lemon juice to clean it of any oil. Add the egg whites to the mixer bowl fitted with the whisk attachment and whip over medium speed until soft peaks form, 2 minutes. Increase the speed to medium-high, gradually add the remaining ¼ cup sugar, and whip until the egg whites are glossy and form stiff peaks, another 1½ minutes. Gently fold the egg whites into the batter until just combined (basically until you no longer see streaks of whipped egg white). Bring a large kettle of water to a boil for the bain-marie.

Place a 9 x 13-inch glass or metal baking dish on the lower oven rack and fill it with the boiling water. Pour the batter into the buttered springform pan over the crust, gently smoothing it if necessary. Place the cake on the higher rack and bake for 15 minutes. Without opening the oven, reduce the heat to 300°F and bake for 55 minutes (it's best not to open the oven during baking, but if you have a glass door and a light, you can see the cake will be a nice dark golden color on top and almost completely set while a little bit jiggly in the center). Turn off the oven and let the cake rest in the closed oven until the oven cools, at least 1 hour but preferably at least 6 hours. Remove the cake from the oven, cool completely if still warm, cover with plastic wrap, then chill in the fridge until the cake has settled into itself, at least 4 hours and up to 24 hours.

Make the plum compote: In a medium saucepan, cook the plums and sugar over medium-low heat, stirring frequently, until the plums soften a bit and release their liquid but you can still see the shape of the slices, 10 to 11 minutes. Remove from the heat, stir in the lemon juice and salt, and cool completely. Covered, the compote will keep in the refrigerator for 1 week.

To serve, loosen the edges of the cake with a knife, release it from the pan, cut into slices, and serve with the compote.

Triple Ginger Persimmon Loaf

Once a week during high season my mother would make her persimmon bread, a dense loaf cake with caramelized corners we'd warm in the toaster oven after school. The edges would almost burn, turning crispy from the combination of sugar and that intense toaster heat. We couldn't spread the cream cheese on top fast enough, so much so that half of it would slide off while we burned the roofs of our mouths with each bite. Here is a slightly springier, lusher version that's great fresh out of the oven, even better the next day—and best toasted, with a schmear of labaneh or cream cheese.

¾ cup vegetable oil, plus more for greasing the pan

3 medium (1 pound) very ripe persimmons, preferably Hachiya variety*

2 large eggs

¼ cup water

1 teaspoon pure vanilla extract

1 cup sugar

1¾ cups all-purpose flour

1½ teaspoons baking soda

¾ teaspoon fine sea salt

¾ teaspoon ground cinnamon

¾ teaspoon ground nutmeg

½ teaspoon ground ginger

¼ teaspoon ground cloves

1 tablespoon chopped crystallized ginger

1½ teaspoons freshly grated ginger

8-Hour Labaneh (page 44), or cream cheese, for serving

○○○○○○○○○○

Makes
1 loaf

Active Time:
25 minutes

Total Time:
1 hour
25 minutes

○○○○○○○○○○

Preheat the oven to 350°F. Grease a standard (4.5 x 8.5- inch) loaf pan with vegetable oil.

Cut off the tops of the persimmons. Scoop the ripe flesh into a large bowl and mash it with a fork or potato masher until very smooth, or puree in a food processor or blender for 10 seconds. Whisk in the eggs, water, vanilla, ¾ cup vegetable oil, and sugar until well blended. In a separate medium bowl, whisk together the flour, baking soda, salt, cinnamon, nutmeg, ginger, and cloves. Stir the dry ingredients into the persimmon mixture until just blended, then gently stir in the crystallized ginger and fresh ginger. Pour the batter into the prepared pan and bake until a toothpick inserted in the center comes out clean and the top is slightly cracked, 55 to 60 minutes. Cool in the pan, slice, and serve with labaneh.

*Longer, tapered Hachiya persimmons get softer—and more quickly—than the rounder, smaller Fuyus, but both can work. Just make sure they're *really* soft. If you need to, blitz the scooped flesh in a blender or food processor.

Shabakia

Zohar means "radiant" in Hebrew, and I can't think of a word to better describe my friend Nofar Zohar, the daughter of Moroccan parents who grew up in the small town of Poriya, near the shores of the Sea of Galilee. She invited me over to her house to cook couscous (see page 286) and, for dessert, shabakia, fried, syrup-soaked cookies in the shape of free-form flowers that her mother makes by the hundreds for family gatherings and holiday celebrations. I had tasted cookies like this before, but they always seemed leaden and cloyingly sweet. She promised a different result as we mixed the simple dough, adding some arak along the way. "It keeps it flaky," she told me. After resting the dough for a few hours, we rolled it into logs, cut it crosswise like oversized gnocchi, then rolled each cut piece into a thin sheet. Using a crimped pastry wheel and then our hands, we lifted the surprisingly pliable dough off the counter, then we pulled the outer strips toward one another in a pastry game of cat's cradle, until the dough tangled into the shape of a free-form flower (see photos on following page). Each flower was dropped into hot oil, a hollowed-out aluminum can helping it maintain its shape. Then, like releasing canaries from their cages, we lifted the cans to let the pastries finish frying in a larger pool of oil. A quick dip in a tea-, honey-, and jasmine-laced syrup, and voilà–the finished cookies were done. They were deliciously flaky and crispy, the effort worth the results.

SHABAKIA

7 tablespoons unsalted butter, at room temperature

1 tablespoon arak

3 tablespoons sugar

3 cups all-purpose flour, sifted, plus ¼ cup flour for rolling

¼ cup cornstarch

SYRUP

2½ cups sugar

½ lemon, rind and pith removed and discarded, flesh quartered

1 tea bag

1 vanilla bean, scraped

Pinch of salt

¼ cup honey

Dash of orange flower water or jasmine extract

Grapeseed, canola, or another neutral-flavored oil, for frying

Makes
16 cookies

Active Time:
45 minutes

Total Time:
2 hours (including minimum resting time)

Make the shabakia: In a stand mixer fitted with the paddle attachment, combine 1 cup water, the butter, arak, and sugar on low speed until slushily incorporated, 2 minutes. Stop the mixer and gradually add the 3 cups flour. Raise the speed to medium and mix until you have a supple, unified, and pliant dough that is no longer sticky, 2 to 3 minutes. Let the dough rest in a lightly floured bowl, covered with a tea towel, for at least 1 hour and up to 4.

Make the syrup: Combine the sugar, 1⅓ cups water, the lemon, tea bag, vanilla bean seeds and pod, and salt in a medium saucepan. Bring to a boil over medium-high heat, then reduce the heat to medium-low and simmer vigorously until the syrup thickens, 20 minutes. Add the honey, raise the heat to medium-high, and return the mixture to a boil, then reduce the heat and let simmer for another 10 minutes. Turn off the heat,

RECIPE CONTINUES

remove and discard the tea bag, add the orange flower water, cover the saucepan with a tight-fitting lid, and keep the syrup warm until you're ready to use it.

Fry and finish the shabakia: Fill a wide saucepan halfway with the grapeseed oil and heat it to 350°F. Remove all paper and glue from 2 clean, empty standard-size tomato sauce cans (14.5 ounces each), then use a can opener to remove the bottom side of each can to create 2 metal tubes. Place the cans in the oil. Line a baking sheet with paper towels and get out a spider, tongs, and a chopstick or thin metal skewer.

Uncover the dough and divide it into 2 equal-sized pieces. Roll each piece into a 12-inch log, then cut each log into 8 equal-sized pieces for a total of 16 pieces. Toss the remaining ¼ cup flour and the cornstarch in a small bowl. A few at a time, toss the dough pieces in the cornstarch mixture, and also use it to lightly flour a clean work surface as you go. Using your hands, shape a dough piece into a 2 x 4-inch rectangle. Use a rolling pin to flatten the dough out into a 5 x 7-inch rectangle, then use a crimped pastry wheel to trim the edges and form an even, symmetrical 4 x 6-inch rectangle; reserve the scraps for frying. Use the pastry wheel to cut lines about ¼ inch apart in the dough, leaving a ½-inch frame all around the dough. Pick the dough up from the counter and separate the rectangle into strands. Working from the outside, pull the outer strands in, cat's cradle–style, then bunch the dough up into a free-form flower.

Drop the dough flower into a can. Using a chopstick, move the dough around in the can for 30 seconds, flipping it, swirling it, and spooning hot oil over the dough; it will begin to puff up like magic. Using tongs, lift the can to release the shabakia into the oil and continue to fry, turning, until golden brown, 2 to 3 more minutes.

Use a spider or slotted spoon to transfer the cookie to the towel-lined tray, drain briefly, then drop into the hot syrup, turning once. Lift the cookie out of the syrup with tongs, shake off any excess syrup, and arrange on a serving tray. Repeat with the remaining shabakia and reserved scraps; these are delicious freshly honeyed but surprisingly good, if not better, the next day; keep them out on the counter, covered with plastic, for up to 3 days.

Thyme-Roasted Apricots with Whipped Goat Cheese

At Amrani (page 81), Noni is always throwing freebies into my bag, offering me little tastes, letting me cut the line if he sees I'm in a hurry, telling me jokes, and generally making me feel like I've been their customer for thirty years as opposed to three. Noni spotted me looking at a jar of halved, roasted nuts. "Guess what those are?" Noni asked me with a sly smile. "And don't say almonds. They're *kwashkos!* Roasted apricot pits," he told me. Bitter and crunchy, I imagined them standing in for almonds in a million recipes until he rained on my parade: "You know, some people think they're poisonous." A little research confirmed that due to laetrile, the compound in apricot pits, these are meant to be eaten in small doses. So if you can find them (at health food stores and online are good bets), mete them out in small portions. I couldn't resist roasting their origin fruit, apricots, with a little honey and thyme, and setting them atop a cloud of whipped goat cheese. It's dessert, for sure, but could be breakfast as well.

Vegetable oil

8 medium apricots, pitted and halved

3 tablespoons honey

1 sprig thyme, roughly chopped, plus more for garnish

4 ounces goat cheese, at room temperature

½ cup heavy cream

2 tablespoons roasted apricot pits (available at some health food stores and online; see Shopping Guide), or toasted almonds

Serves 4

Active Time:
7 minutes

Total Time:
35 minutes

Preheat the oven to 350°F.

Slick a 10-inch round ovenproof dish with vegetable oil, then place the apricots, some cut-side down and some not, in the dish. Drizzle with the honey, sprinkle with the thyme, and roast in the oven until the apricots begin to wilt and brown slightly around the edges, 20 to 25 minutes.

In a stand mixer fitted with the whisk attachment (or use an electric hand mixer), combine the goat cheese and cream and whip at medium-high speed until the 2 ingredients form a fluffy, creamy cloud, 2 to 3 minutes. Serve the fruit with the cream, topped with the apricot pits, and garnished with thyme.

Labaneh Malabi Panna Cotta

This milky pudding, typically thickened with cornstarch, has roots in Syria and Turkey but can be found all over Israel, often roadside, where it is offered in small takeout plastic containers with an artificially colored, rose-flavored syrup on the side. I find the cornstarch version of this dish hard to control. You can either make the pudding too soft or too hard, depending on how long you cook it. My version is a cross between malabi and panna cotta, made with gelatin, because I love the silky texture it creates. Using part labaneh or Greek yogurt gives it a uniquely tart edge. I replace the rose syrup with simple fruit-based toppings that keep the dessert from being too sweet. If fresh passion fruit is in season or available, scooping out the flesh directly onto the malabi is a glorious finish.

MALABI

2 tablespoons cold water

1½ teaspoons powdered gelatin

⅔ cup heavy cream

⅔ cup whole milk

½ cup honey

1 vanilla bean, scraped (reserve the pod for vanilla sugar*)

⅔ cup 4-Hour Labaneh (page 44 or store-bought), or full-fat Greek yogurt

1 teaspoon finely grated lemon zest

FRUIT TOPPING (Makes 1¼ cups)

3 cups halved strawberries or apricots

½ cup passion fruit pulp, if in season

⅓ cup sugar

2 teaspoons freshly squeezed lemon juice

Pinch of kosher salt

○○○○○○○○○○

Serves 6

Active Time:
35 minutes

Total Time:
about
4½ hours
(including
chilling)

○○○○○○○○○○

Make the malabi: Place the cold water in a small bowl and sprinkle the gelatin on top of it. While the gelatin is setting, warm the cream, milk, honey, and scraped insides of the vanilla bean in a small saucepan over medium-low heat until it just begins to bubble, making sure to watch it closely. Remove from the heat and whisk in the dissolved gelatin, labaneh, and lemon zest until fully incorporated. Divide evenly among 6 small cups or ramekins, tapping gently to release any air bubbles. Chill for at least 4 hours. Top the malabi with a small amount of fruit topping or passion fruit pulp before serving.

Make the fruit topping: In a medium saucepan, combine the fruit and sugar over medium heat and bring to a low boil. Reduce the heat to medium-low and cook, stirring occasionally, until the strawberries release their liquid but don't break down, 10 minutes. Remove from the heat, cool slightly, then stir in the lemon juice and salt. Transfer to a bowl, cover, and chill until ready to use.

*To make vanilla sugar, combine the scraped vanilla bean with 1 cup sugar in a jar and seal with a tight-fitting lid. Open 2 weeks later and you've got vanilla sugar.

"Eser" Halvah and Baharat Coffee Cake

I nicknamed this cake after the number ten (*eser*) in Hebrew for more than one reason. First, did you know that in Israel, because being hungry even for a second is verboten, there is often a traditional snack time mandated into the work and school day called *aruchat eser*, or "the ten o'clock [a.m.] meal"? It started out in schools and government offices, where employees punched in early and needed fortification midmorning. I'm all for it. *Eser* is also slang for "great," and this coffee cake, with its labaneh-enriched batter layered with a crumbly mix of coffee, halvah, baharat spice, and walnuts, is perfect for *aruchat eser*, and is also *eser* in the other way. Ten out of ten all around.

CRUMB TOPPING

2¼ cups chopped walnuts or pecans

6 ounces (1¼ cups) finely crumbled halvah (see Shopping Guide)

⅓ cup granulated sugar

⅓ cup lightly packed light brown sugar

2 tablespoons ground coffee

2 tablespoons Baharat (page 24 or store-bought)

¼ teaspoon fine sea salt

CAKE

3½ cups all-purpose flour

2 teaspoons baking powder

1 teaspoon baking soda

1 teaspoon fine sea salt

1 cup (2 sticks) unsalted butter, at room temperature (very soft butter is your friend here), plus more for buttering the pan

2 cups sugar

4 large eggs

2 cups 4-Hour Labaneh (page 44 or store-bought), or Greek yogurt

1 tablespoon pure vanilla extract

1¼ cups whole milk

Serves 6

Active Time:
30 minutes

Total Time:
1 hour
15 minutes

Preheat the oven to 350°F.

Make the crumb topping: In a medium bowl, combine the walnuts, halvah, granulated sugar, brown sugar, coffee, baharat, and salt with your fingers until mixed well, pinching any larger chunks of halvah to crumble them.

Make the cake: Into a medium bowl, sift together the flour, baking powder, baking soda, and salt.

Butter a 9 x 13-inch square baking pan, then line the pan with 2 crisscrossing strips of parchment paper, buttering between each layer and leaving a 2-inch overhang on all sides. Butter the top and sides of the parchment-lined pan.

RECIPE CONTINUES

In the bowl of a stand mixer fitted with the paddle attachment, beat the 1 cup butter and sugar on medium-high speed until creamy, scraping down the sides of the bowl as you go along, 2 to 3 minutes. Reduce the speed to medium, add the eggs one at a time, then add the labaneh and vanilla, beating well after each addition and scraping down the sides of the mixer as needed. Add half of the milk, then half of the flour mixture, then the remaining milk and flour, mixing just until incorporated after each addition.

Spread half the batter (about 4 cups) in the prepared baking dish, then sprinkle half the topping evenly over the batter and gently pat it down. Dollop and spread the remaining half of the batter over the filling, then sprinkle the remaining topping on top of that. Bake until the cake is no longer jiggly and a toothpick or tester inserted into the center comes out clean, 40 to 45 minutes. Cool slightly, cut into 15 equal-sized squares, then serve warm or at room temperature.

Halvah on Challah

One day on set our stylist, Nurit, crumbled a hunk of leftover halvah onto a thick slice of challh she'd slathered with softened, salted butter. It sounded crazy, but it was insanely delicious—and is a new house favorite.

Pull-Apart Knafeh with Honey-Orange Syrup

Many countries can claim their own version (and spelling) of knafeh (or knafe, konafi, kunafi . . .), but the essence of it is a melty, cheesy, creamy filling encased in wispy strands of *kadaif*, thinly shredded filo pastry that looks like very skinny vermicelli and crunches up like magic when baked (there are also versions coated in semolina, and the kadaif is sometimes ground up). Every year during Ramadan, Muslims in Israel fast from sunrise until nightfall to commemorate the holy Quran's revelation to the prophet Mohammed. At night, they break their fast with a festive meal called *iftar*. During a visit to the home of Najah Elshurbagi, who hosts visitors for home-cooked meals in her home in the predominantly Bedouin town of Rahat, we tasted the delicious handheld version of knafeh she had made for the sweet end to her family's iftar dessert. She prepares her knafeh with jibneh, a stretchy cheese reminiscent in both texture and taste to a hybrid of ricotta, mozzarella, and halloumi. Since jibneh and its sister cheese, Nabulsi cheese from the Palestinian town of Nablus, are virtually impossible to find stateside (and often even in the Jewish parts of Israel), I combine fresh ricotta and mozzarella for a pretty decent approximation. Unlike some versions, which are artificially colored an orangey-red, I leave mine *au naturel*. In place of a simple syrup topping laced with rose or orange flower water, I warm honey with fresh orange juice and thin slices of orange, rind and all. The oranges candy slightly in the bubbling honey, creating a bonus element in an already delicious dessert.

KNAFEH

1 cup (7 ounces) good-quality whole-milk ricotta cheese

One 8-ounce ball fresh mozzarella cheese, finely chopped (2 cups)

4 ounces kadaif pastry (see Shopping Guide), defrosted if frozen*

¼ cup (½ stick) unsalted butter, melted

2 tablespoons chopped toasted pistachios

HONEY-ORANGE SYRUP
(Makes about ⅓ cup)

1 small orange (about 6 ounces)

½ cup honey

2 teaspoons freshly squeezed lemon juice

Tiny pinch of salt

Makes
6 knafeh

Active Time:
30 minutes

Total Time:
1 hour
15 minutes

Make the knafeh: Preheat the oven to 375°F.

Line a plate with a triple layer of paper towels, spoon the ricotta onto the towels, top with another triple layer of towels, and press down to absorb the moisture. Scrape the ricotta into a medium bowl, add the mozzarella, and stir to combine. In another medium bowl, toss the pastry shreds with the butter until coated. Form the cheese mixture into six ½-cup balls. Grab a handful of the butter-coated kadaif shreds (about ½ cup). Spread them in your palm, place a ball of the cheese mixture in the center of the shreds, and loosely wrap the shreds around the ball to enclose. Place in an oven-safe baking dish. Bake in the oven until the top is golden brown and the edges are darker brown, 45 to 50 minutes.

RECIPE CONTINUES

Make the honey-orange syrup: While the kadaif are baking, slice half the orange into thin rounds, then juice the other half of the orange (you should have about ¼ cup orange juice).

In a small saucepan, whisk the honey, orange juice, lemon juice, and salt together. Scatter the orange slices on top (it's OK if they overlap). Bring the mixture to a low boil over medium-low heat. Reduce the heat to low and simmer until the liquid thickens slightly and the orange slices appear slightly candied, 10 to 12 minutes. Remove from the heat and cover to keep warm.

When the knafeh is ready, remove it from the oven and invert it onto a serving platter. Drizzle the syrup on top of the knafeh, serve with a candied orange slice if desired, and with extra syrup alongside. Sprinkle with pistachios.

*Kadaif typically comes frozen, in 1-pound packages. Since you're using only 4 ounces here, remove the kadaif from the freezer 15 minutes before using, then use a heavy chef's knife or cleaver to whack off approximately a quarter of the pastry. Return the rest of the kadaif to the freezer and defrost your 4 ounces.

Peach Kuchen

People ask me all the time whether I bargain for my food in the shuk. It's by no means the cheapest place in town to buy produce, meat, or cheese, but the answer is a definitive no. Now that I know the market, I know where to get what I want at the price I want, but, like any premium product, I'm willing to splurge for something I deem worthwhile. So it goes with peaches, which I've used in this version of my favorite cake on earth. My mom had some version of this easy dessert on repeat for my entire childhood. She sometimes made it with canned apple pie filling, sometimes with margarine—nothing could bring this recipe down. There's something about the way the sugary crust, somewhere between cobbler and a shortcake, melds with whatever filling you throw its way that makes it irresistible. I've made it with seedless grapes, plums, apricots, nectarines, apples—even cherry tomatoes—but here I used peaches, because I overbought them in season. Once the cake is prepared, you can do the adult thing and slice yourself a wedge, but more often than not I find myself dissecting it piece by piece, pulling off the crunchy-soft discs on top, grabbing pieces of jammy baked fruit, then finishing with the bottom layer of dough after it has had time to absorb the fruit juices.

1¼ cups all-purpose flour

½ cup plus 2 tablespoons sugar

1 tablespoon cornmeal or semolina

2 teaspoons baking powder

¼ teaspoon fine sea salt

½ cup (1 stick) unsalted butter, softened

1 large egg

4 medium ripe peaches (about 2 pounds)

Vanilla ice cream or Labaneh Whipped Cream (page 320), for serving

Serves 8

Active Time:
25 minutes

Total Time:
1 hour
5 minutes

Preheat the oven to 350°F.

Sift the flour, ½ cup sugar, cornmeal, baking powder, and salt into the bowl of a stand mixer fitted with the paddle attachment. Add the butter and beat at medium speed until partially incorporated, then add the egg. Increase the speed to medium-high and beat until a soft dough forms, about 30 seconds. Press about two-thirds of the dough into the bottom and partially up the sides of a 9- or 10-inch tart pan with a removable bottom (or any round baking dish of the same dimensions), wrap the remaining dough in plastic wrap, and chill both the dough-filled tart pan and the remaining dough for 15 minutes.

While the dough is chilling, pit the peaches and cut them into ½-inch wedges. Arrange the peaches freely on the dough, pressing slightly to adhere them to the dough. Divide the remaining dough into 8 equal small balls and scatter them randomly over the top of the tart. Sprinkle the top with the remaining 2 tablespoons sugar and bake until the peaches look soft and the dough appears golden and crisped on top, 35 minutes. Cool slightly, slide the cake out of its frame, slice, and serve with vanilla ice cream or labaneh whipped cream.

Coffee-and-Cream Icebox Cake

Petit beurre cookies—scallop-edged, mildly sweet tea biscuits that are neither particularly *petit* nor contain any *beurre* (butter)—are the ballast of one of Israel's most beloved no-bake desserts. A distant relative of the flaky, buttery French original, these cookies disintegrate if dipped in coffee or tea for too long, so make sure they soak up only their creamy coffee mixture for a few seconds per side before layering with ricotta-enriched cream. As the cake rests overnight in the refrigerator, the cookies soften and plump, adding distinctive structure and a cakey texture as the layers meld together. If you're not baking for a crowd, the recipe can be halved.

2¼ cups whole milk

Two 3.4-ounce packages of dry instant vanilla pudding mix

¼ teaspoon fine sea salt

¾ cup farmer's cheese

¾ cup whole-milk ricotta cheese

3½ cups heavy cream

⅓ cup sugar

1 cup strong prepared espresso or very strong coffee

1½ tablespoons unsweetened cocoa powder

1½ 8.8-ounce packages tea biscuits, such as Israeli Osem Petit Beurre (see Shopping Guide) or other tea biscuits (54 cookies)

1 ounce bittersweet chocolate

Serves 16

Active Time: 40 minutes

Total Time: about 24 hours

In a large bowl, whisk together the milk, vanilla pudding, and salt, then whisk in the farmer's cheese and ricotta until smooth. In a separate bowl, beat all but 2 tablespoons cream and the sugar to soft peaks, about 3 to 4 minutes, then gently fold the cream into the pudding mixture. Lighten the espresso with the reserved 2 tablespoons cream, then stir in the cocoa until dissolved. Pour the coffee mixture into a shallow baking dish or baking sheet. Working in batches and stirring the coffee-cocoa mixture between batches, dip the cookies in the coffee, letting them soak for 10 to 15 seconds per side (you want them to pick up the coffee flavor but not get so soft that they fall apart). Arrange 18 of the soaked cookies in the bottom of a 10 x 15-inch baking dish. Top with one third of the cream mixture, then repeat until there are 3 layers of biscuits covered with 3 layers of cream. Cover and refrigerate for 24 hours. Remove from the refrigerator, grate the chocolate on top of the cake, and cut into 16 equal-sized squares.

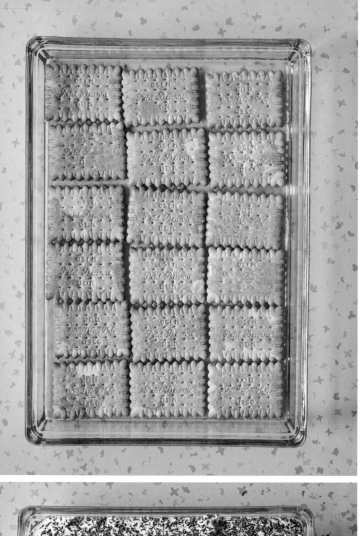

Watermelon, Feta, and Mint

Once *avatiach*, or watermelon, comes into season in July, the shuk becomes a band with an over-populated percussion section as customers and vendors alike hold their heads close to the fruit, tapping and thumping in search of the acoustic equivalent of some sort of hollow solidity that suggests a fresh, juicy specimen. To be honest, I think it's all a bit of a myth: I've done everything I could short of consulting a psychic to predetermine a watermelon's quality and have been disappointed, while other times I'll grab one randomly from an oversized bin and be rewarded with perfection. One thing I can guarantee: If you do find a good watermelon, other than eating it out of hand there's no better way to enjoy it than with a chunk of creamy, salty feta and a sprinkling of chopped mint. To emphasize watermelon's juicy crunch, chill it before serving. Cut the feta with a knife or separate with your hands, and add as little or as much mint as you like. This is more guideline than recipe: Combine the elements to your liking, with the proportions you like, and you can't go wrong.

Spiced Medjool Mandelbrodt
(Israeli Biscotti)

This family recipe comes courtesy of my friend Orly Pele Bronstein, a talented local food writer and editor who calls these her "Israeli Biscotti." Her Bulgarian grandmother on her mother's side, Marika, made these to spoil Orly's father, who had lost his own mother at a young age. Like their Italian cousins, *mandelbrodt* ("nut bread" in German) are twice-baked: first in loaves that are cooled, and then in slices that generate a pleasing crispiness. Bronstein incorporates a version of the warm-spice blend called Hawaiij le Café,* or Coffee Hawaiij, that Yemenites traditionally mix into hot water for a post-meal stomach digestive (for the savory version, see page 27).

2¾ cups all-purpose flour

1⅓ cups sugar

2 cups whole almonds

1 tablespoon ground cardamom

1½ teaspoons ground ginger

½ teaspoon ground cinnamon

¼ teaspoon ground white pepper

¼ teaspoon ground cloves

1 teaspoon baking powder

1½ teaspoons fine sea salt

3 large eggs plus 3 large egg yolks, beaten

1 teaspoon finely grated lemon zest

1 teaspoon finely grated orange zest

3 large (3 ounces) pitted Medjool dates, finely chopped

Makes
50 cookies

Active Time:
15 minutes

Total Time:
1 hour
15 minutes

Preheat the oven to 350°F. Line a large cookie sheet with parchment paper.

In a stand mixer fitted with the paddle attachment, combine the flour, sugar, almonds, cardamom, ginger, cinnamon, white pepper, cloves, baking powder, and salt and beat at low speed until all the ingredients are incorporated, 30 seconds. Add the eggs, egg yolks, lemon zest, orange zest, and dates and fold in on low speed until just incorporated, scraping down the sides of the bowl if necessary.

Divide the dough into 2 equal-sized pieces and place them on the prepared baking sheet. Pat each piece into a 10 x 5 x 1½-inch loaf pan. Bake the loaves until firm and dry, 23 to 25 minutes. Remove the loaves from the oven and let the loaves cool completely (you can transfer them to a cooling rack once they've cooled off a bit). Using a sharp, long knife (but not a serrated knife, which causes the slices to crumble), cut the loaves crosswise into ⅓-inch-thick slices and arrange them flat on 2 baking sheets. Reduce the oven temperature to 325°F and bake until golden and toasty, 15 to 17 minutes. Remove from the oven and cool completely. Store in an airtight container for up to 1 week.

*To make extra hawaiij for stirring into coffee or hot water, simply make a separate batch of the spice blend of cardamom, ginger, cinnamon, white pepper, and cloves called for above; double, triple, or quadruple the recipe and store in an airtight container for up to 3 months.

Olive Oil Chocolate Spread

Israel's own Hashachar Ha'Oleh ("Rising Dawn"), a cheap sugar rush of spreadable chocolate originally created as a way to get calories into young Israelis for breakfast or after school, used to give Nutella a run for its money. But its base of cheap chocolate and vegetable oil has caused it to suffer from a bit of bad PR in recent years. For a kid, the parent-endorsed idea of being able to spread chocolate on any sort of supporting vehicle (my favorite: matzah) holds massive appeal— and it still does for adults (well, at least this adult). This is my version, made with good-quality chocolate, olive oil, cocoa, and a healthy amount of salt. You can use any kind of chocolate you like, from milk to dark, and you need to refrigerate it after cooking for an initial firming up. This also serves as the filling for my Chocolate-Orange Babka (page 352).

⅔ cup sugar

2 tablespoons unsweetened cocoa powder

½ teaspoon kosher salt

1 cup (6 ounces) chopped bittersweet, semisweet, or dark chocolate

¼ cup extra-virgin olive oil

1 teaspoon pure vanilla extract

Matzah, for serving

Flaky sea salt, such as Maldon, for sprinkling

○○○○○○○○○○

Makes
1⅓ cups

Active Time:
10 minutes

Total Time:
about
2 hours
(including
minimum
chilling time)

○○○○○○○○○○

In a small saucepan bring ⅓ cup water, the sugar, cocoa, and kosher salt to a boil over medium heat. Reduce the heat to medium-low and cook, whisking, until the sugar is dissolved and the mixture thickens, 2 to 3 minutes. Remove the saucepan from the heat and whisk in the chocolate, olive oil, and vanilla until the chocolate is melted and smooth. Transfer to a bowl, press plastic wrap onto the surface of the chocolate, and refrigerate until thick but spreadable, 2 hours. Remove from the refrigerator to soften for 30 minutes, or microwave for 10 seconds, then stir before serving. Spread on matzah and sprinkle with flaky sea salt. Refrigerated in an airtight container, chocolate spread keeps for 2 months.

Just One Chocolate-Orange Babka

Here in Israel, babka is called Krantz cake, but the idea is the same: a tender, buttery dough swirled with a rich filling, baked, then soaked with sugary syrup. They've been popular here for years, part of a strong Israeli tradition of yeast-risen pastries, known here as *oogot shmarim*. Most of the recipes I've seen make two or even three babkas, but it's really nice to make just one, either to use as a dessert at a dinner party or to have for slicing and daily eating midweek with coffee. Though the dough starts out a little sticky and needs some time resting in the fridge, it's really not that difficult to pull off. Instead of a stand mixer, which can sometimes be tricky when dealing with a small volume of dough, I experimented with the food processor and its plastic dough blade until I came up with a formula that works like a dream. The orange accents throughout, when combined with the chocolate in the filling, call to mind Sabra, a chocolate-orange liqueur we used to buy from the duty-free shop at the airport on our way home from visits to Israel. The liqueur wasn't great, but that chocolate-orange flavor stuck with me, and the flavor combination works really well here.

BABKA

2 cups all-purpose flour, plus more for flouring your hands and the work surface

¼ cup sugar

1¼ teaspoons instant (rapid-rise) yeast

1 teaspoon fine sea salt

1 small orange

⅓ cup whole milk

1 large egg, beaten

¼ cup (½ stick) unsalted butter, slightly softened, cut into 2 pieces, plus more for buttering the pan

1¼ cups Olive Oil Chocolate Spread (page 350), softened, or Nutella

2 tablespoons heavy cream, warmed

3 ounces plain chocolate wafer-style cookies (such as Nabisco chocolate wafers or Teddy Grahams), pulverized into fine crumbs (about ⅔ cup)

SYRUP

6 tablespoons sugar

2 tablespoons orange juice (ideally reserved from babka making)

⚬⚬⚬⚬⚬⚬⚬⚬⚬⚬

Makes
1 babka

Active Time:
20 minutes

Total Time:
10 hours (including minimum resting time)

⚬⚬⚬⚬⚬⚬⚬⚬⚬⚬

Make the babka: In the bowl of a food processor fitted with the dough blade* (the plastic one you never use!), pulse the flour, sugar, yeast, and salt 5 times. Zest and juice the orange. Warm the milk in the microwave just long enough to take the chill off of it, 15 seconds. Add the milk, egg, 2 tablespoons of the orange juice, and half the orange zest (save the remaining juice and zest—you'll be using them later) to the processor, pulse 5 times, then process until a soft, tacky dough is formed, 1 minute. Add the butter and pulse 5 times, then process until a very soft, tacky, loose dough forms, another 30 to 45 seconds. Open the processor, press some plastic wrap right on top of the dough, and let it rest for 45 minutes.

Lay out a large piece of plastic wrap, scrape the dough into the center of the plastic wrap, flour your hands lightly, and form the dough into a 5-inch square. Wrap it in plastic, and chill it for at least 6 hours and up to 24 hours (the longer you chill the dough, the more manageable it becomes and the flavor of the dough deepens and develops).

RECIPE CONTINUES

Butter a standard (4.5 x 8.5-inch) loaf pan, then line the pan with 2 crisscrossing strips of parchment paper, buttering between each layer and leaving a 2-inch overhang on all sides. Butter the top and sides of the parchment-lined pan.

Microwave the chocolate spread on high for 10 seconds, and stir in the cream, chocolate crumbs, and the rest of the orange zest into the chocolate spread until incorporated.

Clear and lightly flour a work surface. Remove the dough from the fridge and roll it out into a 14-inch square (or as much of a square as you can). Spread the chocolate mixture on the dough, leaving a 1-inch border around the edges. Roll the dough into a tight log, then slice it up the middle lengthwise into 2 equal strips (you should see stripes of chocolate facing up). Pinch the top ends together, then twist the strips around each other, trying not to stretch out the length too much, until you have a lovely twist with the chocolate exposed. Fit the twisted, exposed-chocolate side up, into the parchment-lined loaf pan, cover with a clean kitchen towel, and let the babka rise in a warm place until doubled in size, 1½ to 2 hours. Preheat the oven to 350°F. Bake the babka until deeply golden brown on top, 45 to 50 minutes.

While the babka is cooking, make the syrup: In a very small saucepan, bring the sugar, orange juice, and 2 tablespoons of water to a low boil over medium heat. Reduce the heat and simmer until the sugar dissolves, 2 to 3 minutes. Remove from the heat.

When the babka is done, remove it from the oven and, while still warm, brush it with the syrup, letting the syrup soak into the babka between brushings.

*To Knead by Hand

In a large wide-mouthed bowl, stir together the flour, sugar, yeast, and salt. Zest and juice the orange. Warm the milk in the microwave just long enough to take the chill off, 15 seconds. Add the milk, egg, 1 tablespoon of the orange juice, and half of the zest (save the remaining juice and zest; you'll be using them later) to the bowl and stir together with a wooden spoon or a spatula until a tacky dough forms; it'll take about 2 minutes. Cut the butter into 6 to 8 pieces, then start to knead the butter into the dough by folding the dough over and kneading the butter in with the heel of your hand. It'll be sticky—add a tablespoon of flour if the dough is too wet—and continue to knead until the butter is fully incorporated and the dough comes together in a supple, more evenly textured dough, 6 to 7 minutes. Lay some plastic wrap right on top of the dough, let it rest for 45 minutes, and proceed with the recipe as above.

Almond-Coconut Basbusa Snack Cake

I came up with this recipe, based on the many tender, semolina-based cakes I've had in Arab, Palestinian, and Israeli homes and restaurants, to use up either the ground almond meal left over from making Date-Sweetened Almond Milk (page 302) or Roasted Almond Rosetta Syrup (page 356). I like to bake this up and let it sit around, because it gets even better a day or two later.

¾ cup extra-virgin olive oil, plus more for greasing the pan

1⅔ cups almond meal, or leftover ground almonds from making Roasted Almond Rosetta syrup (recipe follows) or Date-Sweetened Almond Milk (page 302)

1¼ cups fine semolina

¾ cup sugar

½ cup finely shredded unsweetened coconut

⅓ cup all-purpose flour

½ teaspoon baking powder

½ teaspoon fine sea salt

1 cup buttermilk, shaken

3 large eggs

Finely grated zest of 1 lemon

1 teaspoon pure vanilla extract

½ cup Roasted Almond Rosetta Syrup (recipe follows) or store-bought orgeat (almond syrup; see Shopping Guide)

25 blanched roasted almond halves or slivered almonds

Makes
about
40 pieces

Active Time:
10 minutes

Total Time:
30 minutes

Preheat the oven to 300°F. Grease a 9 x 13-inch baking dish or quarter sheet pan (or two 8- or 9-inch round cake layer pans) with olive oil and set aside.

In a large bowl, whisk together the almond meal, semolina, sugar, coconut, flour, baking powder, salt, buttermilk, olive oil, eggs, lemon zest, and vanilla.

Transfer the batter to the prepared pan (or pans) and bake until the cake is set and just firm in the center, 22 to 24 minutes if using almond meal or 26 to 28 minutes if using leftover ground almonds from syrup. Remove from the oven and immediately pour the syrup all over the cake. Using a sharp knife, slice the cake on a 45-degree angle in strips 1½ inches apart. Rotate the pan and make another set of cuts to form diamond-shaped pieces of cake. Press an almond into the center of each diamond. Serve warm or at room temperature.

RECIPE CONTINUES

Roasted Almond Rosetta Syrup

For years I kept a bottle of supermarket rosetta—a syrupy, almond-flavored concentrate with Tunisian roots—at home to flavor seltzer or drizzle over fruit. One day while buying halvah from Linda, the octogenarian shopkeeper of my favorite halvah vendor in Tel Aviv's Levinsky Market, I noticed a few cloudy, unmarked bottles next to the pomegranate and date syrup. "Don't tell me you've been buying that rosetta garbage from the supermarket?" she asked. It turns out the innocuous-looking store brands contain artificial flavors, corn syrup—and even white food coloring. I bought a bottle from her, then tinkered with a recipe of my own to coax out every drop of almond flavor. First, I roast the nuts longer than usual to a deep shade of brown, then grind them and add them to simple syrup with a bit of orange and cardamom flavor for contrast. The result is a surprisingly complex, nutty flavor component that works especially well in cocktails like my Almondy Vodka Limonana (page 310) or simply mixed with seltzer (pictured, right).

Makes 2¾ cups
Active Time: 30 minutes
Total time: 3 hours (including minimum infusing time)

2 cups blanched almonds (sliced or whole are fine)	2 cups sugar 3 cardamom pods	Rind from half a lemon or small orange

Preheat the oven to 325°F.

Arrange the almonds on a large rimmed baking sheet and toast, shaking the pan once midway through, until deep golden and fragrant, 12 to 15 minutes, depending on whether you're using sliced or whole almonds. Remove from the oven, transfer to a plate, and cool completely. Transfer the nuts to the bowl of a food processor and process until fine crumbs form, before you reach the almost-at-almond-butter stage (you want the almonds to be crumbly but not tiny), 15 to 20 seconds.

In a medium saucepan, bring 2½ cups water and the sugar to a boil over medium-high heat, reduce the heat, and let simmer until a syrup forms, 5 to 6 minutes. Add the ground almonds and the cardamom pods, return to a boil, reduce the heat, and simmer for 5 more minutes. Remove the saucepan from the heat, add the orange rind, and let the whole thing sit on the counter for at least 2 hours and up to 8 (the longer it sits, the more almondy it will be). Strain the syrup through a fine-mesh sieve, pressing down with a wooden spoon to extract as much of the syrup as you can. Remove and discard the rind and cardamom pods and reserve the ground almonds for Almond-Coconut Basbusa Snack Cake (page 355), if desired. Decant into a bottle and seal with a tight-fitting cork or top. The syrup will separate, but don't worry; that's just very fine particles of almond solids sinking to the bottom. Simply re-shake before using. The syrup will keep, refrigerated, for up to 6 months.

Shopping Guide

Dairy Products

Labaneh: Whole Foods stores carry labaneh under brand names including Karoun and Arz. They tend to be quite thick, so thin with a little milk to achieve your desired consistency.

G'vina Levana: The Israeli Tnuva brand of this quark-like cheese is available at some kosher stores and at some branches of Costco. German-style quark, made by Vermont Creamery, can be found at gourmet markets and Whole Foods.

Kashkaval: The kashkaval I use and love in Israel is actually a kasar cheese from Thrace, Turkey. Similar cheeses go under the name Kashar and Kasseri, depending on where they're from. Tnuva kosher kashkaval can be purchased at koshercentral.com.

Condiments

Harissa, Schug, Preserved Lemons, and Preserved Lemon Paste: These can be purchased from NYshuk.com and can be found at many kosher stores and Middle Eastern markets. Trader Joe's stores now sell all of these products.

Amba: Galil brand amba is available in some kosher and Middle Eastern markets and on Amazon. Trader Joe's recently began selling amba under the name Amba Mango Sauce.

Herbs and Spices

Spices: All the spices and spice blends called for in this book can be ordered from Kalustyans.com and Pereg.com, a kosher spice company based in Israel. Many spice blends, such as hawaiij and za'atar, can be bought from premium spice blender Lior Lev Sercarz at laboiteny.com and from NYshuk.com.

Dried Lemon Verbena: Abundant and easy to buy in Israel, my favorite tea ingredient is harder to source abroad. Luckily, Klio dried lemon verbena leaves are good quality and available at kliotea.com.

Pantry Staples

Freekeh: Freekeh comes both whole and cracked (cracked is easier to find). Bob's Red Mill and FireGrain cracked freekeh are widely available at supermarkets and online. You'll have to look a little closer for whole freekeh.

Olive Oil: Sindyanna fair trade olive oils, made by a cooperative of Arab producers, and Honey Land, a good-quality extra-virgin olive oil—both produced in Northern Israel—can be bought on Amazon.com.

Tahini: Soom (soomfoods.com), a company run by my friends Amy, Jackie, and Shelby Zitelman, makes its tahini in Israel from Ethiopian sesame seeds imported by Omri Horvitz, Amy's husband. Seed + Mill, which primarily makes halvah, makes a limited amount of tahini as well. Whole Foods 365 brand tahini is also a great choice. Recently one of Israel's best tahinis, Har Bracha, made by Samaritans in the West Bank, can be found at some kosher stores and at makoletonline.com. El Karawan, made by Palestinians in Nablus, can be bought on Amazon. Al Arz, a wonderful tahini made near Nazareth, is also easily found online.

Silan (Date Syrup): Soom Foods (soomfoods.com) recently began importing pure organic silan from Israel. You can also find good-quality silan, made from California dates, from kosher and Middle Eastern shops, and online from thedatelady.com and dvash.com.

Pomegranate Molasses: The most commonly available brands, Cortas and Al Wadi, both Lebanese, can be found at many supermarkets and specialty markets. For a special (and pricier) treat, Mymouné brand pomegranate syrup, made from pomegranates also harvested in Lebanon, has a true, clarion-clear pomegranate flavor without additives or sweeteners. It can be purchased at oliveharvest.com.

Dates: Deglet Noor dates, from California, have been available in supermarkets for decades, but many better supermarkets now sell Medjools; look for ones that are dark brown, plump, and moist; dates with a lot of sugar crystallization may be old or fermented, a result of high sugar content and excessive heat. Good ones, grown in California, can also be found at thedatelady.com.

Barberries: These tiny, tart dried berries can be purchased at Middle Eastern markets and online at persianbasket.com, kalustyans.com, and sadaf.com.

Halvah: The best domestic halvah comes from Hebel & Co. (hebelco.com), and is made in Los Angeles. Seed + Mill (see *Tahini*) works with a private-label Israeli manufacturer to make theirs, which is also excellent.

Kadaif Pastry: This finely shredded filo dough used in knafeh, also called kataifi, can sometimes be found, frozen, at Middle Eastern markets and bakeries. You can buy The Fillo Factory brand kadaif at some Whole Foods markets and online at thefillofactory.com.

Beverages

Arak: The licorice-flavored spirit can be found at some better liquor stores, as well as at liquor-store-online.com.

Orgeat: If you don't have time to make my Roasted Almond Rosetta Syrup (page 00), store-bought orgeat is a great swap-in. Monin, Torani, and Giffard (from France) are the best-known, most widely available brands at stores and online. If you're into small-batch, artisan products, try BG Reynolds, which contains lime and ginger (available at barproducts.com).

Kitchen Equipment

Nut Milk Bag: Porous drawstring bags like these make straining my Date-Sweetened Almond Milk (page 302) and Cardamom-Cinnamon Cold Brew coffee (page 300) a breeze. Find them at health food stores and all over the Internet.

Couscous Sifter (Kish Kash): For making my Easy Homemade Couscous on page 286, you need a tambourine-shaped sifter with extra-wide holes. It can be purchased on Amazon for $25 (search "couscous sifter"). I also discovered a soil- and rock-sifting pan that works like a charm ($15; search for "SE GP2-112 Patented Stackable 13¼" Sifting Pan, Mesh Size ¹⁄₁₂").

Microplane Grater: For finely grating a drift of Parmigiano-Reggiano or lemon zest, search online for the wand-style "Microplane Classic Zester/Grater" or "Premium Zester Grater."

The Pal Ed Falafel Mold: A set of three sizes of this falafel molding tool (page 283) is available on Amazon.

Fermentation Weights: These glass weights, easily found online, are useful for keeping vegetables underneath liquid during pickling.

Sabina Valdman

Uri Scheft, Rinat Tzadok, and Hallel Scheft

Shaily Lipa

Gil Hovav

Ariel Rosenthal

Rottem Lieberson

Roy Yerushalmi

Najah Elshurbagi

Nofar Zohar

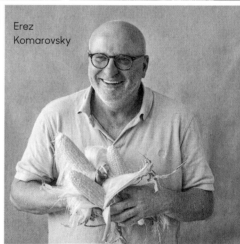
Erez Komarovsky

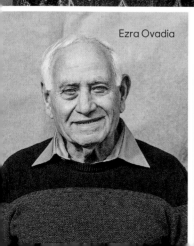
Ezra Ovadia

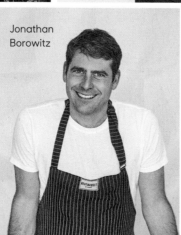
Jonathan Borowitz

Orly Pele Bronstein

Osama Dalal

Acknowledgments

Photographer Dan Perez and stylist Nurit Kariv, for your passion, inspiration, and friendship. Thank you for sharing your vision and that Israeli sunlight. And to the best crew: Boris Korotkov, Noa Castel, Barak Nadav, June Weberman, and Mor Fadlon—you all made our set days as fun as they were delicious.

Tressa Eaton, for cooking by my side and climbing the stairway to heaven (otherwise known as my fourth-floor walk-up kitchen) endless times. Your patience, good cheer, and talent grace every page.

To Lucia Watson, for not simply inheriting but rather embracing and cheerleading for me and this book. Thank you for taking this journey to Israel with me! Thanks to the brilliant Avery team: Megan Newman, Anne Kosmoski, Lindsay Gordon, Farin Schlussel, Ashley Tucker, Suzy Swartz, and Emily Fisher.

To Pam Krauss, for believing in me. I am forever grateful.

To my agent, Janis Donnaud, for everything you do. I adore you!

To Doris Cooper, my neighbor and nocturnal consigliere (with wine).

To Raquel Pelzel, Sara Kate Gillingham, Rosanne Kang, and Catherine Franklin, for your input on this book and for your friendship.

To Amy Klein, Devorah Blachor, and Jessica Steinberg, the original Yerushalmiot. Look at all our books!

To Gil Hovav, for making me an honorary Yemenite. There is no greater distinction!

To Lee Brian Schrager, for your amazing generosity and unparalleled door-opening on my behalf.

To Nadav, Shani, Or, and Yuval, for being my family.

To my late mother, Stephanie Ellen Sussman, for teaching me how to get delicious food to the table and, more important, how to gather people around it.

To Dad and Bette, for knowing that there's nothing a cook loves more than being cooked for.

To Sharon, Ari, Tova, Yaakov, and Akiva, for everything.

To Michal Ansky and Shir Halpern at the Tel Aviv Farmers' Market for your generous advice and emergency loquat deliveries.

To my Israeli food community, thank you for your warm, delicious embrace: Ariel Rosenthal, Rottem Lieberson, Shaily Lipa, Roy Yerushalmi, Efrat Lichtenstadt, Haim Yosef, Jonathan Borowitz, Uri Scheft, Orly Pele Bronstein, Rinat Tzadok, Osama Dalal, Sabina Valdman, Eyal Yassky Weiss, Nofar Zohar, Avihai Tsabari, Erez Komarovsky, and Ayelet Nahum.

To Mike Solomonov, my food brother and champion. Love you and the boys. And to Steve Cook for your friendship. Thank you both for your beautiful foreword to this book.

To Anat Abramov Shimoni and Yishai Shimoni, Ross Belfer, Maya Reik, Rachael Workman, Debra Kamin, Andrew Treitel, and Dina Kraft—the best friends and tasters a girl could ask for.

To Paul Nirens of Galileat (galileat.com) for your expertise in Galilean cooking.

To the team that graciously put my recipes through their paces: Leah Bhabha, Julia Bainbridge, Lauren Bloomberg, Danielle Centoni, Jodie Chase, Danielle Rehfeld Colen, Kristin Donnelly, Robyn Echkardt, Mira Evnine, Rebecca Firsker, Nicole Fisher, Gabriella Gershenson, Gina Hamadey, Israela Levine Kahan, Megan Krigbaum, Meredith Kurtzer, Mari Levine, Michal Levine, Devorah Lev Tov, Adina Lipson, Maggie Mariolis, Katherine Martinelli, Olga Massov, Mandy Morris, Helen Rosner, Emily Rudisill, Shannon Sarna, Kirsten Schofield, Aliza Sokolow, Gayle Squires, Andrea Strong, Stanley Sussman, Yitzi Taber, Kiri Tannenbaum, Julie Tanous, Emily Teel, Rachel Tepper, Lesley Tellez, Marisa Robertson Textor, Tina Ujlaki, and Jeffrey Yoskowitz.

And finally, to Jay, for all that we share and a love that powered this book into existence.

Index

Note: Page numbers in *italics* indicate photos/captions.